Dale Martin Jones

6/23/77

D0045072

Charles Laughton

AN INTIMATE BIOGRAPHY

Other books by Charles Higham

Film Criticism and Biography

THE ART OF THE AMERICAN FILM
    1900–1971

THE FILMS OF ORSON WELLES

KATE—The Life of Katharine Hepburn

Poetry

NOONDAY COUNTRY

THE VOYAGE TO BRINDISI

Charles Laughton
AN INTIMATE BIOGRAPHY

by Charles Higham

INTRODUCTION BY
ELSA LANCHESTER

1976

DOUBLEDAY & COMPANY, INC.
GARDEN CITY, NEW YORK

Library of Congress Cataloging in Publication Data

Higham, Charles, 1931–
Charles Laughton: life of an actor.

1. Laughton, Charles, 1899–1962.
PN2598.L27H5   791'.092'4 [B]
ISBN 0-385-09403-5
Library of Congress Catalog Card Number 75-21228

Copyright © 1976 by Charles Higham and Elsa Lanchester
All Rights Reserved
Printed in the United States of America

Introduction

by Elsa Lanchester Laughton

There is no such thing as a person that nothing has happened to, and each person's story is as different as his fingerprints. Biographers select humans that other humans want to know about. Charles Higham has thought of writing about Charles Laughton for a very long time. The work has been tough, but peaceful; remembering the past may be very therapeutic in a psychiatrist's office, but sitting with Charles Higham, the files, letters, a tape recorder, and of course a pot of tea, has roused memories that I did not know I had. Very disturbing, but better than being indolent . . . with a pot of tea. Then comes the question: Would my husband, Charles Laughton, like me to be working on this book? Probably not. A book about his career and life? No. Will his brother Tom like it? Maybe not. Now, just look here—someone's going to do it if we don't.

This preface, although the first word, is also the last word, since I have written it after the book was finished. I am sorry that the work is finished. Once you start to move into another life it is quite eerie to move out again. As it were, Charles has gone for the second time.

Charles had hoped to become a writer as he grew older, but *not* an autobiographer. He wanted to write something that would help people to understand themselves and find life less tortuous. When Bertolt Brecht asked him why he acted, Charles answered, "Because people don't know themselves and I think that I can show them how they tick." So, in writing, in teaching, in directing, too, his creative drive was in the same direction. But in writing he hoped to probe into his own more personal experiences to help man accept and live with what he is. But Charles insisted that what he had to say couldn't be published. It would hurt too many people. Although Charles became one of the great interpreters of the English language as written by others and spoken by himself, and also became a great editor, carving into dramatic structures the words of great writers, he never really became what he also wanted to be: a writer.

How near Charles got to understanding himself is one of the questions that Mr. Higham and I have tried to probe. I think one can say that perhaps Charles Laughton penetrated human behavior a little more than most people. Certainly as an actor. But then, also, as an actor Charles never felt like a complete or even a real person. If someone had said, "Will the real Mr. Laughton stand up?" he probably would have remained seated.

Once, when Charles was traveling across the United States on the *Super Chief* in the late Thirties, he sat in the dining car opposite a couple. They were a nice middle-aged, middle-class husband and wife, and Charles got into a conversation with them. The husband explained that he was in the wholesale-dolls-underwear business. "And you're a famous actor, aren't you?" he asked.

"Yes."

His wife piped up, "But what do you do in real life, Mr. Laughton?"

Every quest for the real person hiding inside a famous person must be constructed from an intricate collection of facts. This biographical story of Charles, his life, and his films, is a search for the motivations of a career-minded person who became a public figure of his own volition. This book is written not that you may like Charles or dislike him, agree or disagree with him. But that you understand him as an artist and as a human being.

Ambition did not allow Charles to know how to rest. He could not see, or tolerate, side issues when forging ahead toward a project. Like a horse with blinkers, he would rear up and snort if some small object blew across his path. As a relief to this driving ambition, sudden impersonal relationships caught him briefly, here and there. As if after too much discipline and control, the body itself needed the opposite before it could rest. Then came guilts and withdrawals, and loneliness set in.

Today's permissive world would have bewildered him. He needed to be secretive, which apparently sprang from his middle-class British background. Charles was a moral man who was shocked by himself, so that he suffered the painful guilts of the highly moral individual. He could laugh at moral contradictions in others, but he couldn't laugh at the paradoxes in himself. But he could roar with laughter when he told this story:

On another of his trips across the country, talking to a couple in the dining car, Charles asked if they went to the theatre much in New York.

"No, we don't go to plays nowadays," the husband answered. "We don't approve of the immoral language."

Charles inquired, "May I ask, what is your work, your profession?"

"Oh," answered the wife, "my husband is in atomic research."

Mr. Higham analyzes a large part of Charles's life through an interpretation of his acting in films. I have added to this by recalling for Mr. Higham scenes from my personal scenario, as well as supplying letters from Charles's friends and colleagues, and conversations that I have had with his associates.

We were bound, Charles and I, by enforced understanding in the very early years of our marriage. We both married for protection against society, with innocence about the façade that public life and ambition would impose upon us. Together we needed the protection of a house. Although barriers rose up inside this private kingdom, there were at least some areas of total understanding. We did have many perfect days in the country, and months and years in the gardens, and the woodlands and hills surrounding our various houses. I always house-hunted when we made a move, and my rule was to look for the big trees that often indicated the presence of an old house, with the feeling of maturity, and perhaps the end of somebody else's family line. There was Stapledown, the house in the bluebell woods of Surrey, England; the cabin in Idyllwild, California; the cottage in the orchard at Palos Verdes, also in California; the house at Pacific Palisades near Los Angeles, with its garden of oranges, fuchsias, and camellias; the house on North Curson Avenue, in the heart of Hollywood, with its acre of greenery; and finally the Santa Monica cottage and its little tangled terraces with ferns and trees.

Wood fires and sunsets seemed to mark each home that Charles and I lived in over the period of thirty-three years that we were married. There was loyalty to the idea of marriage, there was mutual protection, and tolerance and respect—words that did not at any time pass between us. Charles always had a fear of analyzing or discussing the causes and effects of the marriage, always fearful that the structure would break if words were spoken. So nothing was said. Except very late. Charles hoped to go away with me when all passion, both in art and life, had gone: "I do wish it would all pass, and we could go peacefully to beautiful places and beautiful countries. We've never really been on a holiday, have we?"

In our early days we often took time to walk on the Yorkshire Moors, and once I remember with great clarity being in Scotland in 1938 and spending a day at Loch Katrine. We were on a personal appearance tour for a film, and had a spare day. We spent it chugging round the loch on a lovely, tubby little official reservoir steamer. The day was very beautiful, and I believe typical of the area. It was very clear: ominous gray clouds, yet the sun shining through in bright shafts, we thought on us, and in patches on the green land around the loch. A hundred tiny, tumbling rivulets fell into the loch, jumping through ferns and grasses. We were happy and enchanted. It was one of the few places Charles said he would like to go back to. As we traveled north by car and train, we wondered why so many soldiers were going south—very young boys in badly fitting uniforms. Territorials.

Our marriage endured partly as a result of the places we lived in or even visited. There should have been more trips to the country, to the mountains, deserts, and forests. Work sent us to lovely places: Hampton Court Palace and Kew Gardens; to Brighton,

Sussex, with its glittering pier and South Downs; to Hawaii and to Portmeirion, Wales, to study *King Lear*. These places form a kind of necklace of charms remembered.

As Charles became more involved with work, we missed one spring and then another. Our trips to see the California wild flowers dwindled to nothing by the 1950s. Life went on round the pool at home, and it was quiet. Our banana trees produced good bananas (and still do) and encouraged beautiful yellow orioles to nest in them round the pool. We had flourishing night-blooming cereus that put on a show one or two nights a year. On such a rare night we tried to get friends to drop in to see the show. They did. The huge perfumed flowers came out at nine in the evening and died at 2 A.M. Such an occasion caused all possible kinds of people to meet and mix well.

Creative artists themselves only see the many imperfections in their own art and the impossibility of capturing their dream in the short time allowed to them. But the art collector can build a structure in perpetuity with his knowledge and his taste. If he is faithful to these attributes, he leaves something for others. One little step in the selectiveness of another generation.

The art collection Charles acquired over the years fascinated many collectors and painters. Charles had an infallible eye for what he wanted to reach his own fulfillment. While on tour, Charles wrote to the painter Morris Graves in Seattle in 1943: "I can't get up to see you as I have to get back at once to Hollywood to start a movie. Is it possible you could send me down a few pictures to look at? I am a very prompt guy and won't keep them hanging around. I write a lousy letter. I've somehow never been able to express myself on paper, and I'm just dribbling on trying to say how tremendously stimulated I was by your painting. Very much hope to meet you someday."

Paintings had a direct effect on Charles's acting and his peace of mind, and I cannot put this in better words than Morris Graves's own. He wrote: "Charles told me there was something in my paintings that helped him as an actor. There was a unique trumpet line, something in the style, the shapes, that he was able to translate into his acting. He had the ability to sway people to what he wanted—he didn't *direct* them, but carried them along on his energy. His enthusiasm for painting was an immediate experience as the experience of the theatre. He could see a painting by a new painter, and actually become *animated* by the painting. He would move around, carrying the painting with him in his luggage, acquire a painting, and take it on tour with him more as a living presence than an inanimate object." Later on, Charles wrote to Morris Graves, who was planning to spend some time in Los Angeles: "I suggest when we have something lined up, you come down and stay with us for a weekend or something to look around. Our house is most adaptable to hermits! There is a room with a separate entrance and said hermits need only put their heads out and bark for food or conversation when needed."

Walter Arensberg, the collector, was a close friend who lived near us. It was he, with his preference for pre-Columbian works of a static and geometric type, who said that Charles's collection reflected Charles's "taste for a dancing eye." As a result of this difference in the tastes of the two collectors, there was no conflict between them in choosing works of art. They never wanted to buy the same object. They never clashed—the *dancing* eye and the *static* eye. Every object that attracted Charles was part of a pattern, and the whole effect of his collection was one of unity and one-ness. I would say that Charles sensed the feeling that the painter experienced when he took flight emotionally.

Charles was very sure of his eye—his adrenalin was violently stirred by things that he saw, and this excitement was indescribable when sharing his vision with others. Charles was happy in the role of mentor, and I can never recall at any time his being happier or more grateful than when he introduced his agent to the world of painting. His agent-friend became a skilled and successful collector, and Charles basked in the progress of his pupil. I remember the proud, parental look on Charles's face when this same agent spotted and bought an unsigned drawing in London. It turned out to be a Miró! I could only stand on the sidelines and feel the warmth that reflected from Charles's sense of his achievement. A great pleasure that he was fortunately able to know in his lifetime. On his reading tours, Charles was always looking out for young painters. Partly it was a voyage of discovery, and partly it was the fact that he knew he could help them. If Charles bought one of their pictures, it started them on their way.

Charles's collection, as I said, had unity and I made every effort to keep his collection together, but no one museum or gallery around the country could or would assume the expense and responsibility of touring it. So the collection was sold at Parke-Bernet Galleries in New York during October 1966. His pre-Columbian art, his works by Morris Graves, de Staël, Manessier, Matthew Smith, Siqueiros, and Pierre Soulages. I hope that each buyer added his purchase to a dedicated collection, and that, in the shattering of this crystal-clear collection into hundreds of pieces, the vision of Charles will persist.

Charles once said in an interview, "I've done many things in my life that I didn't want to do, just so I could buy the paintings I loved. I've even done television." One of the things Charles bought with television was time to spend on acting King Lear.

Lear was a recurring theme in conversations with almost everyone Charles knew. He talked about it, read from it and studied it, and wondered when, how, and where he could do it. When the chance to go to Stratford-on-Avon came, the intensive study began. For about a year the intensive study went on. Often he felt the crumbling of his confidence—almost as if he had been deceived by Lear himself.

Charles's Lear was a human man, but painted on a very large canvas, a king-size canvas. The theme of remorse and guilt, which was contained in his interpretation of the role, was part of his own nature. He had been magnetized by the part all through his life, it seemed, in the spirit of a conqueror out to cleanse himself. Lear was Charles and Charles was Lear, and this identity with Lear was not a comfort. He had endlessly wakeful nights and nightmares about death all through the Stratford run and always afterward. At every performance he really reached out and stretched to solve the mystery of the crucifixion of Lear, but he never did quite touch on that ecstasy. Life is not long enough for an actor to untie and reweave the intricacies of the King Lear warp and weft. Nor could Charles untie and reweave all the intricacies of his own warp and weft.

The vast set for *Lear*, with its larger than practical throne, was primitive and impressive, and gave one a feeling of prophetic doom that was just right. Charles climbed to his throne like a tired giant—wearing a great green robe. With his long white hair and beard he certainly dominated the cast on stage, as a William Blake figure can dwarf a sea of people. The sculptor Henry Moore, after seeing a performance, said: "His interpretation of Lear was entirely different from any I had seen before—it was very warm, human, and deeply tragic. He was exhausted after it and we did not stay long in his dressing room, but even though tired, he was very sweet to Mary, my daughter. I think he was then already ill, but his spirit was tremendous. He was a great actor, and his death was a big shock and sadness to me."

If his own personality resembled Lear's, Charles often associated me with Cordelia. I would speak my mind, as Cordelia did, to the point of hurting—but being quite truthful, too. Charles often said he wished that I could play Cordelia. But Cordelia was a young girl, and when the time came I wasn't that. He would sometimes quote to me Lear's speech when he and Cordelia are led away to prison: "We two alone will sing like birds i' the cage."

Before *King Lear* opened, Charles was already playing Bottom in *A Midsummer Night's Dream*, and he was superb in it. In contrast to the tragic *Lear*, I do not think that he had one unhappy moment with *Dream*. The performance of Bottom brought out the antic side of Charles and he was uproariously funny. On days Charles had off, I would drive him slowly round the countryside in our Rover to little towns and villages in Warwickshire, and we would have dinner in a pub or small hotel. We often walked in the woods and fields and always came back with wild flowers. In Act Four, Scene Six of *Lear*, Lear enters "fantastically dressed with wild flowers," and for this I made Charles many a wreath of various flowers we would find—speedwell, bryony, and vetch, bound together with grasses.

The death of King Lear cannot but give the audience a feeling of elevation and relief that such self-inflicted torture should have ended for him. It is almost as if the scene of Lear's death were written from the other side of the grave, and it was at this moment that Charles's performance, retroactively, made its power felt. The audience's sympathy reached back and back for his King Lear. I mark this moment well; for, looking back on Charles's own life, I am forced to feel, also, the relief at the end of his own self-inflicted burden.

Charles died determined that he would try Lear again.

I am still angry that Charles died. Who can there be to look at things with? The garden, the paintings. To discuss food with? Should we have a stew tonight? Did he know that Mickie (his cat) caught a garter snake on the hill? Everyone misses these little things more than the big ones. When Charles was alive I always sang in the bathtub, went upstairs two stairs at a time. But not now. I mean, not particularly because of growing older, but because after Charles died it never did occur to me to dash around the house.

The passage of time reaches a high speed as you get older. All older people know this, and constantly say, "Well, Christmas is here again . . . so soon." You learn that life is not long enough to plant a tree. It will grow, but you will never see it become a great tree. You feel like the White Rabbit in *Alice in Wonderland*—no time, no time.

I live in the same house with the pool, the bananas, orioles, and cereus; and from day to day quietude and peace are pleasant. Raucous noise and violence are avoided. But in this I only join many millions of people of all ages. And at this point I realize what Charles must have felt from his childhood on. No time, no time.

Author's Prologue

The first film actor I ever saw was Charles Laughton. Or half-saw.
My mother had taken me to a movie theatre—I can still smell the
damp linoleum and the faint scent of moldering plush—sometime
in the first five years of my life, to an innocuous comedy with Virginia Bruce and Melvyn Douglas, and we came in at the tail end
of the bill's first half. My eyes focused, without much interest, on
this old picture, crossed through with lines as though the celluloid
had creased, like the human skin. I saw the engine room of a submarine (I knew all about submarines, as I had built a model one
at home), a sudden flood of water from a dozen valves (I knew
the details were wrong, and told my mother so). Inside the cabin
was a doughy man in a uniform, his face the color of lye; he was
struggling in the water, striking out feebly at a portrait of his wife
on a bureau; the water went up over his head, and he began
gurgling in a death agony. My mother's hand fell across my eyes,
to protect me from the sight—how little she knew about the
chilly realism of children!—and I remember her black kid gloves,
ribbed along the finger like Minnie Mouse's, trying this sentimental protection. I fought their guardianship; and peeked

through the fingers at the screen, which was now divided into silver slivers. I got my sadistic wish: I saw Charles Laughton drown.

For years after that, I was fascinated by this actor. The virus of buffomania in my veins, lingering in the bloodstream like the malaria parasite, drove me back again and again to see his homely, cunning, sleepily observant face, mugging away in bad World War II films. It was not until adulthood—or are all movie maniacs perpetual adolescents?—that I began to see his good films, to realize his powers as an actor. Drastically uneven, he was capable of being a raw Yorkshire ham, when the part didn't attract his intellect; but often, he could be among the purest and sharpest of actors, devoid of tricks.

It was, therefore, a surprise and a pleasure when Elsa Lanchester asked me to write this book. I had admired her often: her daffy Greenwich Village artist in *The Big Clock* (1948) had been as memorable, in its way, as Laughton's flabby, malign business chief in the same picture, and there was a moment of confrontation in the action I had always treasured, when she painted a witness to a crime for him, and it turned out to be a sub-Picasso still life. She was very funny, too, in *The Spiral Staircase* (1946), as a servant constantly squabbling with a gruff old bulldog; she was touching in *Tales of Manhattan* (1942), as a considerate anxious wife to Charles's struggling pianist; she was enjoyably horrendous as the *Bride of Frankenstein* (1935).

Meeting her then, was like meeting an old friend; and in our months of working together, she did not disappoint. As in her movies, which she could almost have written herself, she is full of quirks of humor, unpredictable little barbs designed to puncture any balloons of self-esteem one might optimistically set afloat; and she has a view of life that goes wittily widdershins, i.e., anticlockwise. She tends to judge people, I soon found out, by their honesty; a point of view which has left her with very few to admire in the history of Hollywood. Each day, at 2 P.M., I would arrive by car at her odd, pre-World War I house, with its turret and bristling garden, its large, pallid rooms, rather resembling a small monastery, and make my way through Scotch mist or rain or feeble winter sunshine to her door. Sometimes her Irish maid opened the door to my ring; at other times she herself greeted me, small, with an impish iconoclastic smile that at once told the visitor not to take himself too seriously, and welcomed him cheerfully in. The dimpled chin, clever mouth, sharp, observant eyes, and surprised red hair were very much as I had always seen them. Upstairs, there was Charles's study/library, and next to that, his somber bedroom; between, a small bathroom, the whole exuding a melancholy charm. I would sit there for a couple of hours each day fortified by strong black tea and marzipan cake, rummaging through the metal cabinets in which Elsa had stored her many files of interviews, clippings, letters, and photographs; my task was to render the mass of material coherent, to give what we hoped would be a clear and consistent portrait of the extraordinary actor, half genius, half ham, that she had married. She would read through my bad typing, the annotations and corrections in a handwriting closer to Chinese than to English, with quiet patience, sharpening a phrase here, cutting another there, suggesting additional material when a paragraph seemed too thin; she was never censorious, never evasive, when the serious question of Charles's homosexuality came up. Her mind was needlingly acute, sometimes pricking the vanity of the author, which was no doubt good for him, sometimes offering a small amount of praise, which was just enough to stimulate without inflating his silly ego, and at all times effectively concise and precise. Really, she should have written the book herself. But she is as painfully honest with that self as she is with others; she knew she could not be objective.

She did not want her name on the book, except as author of the introduction. Yet much of the book owes its existence and nature to her attentiveness and her influence. She did her best to temper my chief weakness as a writer, my hyperbolic effusiveness; she channeled my excessive energy; she metaphorically tied my hands when they tended to run too fast across the typewriter. Those months in the Hollywood Hills were often painful and tiring; writing about Charles's miserable emotional life and severe final illness exhausted me spiritually and physically, so that the last weeks of work were like carrying a thornbush on my back. But she sustained me: her generation—she is now in her seventies— was made of sterner stuff. And above all, I was sustained, as I had been in writing a previous life of Katharine Hepburn, by the account of a great love affair which the book would expose for the first time. Elsa's love for Charles Laughton, and his for her, was an affair of the intellect and of the heart which was asexual, which did not depend on the bed as its foundation. When Elsa had her lovers, all men, Charles accepted them; and she accepted his male lovers as well. True, there were moments of severe tension and unhappiness between them, as a result of their separate and sometimes conflicting sexual lives; but on the whole they enjoyed great happiness together, in their love of nature, in their love of houses, in their shared readings, and especially toward the end in their working together on Charles's performance as King Lear. Their lives, both energetic and creative for all their suffering, enlivened by a very British sense of the ridiculous, filled with a love of America, were, in the last analysis, valuable and good. That is the reason I was drawn to writing this book; and that is the reason I gained much from writing it, learning, more than ever before, of the resilience, courage, and strength of the human spirit.

Dedicated to Jane Wilson.

*Special acknowledgment to
David Bradley.*

Charles Laughton

AN INTIMATE BIOGRAPHY

ONE

In 1899, when Charles Laughton was born there, the ancient Yorkshire town of Scarborough had a population of just over thirty-eight thousand people. The newfangled automobile was rarely present in the streets, which still echoed with the clop of horses' hooves, the creak and roll of carriages, carts, gigs, and broughams, and the crack of drivers' whips. The town was a fashionable seaside resort, and along its fine esplanade, developed into a handsome marine drive some eight years later, there was a bright parade on sunny afternoons of men in tall hats and cutaways, and ladies vivid with bonnets and ribbons and bows. The sea-bathing was good, and at weekends, when the weather was clear, men and women and children appeared in all their finery of zigzags or polka dots, stepping down from the candy-striped bathing machines onto the pebbles of fine golden-white sand for a dip in the Atlantic. Slicing the smooth half-moon of the coast, a bold peninsula, shaped like a hammer, divided the North and South Bays. On the peninsula's highest point stood the twelfth-century ruin of Scarborough Castle, with a high sturdy keep, a moat, and turreted walls.

Scarborough was then, as it remains, a watering place, noted for its two mineral springs, and the elegant Spa House with wide and formally elegant gardens. The town, windy and spacious and sparkling in the light, boasted a handsome aquarium, a museum—a Doric rotunda with a great natural history collection—theatres, and pompous Civil Service buildings. Nearby, the Derwent bubbled up from its rocky spring before flowing southwest to the Ouse and then on to the Humber. Scarborough was noted for its temperate climate—seldom above sixty degrees or below thirty at any point in the year, though the wind could drive the rain as fiercely across The Esplanade, scattering pedestrians and turning umbrellas inside out, as any wind in the Orkneys. Anybody walking along the peninsula or the beach front could see, in rain or shine, a scattering of fishing boats out in the bay, and sometimes a handsome yacht, owned by one of the richer families.

Robert and Eliza Laughton were among the shrewd couples who shared Scarborough's growth in popularity at the end of the nineteenth century, and flourished there in the hotel business. Robert's father, portly and jovial, had spent his life as a Jeevesian butler to a family in Derbyshire. When he had saved a sufficient sum to retire, he had moved to Scarborough, and bought a small inn. Robert Laughton grew up at the inn, where in his early twenties he met a spirited Irish girl, Eliza Conlon, who came from Irish farmfolk living in Seaham Harbor, Durham. Eliza had run away from home to escape an arranged marriage to a farmer. She had found a job as a barmaid in the Laughtons' inn. She broke off an engagement to another man when she met and fell in love with Robert.

After Grandfather Laughton's death, the couple bought the shabby Victoria Hotel, which had seen better days, and worked hard to clean it up and redecorate it. Two years after they moved in, with business thriving, Charles was born, followed in later years by his brothers, Tom and Frank.

Neither parent was particularly attentive to Charles during his formative years from one to twelve. His father was constantly spending his free time hunting and fishing, and his mother worked relentlessly on the accounts, taking care of the guests, and building up a staff. Most of the time, Charles and his brothers were in the care of a succession of maids; Charles would frequently corner one or another of these maids in a linen closet, dressed up in sheets and pillow cases, declaiming from various plays and poems.

At three years old, he was certainly too young to note the local South African War riots or the return of the veterans through the streets which that notable Scarborian, Sir Osbert Sitwell, so vividly recalled in his memoir *The Scarlet Tree*. But Charles must have remembered the Scarborough Pageant of 1912 in which the history of the city through twenty-five centuries was given in marvelous tableaux: Prehistoric Incidents (the programme went), Romans and Druids, the Sack by Hardrarda and Tostig, Henry II and Albemarle's Castle, Friars, Edward I's Court, Gaveston, Richard III, Stafford, the Siege of Scarborough, the Release of George Fox, the Tossing of the Mayor, a Miscellany (Gabler's Fair, Press Gang, Smugglers, Pirates, Visitors, Celebrities, and Eccentrics).

This vivid event, held in the grounds of the great Castle, must have appealed strongly to young Charles's sense of drama. He loved a traveling show, George Royle's *Fol-de-Rols*, and the Punch and Judys in the small striped theatres at the beach. He loved the pierrot troupes which performed on the sand, the pantomimes at a local theatre, particularly *Mother Goose*, and the locally famous Mirrorama, a scenic "world voyage" achieved with revolving back cloths. He also loved the early film comedians John Bunny and Flora Finch; and he created his own tiny model theatre with marionettes.

Fat and awkward, Charles found a wonderful escape in the magical world of theatre—a general term which he knew even at that early age could encompass many kinds of performance. He also found release in his sweet and devoted Aunt Mary, who took him for magical walks in the Yorkshire Moors, showing him varieties of wild flowers. Liking flowers, and learning their botanical names, liking to dress up and play-act, and hating to go hunting with his father—he never forgot the horror of a golden pheasant, its wings glittering in the sun, swooping into death from a well-aimed bullet—Charles showed early what the world condemned as feminine traits. Though he never talked about his suffering as a child, one can easily imagine that his fellow pupils at the local preparatory school tortured him for his fatness, his fondness for beauty, and his disinterest in boyish games. It was typical of him that when he went hunting for bird's eggs in the high cliffs of Scarborough, he never disturbed the nests, only observed the delicate colors and marveled at the movement of the birds' wings.

By the age of thirteen, he had already indicated to Aunt Mary —and to others who could see—a poet's soul. Quite unkempt, he was deeply private, hypersensitive, tortured, and terrified. Yet, like many nervous and sensitive children, he saw deeply: his mind stripped away pretenses and pierced through to the truth. He knew that the Roman Catholic Church in which his parents worshipped was not for him. Yet he was schooled first at a convent of French nuns, where he learned perfect French, and later at Stonyhurst College, the famous Jesuit school.

Stonyhurst must have seemed to his mother the anteroom to a pure and holy Life Everlasting, but for Charles it must have resembled an anteroom to Hell. The histories of the College, filled with praise for so many pupils distinguished in the arts, the army, or the priesthood, characteristically omit any mention of the College's most gifted pupil since Arthur Conan Doyle in the 1870s. In its echoing and cheerless halls, Charles was directed through a life of cold discipline. For six years, from 1912 to 1918, he endured this ordeal. There was no system of half-yearly "removes" or short vacations as there was in other colleges; holidays were briefer than elsewhere; and until shortly before Charles's arrival, there had been no Christmas holidays at all. Watchful Jesuit officials were in charge of the boys every second—on or off the playground, in or out of the classroom—and worked in night shifts in the dormitories to suppress the slightest show of sexual feeling. They were grim plainclothes policemen, not permitted to smile while on duty, or to talk to their charges.

Each day began with the public recital of morning prayers and the ceremony of the Mass. Prayers were spoken before and after each class, and in the evenings there was a visiting of the Blessed Sacrament, the Rosary was recited, and other duties performed. Each day closed with night prayers, said publicly in the boys' chapel, or with Benediction in the school chapel. Each May the boys gathered solemnly around the statue of Our Lady—the patroness of all sports and studies of the boys—in the gallery between the boys' chapel and the refectory.

Since Charles is not mentioned in any of the football or First XI teams for the whole of his stay, we can find firm support for the conviction that he must have been less than good at games. Since he would also have been revolted by the religious rituals of the College, we can assume that he was regarded as something of a freak and an outsider, as well as the traditional Ugly Fat Boy, by the other pupils. We do know that he excelled in the school debates, held in the Community refectory during dinner, with the boys pitted against each other in pairs, and at the "Academies," or school concerts, in which he is reported to have recited Latin verse while the orchestra played Schubert's *Military March* and J. T. Hall's *The Wedding of the Winds*. He also appeared in a school play, *The Private Secretary*, typecast as a rotund innkeeper, drawing his interpretation from a study of his father. "We hope to see more of C. Laughton," the *Stonyhurst Magazine* dramatic review said.

An unhappy memory of Charles's later years concerned what a Jesuit priest told him about committing sin: "If you do this, my boy, you will be punished through all eternity, through all eternity, *through all eternity*. Do you know what eternity is? It is as if this world were a steel globe and every thousand years a bird's wing brushed past that globe—and the time it would take for that globe to wear away is all eternity."

So far as we can determine, Charles left Stonyhurst without taking the London Certificate which might have led him to a university, perhaps even Oxford or Cambridge. He refused a commission, enlisting as a private instead in 1918, in the Royal Huntingdonshire Regiment. He was sent to France to serve at Vimy Ridge. He never wanted to discuss what happened there. But official records of the war show that the Royal Huntingdonshires were involved in a major bayonet attack, and Elsa recalls that Charles once told her he had to stab men to death with a bayonet. For so sensitive a boy, so aware at nineteen of the preciousness of life, this must have been a horrifying experience. He was demobilized with the Armistice. But only a few days before, he had been gassed. For most of his life after that, he broke out in severe rashes on his back as a result, and for a time the gas affected his larynx and trachea.

He returned to the Pavilion Hotel, which his parents now

owned, still dressed in khaki and suffering from the physical, emotional, and mental effects of the war. His father completely failed to grasp what Charles had suffered, and when Charles started to talk about it, he simply told him briskly, "All right, my lad, now that's all over you're going to get down to some real work!"

Charles was packed off to London to learn the hotel business at Claridge's—in turn as bill clerk, control clerk, and cashier's clerk. He had just turned twenty. His collar frequently went dirty because he spent all of his money for tickets to the gallery of various theatres. He saw *Chu Chin Chow* thirteen times, *A Kiss for Cinderella* ten times, and the Drury Lane revue *Razzle Dazzle* nine times. His favorite actor was Sir Gerald du Maurier, whose brilliant style and great elegance appealed to him and influenced him later on. And at the front desk at Claridge's he marveled at the procession of stars, including Hilda Trevelyan, Ellaline Terris, and Ethel Levy, who passed through the famous lobby.

He returned after a year determined to bring the Pavilion up to date. He removed the somber, flock-sprayed wallpapers from the public rooms, had them repainted and redesigned, and hired a dance band; as a result, the wealthy people of the nearby Midlands came there for their summer holidays, and the hotel flourished splendidly. In between heavy duties at the hotel, he put on and acted in amateur theatrical productions for the Scarborough Players. These included *Trelawney of the Wells*, *The Dear Departed*, *Hobson's Choice*, and *Becky Sharp*—all at the Scarborough Amateur Dramatic Society, and favorably reviewed in the local papers. Finally Charles, at twenty-four, decided to enroll at the Royal Academy of Dramatic Art in London. Only his father supported him in this desire; everyone else joined his mother in warning him that an actor's life was hard and penurious. It was tragic that, in 1924, just when Charles needed his father's help and encouragement most, Robert Laughton died.

Charles moved to London later that year, after redecorating and redesigning his father's farm at Lockton for his mother to stay in, and choosing new managements for the family hotels. He had to experience the ordeal of his entrance examination at the academy: Shylock's speech about Jewishness from *The Merchant of Venice*. He studied the part desperately, day and night, for sixteen days, gazing into the mirror in his room in Holborn, trying on false beards and costumes, pacing the Strand reciting the lines.

When he finally arrived for the test he was shaking with terror. He put his hat down on the seat beside him. Somebody sat firmly on it, but he was much too nervous to say anything. Finally, he performed the test in front of a distinguished group of judges, all of whom unanimously agreed that he was very promising indeed.

Charles trained with the great Russian director Theodore Komisarjevsky, a gentle, mouse-colored man with a charming personality, who had had a tremendous effect on operative and theatrical productions in Moscow, introducing revolving stages and avant-garde set design. Charles made an immediate impression at RADA, and Kenneth Barnes, the genial director of the academy, noted his solidity, force, and skill in students' productions. Barnes said later:

> He was a student of infinite curiosity, always searching for a new and meaningful approach to whatever character he was studying . . . sometimes, unobserved, I would watch him as he moved round one of the Academy's rehearsal rooms. He could people the room with his impressions and many variations . . . it was magic. Other students would take time to drink coffee and chatter, but Laughton used this time alone, creating.

Charles appeared in French plays directed by the famous, intelligent, and sensitive teacher Alice Gachet, who took him under her wing and greatly helped his career, and also as Falstaff in *The Merry Wives of Windsor*, a part he failed in because he had drunk too much champagne to steady his nerves before the performance. His RADA report card for the autumn term of 1925 read:

> *Voice Production:* Has only attended a few classes with careful work when he came. Diction very fine.

> *Acting:* Laughton is sometimes too brilliant. He is handicapped and knows it. He'll persevere and prosper.

> *French:* Knows what he wants. Gives everything to it. Breaking bad habits.

He made his London debut at the St. James's Theatre on March 24, 1926, in a RADA students' competitive performance, which included scenes from Molière, Shaw, Shakespeare, and Chekhov. Charles appeared as Dr. Sutcliffe in Tom Robertson's *School*. The *Times* critic wrote, "Although the part is not a very promising one, Charles played it with assurance." He was highly praised for his appearance as Sganarelle in Molière's *Le Médecin malgré lui*, and as Falstaff in *The Merry Wives*. The judges— Irene Vanbrugh, Henry Ainley, and Allan Aynesworth—awarded Charles the Bancroft Gold Medal as the finest actor the academy had produced in a period of one year.

As a result of this honor, Charles could enter the professional theatre with a degree of confidence. But already at that early age he was insecure, afraid of the very thing he wanted most: public success. He was painfully aware that his heavy body and unhandsome features would preclude him from a career as a romantic leading man—that he would be condemned to act unattractive human beings for the rest of his life. We can only imagine what suffering, at the outset of his career, this certain knowledge caused him.

Charles's first professional role in the theatre was as Osip in Komisarjevsky's production of Gogol's *The Government Inspector*, opening at the Barnes Theatre on April 26, 1926. Komisarjevsky's work was generally praised: he made a roundabout of the stage, with multicolored streamers, a brass band, and stock-still police officers like toy soldiers, all conveying a vivid abstract of Russian village life. Often, the stage revolved with the players on it; they changed into refreshing patterns, eye-catching and iridescent, as the scenes spun about, and the director even allowed the stage itself to show up weaknesses of character: one pompous man trips over it, a stupid man is rendered even dizzier by it. Claude Rains as Ivan Alexandrovich, the ordinary man mistaken for a government inspector, was widely admired; and Charles's acting as a lazy old servant was said to have had flair. He was on his way.

In July of the same year, Charles appeared in Ibsen's *Pillars of Society*; in Chekhov's *The Three Sisters*; in Chekhov's *The Cherry Orchard*, playing the clerk Epihodov; and in Ferenc Molnár's *Liliom*.

Gradually, through an accumulation of these stage appearances, Charles had begun to establish a reputation by the middle of 1927. His heavy, powerful face—which he thought ugly but which was in fact an expressive and sensitive instrument of his will and his spirit—his effectively used, massive body, his voice with its sudden unexpected emphases on certain words, his characteristic sidelong blinking glances—all these were marks of a highly individual actor in the making. The fact that he doubted his talent made him more of a perfectionist than ever, refining and again refining his technique. The pain of his own existence—his awareness of his lack of looks, physique, elegance—could be quenched in his guises as an actor. The fat boy at school, butt of all jokes, could stand on a stage and feel the applause soothe him like a balm.

How much he learned from Komisarjevsky we cannot now determine. Probably the richness, the fluidity, the sense of vivid color that make the Russian's productions so famous in their day, and which so tragically are not preserved for study on film, impressed Charles and gave him much inspiration for his own stage productions years later. Also, on the evidence of Komisarjevsky's own books, we know the director's emphasis on freshness in a performance, the sudden surprising thrusts of observation which could bring a character to life, and which became characteristics of Charles in performances throughout his life.

Charles's career continued purposefully. He was a powerful General Marskoff in J. B. Pagan's *The Greater Love*, a play about the French Revolution staged at the Princess Theatre, of which Basil Gill was the magnificent star. He was amusing as the cuckold in Harrison Owen's *The Happy Husband* at the Criterion, and ruthless and unscrupulous as Count Pahlen in *Paul I* at the Court Theatre. None of these productions enjoyed long runs, but it did not matter: Charles was gaining experience, learning with painful slowness the timing, the delicacy of gesture, which were to mark him as an actor. Studying the lines in relation to the work as a whole, and in terms of their innermost intention, was agonizing; but nothing could stop his drive.

After *Paul I* closed, Charles was at last offered a major starring role—Mr. Prohack in Arnold Bennett and Edward Knoblock's version of Bennett's popular novel, of the same name. *Mr.*

Prohack is the story of a lower middle-class Treasury official, hen-pecked and family-ridden, whose salary is moderate and whose prospects are dim. He pads about in velvet smoking jacket, baggy trousers, and carpet slippers, blinking sleepily—a perfect image of mediocre obscurity. Suddenly he becomes heir to £100,000. His life changes spectacularly overnight. He engages a secretary, gambles in the Romanian oilfields, flirts with a member of the aristocracy, Lady Massulam, and gradually shows how tragicomic the life of a rich man can be.

Arnold Bennett was far from happy with Charles's selection as Prohack, and he did not realize that Charles was imitating him wittily at rehearsals. Not recognizing himself in the portrayal, he would sit in the orchestra and yell out, disconcertingly, "Not a bit like Prohack! Not like him at all!" Charles acted the role with all of his now considerable technical command. A characteristic touch, introduced by him, occurred when Prohack learned he had inherited his fortune. Most actors would have insisted on leaping about and tossing hats in the air. Charles simply sat, blinked, and quietly absorbed the good news—a cool clerk to the last. The reviews were encouraging to Charles, but not to the play, which critics thought much too insubstantial. Charles enlivened the performance on the first night by making himself up and dressing to look exactly like Arnold Bennett—moustache and all. The press recognized this immediately. Bennett was furious and called Charles up to say, "Who do you think you are? How dare you do such a thing? A piece of gross impertinence . . . unwarrantable effrontery . . . Goodbye." But later he realized he was wrong. He accepted the point of the joke, the play turned out to be a success, and Charles's performance became most popular.

Mr. Prohack was important to Charles for another reason. Early in the rehearsals, he met a young woman who was to be the most important figure in his life.

TWO

Elsa Lanchester, cast as Mr. Prohack's impish secretary Mimi Winstock, was already established as a remarkably gifted star in her own right. She was famous for her red hair, huge surprised eyes, tiptilted nose, witty mouth, dimpled chin, and Bohemian cloak and sandals. Her parents were vegetarian pacifist socialists who had chosen never to marry. Her father was an accountant, and the family had to struggle along on a tiny income, constantly moving from one depressing home in Clapham Common to another. She was selected for Isadora Duncan's free school of dancing in Paris; her refusal to be impressed by Miss Duncan's posturings made her unpopular there. Already, as a child, she had developed a deeply irreverent attitude toward pretentiousness, pomposity, self-importance, and complacency—sitting targets for her accurate satires in later years.

At eleven, she started a Classical Dancing Club in London, made up of neighborhood children, with a tiny magazine, *La Danse*. Even before her teens, she was being called "Bohemian" by snooty ladies—in her hand-woven clothes, her sandals, with her red hair sticking straight up, resisting all combs and definitely not succumbing to hats. She was delighted when people called her mad, and she trained her parrot to scream at them.

At the Margaret Morris School in Chelsea, Elsa became an assistant teacher of dance. At fifteen and a half, she began taking private pupils, and gradually developed an organization called the Children's Theatre. The theatre presented songs, dances, and plays, including *Tom Thumb*, by Henry Fielding, and Jane Austen's *Love and Friendship*.

In her late teens, Elsa started a nightclub in Charlotte Street with Harold Scott and Matthew Norgate, called the Cave of Harmony, offering plays and a midnight cabaret—and no drinks. Many important players appeared at the Cave of Harmony's famous midnight show, and Elsa and her colleagues, Philip Godfrey, Harold Scott, and Helen Egli, used to present Victorian songs, including "The Rat-catcher's Daughter" and "True Friends of the Poor." The Cave of Harmony flourished, and moved to Gower Street. The tall, physically fragile, and witty John Armstrong, the great costume and set designer, wrote funny lyrics, painted the scenery, and ran the coffee stall.

The Cave of Harmony became very popular in intellectual London, and Elsa enjoyed great personal success. She not only revived the music hall songs of the Victorian era, her training in dance made her body a startling and funny instrument of her satirical nature.

She appeared for Sir Nigel Playfair as the Larva in Karel Čapek's *The Insect Play*, in Congreve's *The Way of the World*, Sheridan's *The Duenna*, and *Riverside Nights*, mostly written by A. P. Herbert, a revue in which Charles saw her. She wore a top hat, a short ballet dress, risqué for its time, and bare legs—and caused a sensation. She sang her vintage songs, filled with doubles entendres, in the Midnight Follies at the Hotel Métropole, the Cavour, the Café Anglais, and the Café de Paris. She sang at parties given by Lady Cunard, who admired her version of "I've Danced with a Man Who Danced with a Girl Who Danced with the Prince of Wales." It was typical of the snobbery of the period that Elsa was not treated like a guest at these aristocratic soirées, but often was given her meals on a tray in a secretary's room. When somebody mentioned Charles Laughton's name to her at the time, she said, "Who's Charles Laughton?"

By the time Elsa played the secretary in *Mr. Prohack*, she—like the rest of London—emphatically knew who Charles Laughton was. The stage at their first rehearsal was almost bare and lit only by two working lights on iron standards. Charles made almost no impression on her. His face was pale, his hair was mousy, his suit was pale gray and badly pressed, and his arms were loose at his sides. He looked like a floury baker's assistant. Elsa said to him, as they sat on wooden stools for the reading:

"James Agate[1] talks about you a lot. He said that you were the only actor who should play with me in *The Pool*.[2]

Charles replied: "So we nearly met before this play."

"Yes, I suppose so. Tony Bertram, who wrote the play, is a friend of Jimmy Agate's. It wasn't a very good play. *I* don't think it was very good, anyway."

The conversation continued desultorily. The "cold" reading went on. Charles stumbled over his lines, Elsa was awkward and, in her own estimate, "appalling." At the lunch break, Charles, Elsa, Lydia Sherwood, and other members of the cast went to a cheap restaurant in Sloane Square for cold roast beef and pickles. Then, one evening, Charles asked Elsa to have dinner with him at a French restaurant, also in Sloane Square. They ate sole véronique. Later, they had lunch there, and divided the cost of the meal. They discovered that they both had Aunt Marys who loved flowers—Elsa's was a gifted painter of flowers. They discovered a mutual rapport, a dislike of pompous and pretentious people, honesty about life, a mutual disrespect for high rank, for religion, and for the aristocracy which ran England. They were mavericks, freethinkers, and, for all their open skepticism, basically idealistic. Moreover, they were strongly attracted to each other. Elsa was deeply drawn to Charles's personality, and never found him physically unattractive. He was clearly drawn to her refreshing, unpredictable, eccentric beauty.

One weekend they managed to meet at Waterloo Station and slip away by train for a Sunday in the country. They visited a house built by Clifford Allen, who had been a socialist conscientious objector during the war, and who had Sunday literary-polit-

---

[1] A famous critic of the period.
[2] A play in which Elsa, but not Charles, had recently appeared. She acted as a Thameside tavern girl, Harriet.

ical gatherings, attended by intellectuals of the time, including C. E. M. Joad. Charles did not care for Allen, whom he thought a dull, high-minded intellectual snob, but he enjoyed the seven-mile walk from the station that chilly day, along a stream, picking bunches of flowers with Elsa—king cups and forget-me-nots and daisies. They scarcely spoke a word—just silently enjoyed the experience together. They had become fast friends, and more than that. They had no sense of calculation toward each other, of what one could do for the other, or what their relationship might become.

Toward the end of the run of *Mr. Prohack*, Elsa invited Charles to a party given by the editor Gerald Barry at his flat. Maynard Keynes, Lytton Strachey, Frances and Vera Meynell, and members of the Chauve-Souris Company were present. Elsa danced with several people and even executed some solo dances, wearing an evening gown with a silver lamé bodice and a mauve taffeta ruffled skirt, and an amethyst necklace. Charles sat glumly and palely at a buffet table, hardly speaking. She went back to him often, but more often left him to resume her dancing. He did not join in.

After the party broke up, Charles and Elsa took a cab. He was to drop her off at her flat and then go on to his own. It was 3 A.M. When he opened the door for her, took her to her apartment door and said good night, he rather clumsily kissed her on the lips. He was as surprised by himself as she was. They looked at each other, astonished by what had happened. They clung together for a moment. She asked Charles in.

They sat and talked for about an hour in Elsa's room with its wicker armchair, box spring bed, gas fire with its shilling meter (if the meter ran out, the gas did too), hand-woven rug, and green-painted wheel-back chairs, a typical "Bohemian" bed-sitting room. Elsa often had friends dropping around when Charles was there, including James Agate, John Collier, Agate's gifted protégé the drama critic Alan Dent, and Anthony Bertram. Charles's landlady objected to ladies after hours, and they both moved: he to the Garlands Hotel, and she to a room in Bloomsbury Square.

One evening, Charles's mother came to dinner at the Garlands Hotel. The conversation in the small, mahogany-paneled, drab dining room with its white tablecloth, was nerve-racking. Elsa tried to keep it going, without much success. She wore a simple black dress and green amber beads, Charles's first gift to her. They went up to Charles's rooms still talking awkwardly, with many pregnant pauses by a coal fire in his sitting room. Finally Elsa said, "My eyes pop out so much that I have to make a hole in my pillow at night to be comfortable!" At last Mrs. Laughton laughed. The ice was more or less broken.

While Charles and Elsa's relationship continued, in February 1928, *Mr. Prohack* closed. Charles almost immediately went into a production of Benn W. Levy's play, A *Man with Red Hair*, based on the novel by Hugh Walpole. It was his first meeting with Levy—a dapper, smallish, smartly amusing man just under thirty. They became friends.

Hugh Walpole had written *Portrait of a Man with Red Hair* in the early 1920s. Scribbled on notepads on a train in Switzerland, it was a shameless potboiler in which Walpole took little pride, although the reviews when the book appeared in 1924 were surprisingly glowing. Dubbed by Walpole "a penny dreadful" it went into rehearsal at the Little Theatre in February 1928. Although the play ran only two months, it became somewhat of a *succès de scandale* for Walpole, Levy, and Charles.

Charles's part as the sadistic Mr. Crispin, who imprisons a young girl (Gillian Lind) with the aid of his insane son (James Whale) and a group of sinister Japanese servants, provided a field day for Charles. It was his first chance to be a monstrous villain. The *Times* critic summed up London opinion with: "Mr. Laughton has made so subtle, so revoltingly brilliant a study of sadistic obsession that the man, and through him the play, is well-nigh intolerable. Mr. Laughton by face, by voice, above all, by imaginative bodily movement, compels suspension of disbelief."

Hugh Walpole was pleased with the performance, writing to a friend, "He brings my terrible man to sickly life—marvelous!"

In preparing for his part, Charles spent many hours under the arches of Charing Cross practicing with a bull whip for the play— later, he duplicated the use of the whip in his film *Island of Lost Souls*. Elsa became rather sickened by the whip practicing, much preferring their weekends together at a pub in Sussex called the Dog and Duck, where they registered as husband and wife. The pub's owners rather proudly thought they were the only people in the world who knew the secret of the Laughtons' marriage. They must have been surprised when the real marriage actually took place.

Charles and Elsa's nights at the Dog and Duck were enjoyable but uncomfortable. They had to put up with lumpy feather mattresses, and a cheerless journey to the bathroom, which was down a narrow hallway, up a few steps, and then down some more. The hot water was disconnected at night and the lock on the bathroom door refused to work. But, despite the discomfort of the inn, Charles and Elsa were happy, sitting up until all hours talking about plays, about getting a flat, about marriage. Finally, they moved into a beautifully furnished flat together—in Dean Street, Soho, in a house that had once belonged to Karl Marx. The flat was back to back with another rented by Kenneth Grahame, author of *The Wind in the Willows*, with whom they had a waving acquaintance.

After *A Man with Red Hair* closed, Charles opened immediately in May 1928 in Michael Morton's play *Alibi*, based on a novel by Agatha Christie. It was a Hercule Poirot story: the Belgian detective investigates the murder of Roger Ackroyd, stabbed to death in his study after dinner. Given the difficult challenge of making a real human being out of Miss Christie's pasteboard figure of Poirot, Charles gave an excitingly detailed performance, his Belgian accent flawless, his cross-examination of the various witnesses quietly deadly, his final pointing at the killer electrifying in its impact on an audience. Henry Daniell, later to play in Charles's films *The Suspect* and *Witness for the Prosecution*, appeared as an icily detached butler in the production.

Alibi was a critical and commercial hit, and ran for several months. Charles and Elsa decided to move once more during the run, eventually finding a small top-floor flat at 15 Percy Street off Tottenham Court Road. Originally the servants' quarters, it was a modest place for two such celebrated professionals, but salaries in those days were not high. They had two rooms made into one, a very small extra room, a tiny kitchen, and an equally tiny bathroom. They liked living there.

On Sundays, they sometimes traveled up to Scarborough and stayed, very prim-and-properly, in separate rooms at the Laughtons' Pavilion Hotel. They walked through the heather of the Yorkshire Moors, explored antique shops, and bought furniture at incredibly low prices.

During the run of *Alibi*, Charles and Elsa diverted themselves with a lighthearted venture into moviemaking. Ivor Montagu made a series of three short films[3] in which Elsa starred. Amusing two-reelers, they offered Charles tiny supporting roles. Their only historical value is that they were written, in a mood of cheerful abandon, by H. G. Wells. They reflected much of the spirited fun which had marked the heyday of the Cave of Harmony, and rapidly became collectors' items.

Following *Alibi*, Charles appeared with great distinction as Mr. Pickwick in Cosmo Hamilton and Frank C. Reilly's adaption of Dickens' novel. Charles made a wonderfully jolly, indignant, myopic, and potbellied Mr. Pickwick, and the reviews were excellent. Just after the run ended, Charles and Elsa made up their minds. They were married in a London registry office on February 9, 1929. They decided to get married on a Sunday to avoid the press. But a few groups of journalists stood huddled in the rain outside their flat, and they had to run a gauntlet, racing out separately—Charles going first—and taking off to the Registry Office in separate cabs. In pouring rain, they reached their destination, with John Armstrong and another friend, Iris Barry, as witnesses. Elsa wore the same ring for the ceremony she had worn for several months—but after the marriage she never wore it again.

They left at once on the boat train, taking the channel steamer from Folkestone to Boulogne, and changing to the overnight train for Switzerland. In Arosa, they joined Charles's mother and Frank Laughton at the Seehof Hotel, where they stayed two weeks for the skiing. Charles proved to be very expert on the icy slopes, but Elsa was all arms and legs, and fell over, bruising herself; she also felt a little hurt by Charles's mother's rather cool attitude toward her during this odd honeymoon *en famille*.

Continuing with the tour, the Laughtons left by train for Naples, where they luxuriated in a splendid salmon-pink suite at the Grand Hotel. They picnicked at Paestum, explored the ruins, and returned to the hotel so covered in white dust they looked rather like two snowmen. At Ravello they climbed hills, picked vi-

---

[3] *Bluebottles, Day-dreams,* and *The Tonic.*

olets, wild crocus, and green iris, and ran into Osbert Sitwell and William Walton, who were staying at Amalfi.

At the end of the honeymoon, they hurried back to London, where Charles began rehearsing at once for his part as Jacques Blaise, a Renaissance astronomer, in Jacques Deval's play *Beauty*. The play did not succeed. Charles's performance was not particularly admired, even though some aspects of it appear to have re-emerged almost twenty years later in his performance as Galileo in Brecht's play. He suffered from laryngitis during the brief season; and the throat, caused by inflamed tonsils, worsened during the run of Sean O'Casey's play *The Silver Tassie*, in which he was miscast as a powerful Irish athlete, injured in the war, who becomes possessed of a fiery poetic spirit in the wake of the Armistice.

Despite his miscasting, Charles gave a striking performance in the play, which was directed by Raymond Massey in an impressionistic style that apparently owed much to Komisarjevsky. Critics agreed that Charles delivered Harry's great speeches with an impeccable Irish accent and bravura attack: the speech about being a cripple ("Legs were made to dance, to run, to jump, to carry you from one place to another; but mine can neither walk, nor run, nor jump, nor feel the merry motion of a dance"), the speech about wine ("Red wine, red like the faint remembrance of the fires in France; red wine like the poppies that spill their petals on the breasts of the dead men"); and above all the speech about the loss of ability to be part of nature ("I'll say to the pine, 'Give me the grace and beauty of the beech'; I'll say to the beech, 'Give me the strength and stature of the pine.' In a net, I'll catch butterflies in bunches; twist and mangle them between my fingers and fix them wriggling on mercy's banner").

Knowing Charles's love of trees, flowers, and butterflies, one knows what it must have cost him to utter those words. The scene of the trenches in Act Two must have been another anguish, bathed in blue light, and directed with powerful realism by Massey: Charles had never been able to endure the slightest reference to his own "going over the top." Feeling his way into the part of a crippled veteran, he must have agonized over what it would have felt like if his own body had been shattered, if he had been left broken and impotent by the war.

Emlyn Williams, who played a small part in the production, never forgot Charles wheeling himself around backstage wrestling with O'Casey's lines like a maddened baby. Williams wrote to Elsa:

> *The Silver Tassie* had an enormous company and I never got to know Charles, just "Good evening" in the wings. He was seriously miscast as a young Irish footballer, knew it, and looked miserably tormented unless (characteristically) he was chuckling like a schoolboy at the humor of the genuine Irish actors in the play. In the last scene, though, he suddenly became free. I have never forgotten, walking in on that dance hall, the sight of Laughton, in an invalid chair, careening wildly among the couples. Whenever I hear the tunes "Avalon" and "Over the Waves" I see him panting around like a maimed bull on wheels, enraged, tragic.
>
> In the late 1920s, when any male star in London was inevitably tall, slim, handsome, debonair and—to the naked eye—well bred, Charles Laughton was something. How could a young man (young? when he was not looking like a slow-witted baby he could be taken for 50 instead of 30)—how could a character actor like this one, patently built to support the stars, short, fat, moonfaced —how could *he* be a star? But he was, and he became the talk of London.

It was the beginning of a happy professional association with Emlyn Williams, who was at the outset of his career as both actor and dramatist. Williams appeared also in Charles's next play, Reginald Berkeley's farce *French Leave*, in which Charles had a high old time as a red-faced, mustachioed, brass-buttoned old brigadier-general.

While Charles was appearing in *French Leave*, which closed after only a few weeks' run, Edgar Wallace, the panjandrum of thriller writers, was preparing a production of a new play he had written, and which he would direct himself. The title was *On the Spot*, the subject Al Capone and the Chicago gang wars. In the autumn of 1929, Wallace had followed the suggestion of his American publisher, George Doran, that he should visit New York and appear before his vast American public. Characteristically engaging the royal suite on the S.S. *Berengaria*, he sailed to New York. By his own count he gave 98 interviews at the Hotel Marguery, and shook 1,250 hands. In twenty-four hours in Chicago he undertook a tour in which he was shown by his hosts Al Capone's house, the flower shop where Dion O'Banion was shot down, and the St. Valentine's Day garage. He came home to England with vivid memories and a large folder full of police photographs of Capone and his men.

He closed himself up in his study and wrote *On the Spot* in four days. He sent the play to Charles the moment his secretary Miss Reissar had typed it. The small parcel made its way from Wallace's luxurious home at 31, Portland Place, to Charles's modest digs at Percy Street. Charles liked it, and, though suffering from severe tonsilitis, with an operation imminent, went over to Portland Place to see the great man.

It was rather like an audience with the Pope. Wallace, frog-mouthed, haughty, and self-important, sat behind his study desk in a sumptuous purple dressing gown with gold tassels, worn over a Savile Row gray suit, shod in monogrammed carpet slippers, and brandishing a very long cigarette holder. He had three dictaphones, two secretaries, and three glass screens which framed him dramatically.

Wallace described to Charles his Capone-ish central figure's ornately vulgar life-style, unwittingly delineating someone who resembled himself. He spoke of Perelli's pipe organ, stained-glass windows, scarlet carpets and divans and Chinese mistress, his tongue wrapping itself around the verbose descriptions. Charles left feeling slightly dizzy, too exhausted to refuse the role.

A week later, Charles went into the hospital to have his tonsils removed; he and Elsa decided to affect his recovery by taking a brief holiday in the hotel where they had spent their honeymoon at Ravello. There, Charles read and reread Wallace's expert pages, studying Italian types and the Italian accent in order to be able to master the part of Tony Perelli, Wallace's copy of Capone.

Back in London, Charles went into rehearsals, with Emlyn

Williams cast, at Charles's suggestion, as his chief henchman. Dark and swarthy, Williams could easily be made to resemble an Italian. Edgar Wallace, assisted by Carol Reed,[4] handled the entire production himself with an air of imperial grandeur. Williams writes of a rehearsal:

> In the center of the stage, Laughton. He was alone, absorbed, mouthing lines to himself, pacing to and fro like a caged schoolboy, growling, glaring, totally dedicated. Then the schoolboy would stand stock still and peer into space with a slight scowl as if he had just been turned down for the part of Cupid in the school play and was settling for a sulky Bacchus.

The play opened on April 12, 1930, to a chorus of approval from both audience and critics. Charles Morgan wrote for the New York *Times:* "Perelli . . . an evil, callous, vain and hypocritical man, is a portrait far above the average of those seen in crook plays, partly because Mr. Wallace has troubled to get into his mind, partly because Charles Laughton's study of evil is extraordinarily accomplished." The London *Times* critic said: "It is Mr. Laughton who gives the evening a distinction beyond the ingenuity of its contrivances. The insolence, the vanity, the weary skill of a masterly criminal are all in his study of Perelli."

On the Spot ran for just under a year and confirmed Charles's position as one of the greatest actors of his generation. He went on tour with the play. One night in Manchester something went wrong. He was walking toward the pipe organ, on which he would appear to be playing "Ave Maria"—actually a record was being used backstage—when the organ started to play before he touched it. The audience yelled with laughter.

At the final curtain, Charles said: "Ladies and Gentlemen of Manchester, you are the only people in the world who know that I cannot play the organ. Will you keep my secret?"

For months, during 1930, Charles and Elsa were almost continuously in search of a little house in the country. Every Sunday they explored Surrey, Kent, Essex, the Chilterns, and the Thames

---

4 Later to become famous as the director of *The Third Man* and *Oliver!*

Valley without finding exactly what they wanted. Then, about six weeks after the run of *On the Spot* began, Elsa went to dinner at the home of the architect and town-planner Clough Williams-Ellis, a vibrant, energetic man with a handsome, weathered face, and his wife Amabel in Hampstead. Elsa told them of her problem. Clough had just the place they needed: a cottage in Surrey he was about to give up because he was going to spend much of his time at his new and subsequently celebrated experimental model village, Portmeirion in Wales.

As soon as Elsa heard the description of the cottage, her heart skipped several beats. She telephoned Charles excitedly at his theatre. The cottage was called Stapledown, it was only twenty-eight miles from London, and was built 625 feet up in woods with bracken growing all the way to the front door. It was about two miles to the nearest village, and was surrounded by pine trees and bluebells.

That Sunday, Charles and Elsa took the first available train with Clough to see the cottage. They fell in love with it at once. It was thatched, built of wood, and supported by pine-tree trunks about one foot off the ground. They bought it quickly.

For the next few years, Stapledown was a constant pleasure, a binding factor in the marriage. Clough Williams-Ellis was to build the Laughtons a brick cottage on the grounds, but in 1929 there was just the wooden house lit by kerosene lamps, with a hole in the garden doing service as a toilet. Later, they had an "Elsan" outdoor septic tank, which unfortunately became known as "Elsa" when the "n" was rubbed off.

A man called Burns used to drive up from the village of Clandon to cook the vegetables for them on oil burners—which took two hours to boil potatoes—to grill steaks or fry them on iron griddles over the wood fire. They washed with tin jugs of water and tin basins; often they used cold water, because it took an hour to make it even lukewarm on the burner. But the Laughtons didn't think of it as primitive. They enjoyed the blazing fires, with an endless supply of wood for kindling, and the quiet nights, even when it was so cold they had to heap six blankets on the beds.

They enjoyed the passage of the seasons—a panorama of color in those woods. The first flowers which appeared after the frost melted were the wild anenomes; then banks of primroses broke through; a sea of bluebells; wild crab-apple; wild daffodils; bracken growing so high they could walk under it; buttercups and cuckoo flowers; butterfly orchids and bee orchids; poppies and miles of foxgloves. They made sloe gin with sloes picked from the hedges and barley sugar each fall. Later, they made a circular garden around the brick house, where they planted vegetables and flowers. Charles became ecstatic when he saw the Michaelmas daisies at Christmas time. The daisies attracted butterflies, and one year he and Elsa saw an unforgettable sight: thousands of butterflies with saffron and russet wings covering the pale blue of the flowers like a tide.

Driving in the country with Charles could be a hazard. Unable to drive, he would thrust his arms across Elsa in the driver's seat in order to point out some tree or flower, often blocking her view and almost causing an accident. If she didn't stop the car so they could pick the flower he had admired, he gave her serious trouble. The sight of a double rainbow against black clouds on the South Downs of Sussex threw him into transports of joy.

In London, during their days together at the time, they found a continuing mutual love of painting. They went to the Tate and the National Gallery a great deal; in later years, they were frequent visitors at the Lefevre Galleries, where John Armstrong exhibited.

After *On the Spot* ended its tour, Edgar Wallace wrote from 31 Portland Place asking Charles if he would take on a new thriller, *The Mouthpiece*, about a crooked lawyer. Charles was disappointed with the play, feeling it had none of the dash of the earlier work, and he declined it. He also turned down a subsequent Wallace concoction, a play about a Chinese swordsman, despite the most earnest pleas by its author.

During the hiatus that followed his rejection of this last part, Charles appeared unhappily in three best-forgotten films of the period[5] and acted a bit role as a greedy old diner in a nightclub scene of E. A. Dupont's famous picture, *Piccadilly*. More auspiciously, he took on one of the best stage roles of his career: William Marble, the unhappy murderer of Jeffrey Dell's version of C. S. Forester's novel, *Payment Deferred*. He and Elsa became

[5] *Down River, Wolves,* and *Comets,* a "talkie revue."

friendly with the gentle Jeffrey Dell and his friend Eileen during rehearsal; Elsa appeared as Charles's daughter in the play. Charles was in good spirits while reading and discussing the script; but as he began to rehearse, the character of Marble began to obsess him. He became irritable and touchy and depressed. He blamed the director, H. K. Ayliff, for making his life miserable. He searched Marble's character so deeply to discover his motivations in killing an Australian nephew for money that he began to feel like a murderer himself. Elsa began to sense, for the first time in two years of marriage, an acute sense of strain in Charles.

It was during the rehearsals of *Payment Deferred* that Elsa suffered a severe shock. Late one night, a young man was stopped by a policeman and questioned for loitering outside the Laughtons' address on Percy Street. While the policeman was talking to the youth Charles arrived with Jeffrey Dell. The policeman told Charles that the boy claimed Charles had picked him up in a park the previous day and had taken him home, promising him money, which he had not given him. Now the youth had come back to get the money from Charles. Charles denied this whole story to the policeman, who took the boy in custody.

Charles and Jeffrey Dell went upstairs to the flat. Charles was in a state of shock, pale and trembling. Elsa asked him what was the matter. He was barely able to reply. When Jeffrey Dell went into the kitchen Charles told her, forcing each word out, "Something awful has happened. I have something to confess."

It was the most difficult moment of his life. He had had relationships, brief and futile, with boys or men, for some time now, and had never dared tell Elsa about them. Knowing that the arrest of the boy would certainly lead to a court case and there was no alternative but to admit the truth, he told her of the episode in the street a few minutes before and that in fact he had taken the young man home from the park.

Elsa could have burst into tears, collapsed, or struck Charles. But instead, her compassion fighting her despair, she simply said all she could say in the circumstances: "It's perfectly all right. It doesn't matter. I understand." Charles might have been able to tolerate her anger, but her pity and consideration for his plight caused him to break down completely. He started to cry.

Jeffrey Dell came out of the kitchen and they sat drinking silently in the living room, the tears running down Charles's cheeks.

Later, the case came to court, but Charles escaped being prosecuted: the judge simply warned him against "misguided generosity," and the matter was allowed to drop. Just before the opening of *Payment Deferred*, what might have been a major public scandal was thus narrowly avoided.

Elsa became psychosomatically deaf for a week as a result of the shock, and had great difficulty continuing with rehearsals for *Payment Deferred*. She says:

> I suppose I shut my ears off. I have since realized, or was told, that it was probably a sort of reaction to some news I really didn't want to hear. Later on, I asked Charles what had happened. And he told me he was with this fellow on our sofa. The only thing I could say was, "Fine, OK. But let's get rid of the sofa."

Weighed down with this episode, which he and Elsa never discussed again, deeply guilty because of his homosexuality, Charles opened in *Payment Deferred* to a good press and to a very enthusiastic public reception. His William Marble, terrified, distraught, filled with guilt, became all the more real because of the harrowing events that had occurred during rehearsal. It was one of his most realistic performances—the American producer Gilbert Miller signed him and Elsa to appear in the play on Broadway as soon as the run was over.

By the time he and Elsa left England, Charles was beginning to stand head and shoulders above his contemporaries. It was a great age of matinée idols in musicals—wasp-waisted, slightly effete, tending toward white tie and tails—figures like Ivor Novello and Jack Buchanan. Charles was a startling new phenomenon: the character actor as star. Simultaneously, in the movies, Emil Jannings was emerging as an unglamorous leading man. Charles had already begun to occupy a similarly eminent position on the stage. The influences on his style were clear: George Robey, the greatest music hall star of his day, with his famous eyebrows and heavy emphatic voice, and Sir Gerald du Maurier, whose marvelous refined technique was a constant astonishment to Charles.

Charles emerged at precisely the correct moment. Naturalism had begun to be a feature of the English theatre, and the talkies had just begun. The demand for actors with fine voices and forceful stage presences was increasing steadily. Within a year he would begin his most widely admired career—as a movie actor.

The events of Charles's career in the Twenties were so swift, the rush into play after play so extraordinary, that he scarcely had time to get his bearings before departure. In the five years since he had left the Royal Academy of Dramatic Arts, he had appeared in several major productions, of which only the most outstanding have been mentioned in these pages. Many of these had had limited runs, had been transferred quickly with different casts to Broadway, or had collapsed, for one reason or another, after a few weeks. Yet, in this period of strain and speed, Charles had rapidly and certainly developed as a master of his art. His versatility alone would have marked him as a great actor. He had played simple villager, treasury official, sadistic murderer, Belgian detective, and Italian gangster with equal flair, daring, and attack, his sheer presence an overpowering force in the English theatre. His sleepy sidelong glances, combined with slow, ashamed, nervous blinks, his odd, crablike sidelong walk, his round shoulders and head thrust forward, his sudden unexpected looks of darting suspicion, his hearty guffaws and frightening enigmatic silences were the talk of London. He could be angry bull or docile lamb, naughty child or vicious parent; he could look like a schoolboy just caught robbing a piggy bank, seated awkwardly with hands folded, thumbs up, knees touching, eyes blinking heavily, or he could be an overwhelming monster with a whip, authoritative and icily cruel, like every evil schoolmaster rolled into one.

Charles and Elsa continued to live as they had before—a life of what today seems to be considerable austerity, in their tiny flat in Percy Street and in their simple country cottage among the trees. For Elsa, with her background of poverty, the life seemed actually luxurious. They very seldom quarreled; they were comfortable.

1. Charles aged five. They hoped he would go in the Navy.

2. Charles about twelve years old. Scarborough.

3. Charles, nineteen, in the Royal Huntingdonshire Regiment.

4. Charles in *Hobson's Choice*. Scarborough Players, early 1920s.

5. Pictured with his mother, outside Pavilion Hotel, Scarborough, early 1930s.

6. With Elsa in *Rembrandt*. (London Films)

7. Bedroom scene with Elsa as "Anne of Cleves," *The Private Life of Henry VIII*. (London Films)

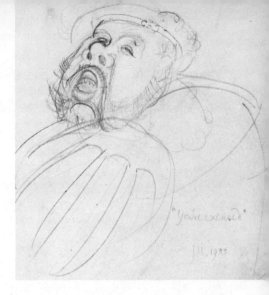

8. Sketch by James Mason. Old Vic production of Shakespeare's *Henry VII*, 1934. (James Mason)

9. Josef von Sternberg (left), Merle Oberon, and Charles on the set of the unfinished *I, Claudius*, 1936. (London Films)

Their parents accepted the marriage with pleasure. Elsa's mother saw security for Elsa's future in Charles, and she adored him. Charles's mother was also friendly after the ice was broken. Charles's brother Frank was very close, but Tom never particularly liked Elsa.

Though Elsa never brought up the subject of Charles's homosexuality, it ate into her. It ate into him as well. Charles said that Elsa did not want to have children, because she didn't want the father to be a homosexual. The real reason was that she didn't feel fond of children herself, and she disliked Charles's "talking down" baby talk to children. But Elsa felt a maternal instinct for Charles take over: she felt great compassion for him. Their sexual life together gradually ceased to exist. He was deeply in love with her, and she was deeply in love with him. It was a love that survived the loss of sexual communion, a binding emotional and intellectual force which nothing could shake.

THREE

Despite fairly good weather conditions, Charles was seasick during part of the crossing to New York for the Broadway production of *Payment Deferred*. While he lay in his berth, Elsa enjoyed walking round the decks, and she went to all meals, Charles joining her when he could. The Laughtons were met in New York by the writer Helen Deutsch, who was working for Gilbert Miller at the time, and by several photographers and reporters. Elsa sat on deck posing for cheesecake shots, her skirt pulled up above her knees, with a lifebelt in the background. At the Chatham Hotel, they met Iris Barry, the stimulating, enthusiastic founder of the London Film Society and later the Curator of the Museum of Modern Art's motion picture library, and they flipped through a pile of telephone messages, including one from the journalist Dorothy Thompson. As they watched, appalled, Iris, temperamental and talking incessantly, grew drunk on bathtub gin, and by sunset she was completely out for the count.

Payment Deferred opened out of town in New Haven and moved to the Lyceum Theatre on September 30, 1931. Charles and Elsa appeared at women's club luncheons, sitting on a dais while people stared at them and drank tea. They were annoyed by the inquisitive celebrity-hungry stares, the ugly hats and veils and piqué gardenias, and Elsa, acting in self-defense, used the back of her programs to draw witty, spidery caricatures of the spectators.

Too grim for Depression audiences, *Payment Deferred* closed after only three weeks, despite excellent reviews. Burns Mantle in the *Daily News*, Percy Hammond in the *Herald-Tribune* and Brooks Atkinson in the *Times*, led the chorus of praise for Charles's performance, which earned a standing ovation on the first night.

Gilbert Miller sent the Laughtons to Chicago for a limited three-week run. Though nervous about reports of gangster mobs, and forced to attend a horrible party in which pornographic and gynecological films were shown, they generally enjoyed their stay. Venturing out in the icy winds off Lake Michigan was a quite hilarious experience, involving hanging on to ropes strung between the sodium lamps to prevent being blown over by the powerful gusts. They took pleasure in their hotel, which had a convenient market in the basement, and Elsa prepared many of their meals in the suite.

Charles and Elsa were about to leave for London when Jed Harris, the acrid "boy wonder" of the Broadway theatre, came to dinner in New York and suggested that he should produce a Broadway version of *Alibi*. Charles was delighted to sign with this young, brilliant, and already legendary producer, but he soon had cause to regret his decision. Theoretically letting Charles direct the rehearsals, Harris in fact differed violently with Charles's interpretation until Charles felt destroyed, plunged into despair. Elsa's only defense was to draw acid little sketches of Harris on the hotel stationery.

Although Charles was well received, and again enjoyed a first-night ovation, the play failed after forty performances. But those who were lucky enough to see him were as enthralled by his witty, relentless Hercule Poirot as London audiences had been. He electrified audiences once more in the great climactic scene when he exposed the murderer.

Charles and Elsa returned briefly to England. Very short of money, they moved into a couple of small, slightly decayed Italianate rooms above a restaurant, l'Étoile, in Charlotte Street, where they arranged for their cabin trunks to be pulled laboriously to the top of two very steep flights of stairs. The ceilings were painted with cherubs, cloudy porticoes, and pink roses. No sooner had they settled in than telegrams began arriving from their friend Benn W. Levy in Hollywood, announcing that Paramount wanted to sign Charles to a long-term contract, and that Levy had written a script especially for Charles. It was entitled *The Devil and the Deep*, and Charles's role was to be that of an insanely jealous submarine commander married to Tallulah Bankhead. Although the idea scarcely appealed, and Charles dreaded succumbing to a long multipicture contract, he had to face up to economic reality. After many anguished discussions with Elsa, he finally accepted.

Once more the Laughtons crossed the Atlantic. After Charles signed the Paramount contract in New York, they set off by train to California, stopping in Flagstaff to see the Grand Canyon, where they took photographs of each other, and alighting at Albuquerque to note the oddity of Indian traders commercializing their own handicrafts. Benn W. Levy met them at Pasadena with the photographer John Engstead. Levy drove them to the Beverly Wilshire Hotel for a couple of nights' stay. Looking out of the hotel window, they weren't impressed by the view: a sea of white clapboard houses almost unrelieved by trees. They commented to each other on the contrast between this banal work of man and the God-given beauty of the Grand Canyon.

The people at Paramount had found them a home: the last house on La Brea Terrace in the Hollywood Hills. It wasn't very inspiring. It was somewhat run down, made of stucco, with broken screens in the living room, and neither Charles nor Elsa felt particularly comfortable in it. Luckily they had a chauffeur-houseman named Rogers, an excellent cook, who drove Charles to work early in the mornings, cleaned, made the beds, shopped, and prepared meals. Elsa was depressed during Charles's absences. Hollywood ignored her, despite her British success, and she worried Charles with her despair, spending her days wandering about, lost in an alien environment. She would walk up the hill to the Outpost sign behind her house, through scrub and yuccas, coming home with armfuls of wild sage and mariposa tulips to liven up the rooms; but these did not compensate her. She was aware of the spring, the time of arrival of the first bluebells in English woods, and she was desolate. She worked off her depression and homesickness only partially by writing to friends in England, and by taking trips with Charles into the desert, to Lake Arrowhead, or to the still lovely Japanese Gardens.

The Devil and the Deep was delayed by Tallulah Bankhead's illness, and Charles first made *The Old Dark House* for James Whale, at the behest of Benn W. Levy, who had written (with R. C. Sherriff) that horror film's script as well. Based on a novel by J. B. Priestley, *The Old Dark House* was an outrageous old-fashioned barnstormer about a group of travelers stranded in a crumbling mansion in Wales. With his passion for Gothic excess, Whale, aided by his writers, created a gallery of bizarre characters played by a predominantly British cast: the attenuated, epicene Ernest Thesiger, with his bird bones and spinster's voice, acted Roderick Femm, a tippling scion of a mad family; Brember Wills played his dwarfish, evil brother; Boris Karloff was a growling bearded butler with a scarred face; and an anonymous woman—a typical Whale joke—played a 102-year-old-white-bearded man piping away sagely in an attic. Charles, cast in one of the very few "normal" roles, as a tweedy, plus-foured Lancashire businessman in love with a Cockney waitress—Lillian Bond—acted with warmth and sympathy, touchingly playing the brief scene in which he reveals his profound affection for the girl. But generally speaking he was wasted in this nice funfair spookhouse of a movie.

He had mixed reactions to his director and his fellow players. He was irritated by Whale's touch of vulgar greed, the habit he had of talking about "running [Hollywood] gold through his hair," and he and Elsa, with their plain tastes, did not appreciate the excessive Italianate baroque style of Whale's house. But they both admired Whale's pictorial and dramatic skill as a picture-maker. Lillian Bond came over to La Brea Terrace in her pretentious automobile, with a mother the Laughtons never really warmed to. Ernest Thesiger was rather aggravatingly mannered, talking shrilly about "arsenic apples" when Rogers served tinted mint-flavored apples with dinner, and walking down Hollywood Boulevard carrying a yucca wrapped in a newspaper. Boris Karloff didn't greatly appeal to Charles either. Whale, though from a poverty-stricken background, had become a cool, elegant, and terrible snob and spoke contemptuously of Boris, calling him "a coal-heaver, a truck driver." While Charles hated that kind of class consciousness, he still didn't warm to Karloff.

When work finally began on *The Devil and the Deep*, Charles wasn't in a good mood. He had little or no time for the director, a slight, mild-mannered contractee, Marion Gering, or for the visibly bored, world-weary Tallulah Bankhead, who played a sentimental hit of the period over and over again on a phonograph between scenes. He had never liked Bankhead. At a party in New York she had drunkenly called him "a big, fat slob" in front of everyone, and now, on the set, she was far from charming.

Bankhead, lank-haired and languid, also had an infuriating habit of breaking up on her own lines. In one scene she asked a radio operator, "Have you tried the radio?" and he replied, "The oscillator isn't working." Bankhead roared hoarsely with laughter every time she heard the line, exasperating not only Charles but Marion Gering as well. The actor playing the operator was so upset he stumbled into a water cooler; it shook the lights and a camera filter fell on his head.

Making the picture was an ordeal. Scenes stretched into the night. The water in which the cast was frequently submerged was very cold, and Bankhead drank hard liquor heavily. Actors who worked on the picture—as well as the cameraman, Charles Lang —noted that Charles would stand behind the flats, working himself up with agonized concentration for every scene. In sequences in which Charles was seated at a dinner table, talking jovially, his legs under the tablecloth shook violently.

By contrast, Charles worshipped Gary Cooper, whose effortless, almost invisible technique impressed him deeply. People despised Gary Cooper, feeling that he wasn't acting at all, that he simply played himself. But Charles—and Elsa—felt that he had exquisite technique, making the lighting of a cigarette a marvelous thing to watch. Years later, when Gary was dying, Charles was too deeply disturbed by his own fear of death to go and see him; but he mourned him, and always felt guilty that he had not plucked up enough courage to visit the sickbed.

The Devil and the Deep's final scene—in which the demented commander sinks his own submarine and drowns—was very difficult to shoot. The entire set had to be submerged in a tank filled with hundreds of gallons of water; there were two takes of Charles wrenching open an iron door to flood the vessel, floating along a companionway on a rush of water, and falling down in the final engulfment. In the first shot, the water came over Charles's commander's cap and it floated off, creating a comic effect. So the director ordered the set drained; Charles had to change his clothes —he was shivering with cold, sopping wet, and forced to drink neat whiskies to keep his circulation going—and then go through the whole scene again at four in the morning, with the cap taped to his head.

In this sequence, Charles worked exceptionally hard for the director. He rejected the use of a double as the Commander is swept down a companionway on a flood of water. Later, he is seen striking futilely at Bankhead's picture on the wall as the water swallows him up, screaming with hysterical laughter in a frightening revelation of a man dying insane.

Charles was not especially enthusiastic about his role of Charles Sturm in *The Devil and the Deep*. But Benn W. Levy wrote an effective screenplay, and the part of Sturm was a gift to an actor. Shown in the opening scene picking up one of his wife's love letters, Sturm is established from the beginning as an oily, menacing monster, constantly telling an Irish fishing joke to anyone who will listen, haw-hawing with laughter at its vulgar denouement, humiliating his wife, and dwelling with sharp jealousy on the handsome face and figure of his rival, the naval lieutenant Cooper played.

The streak of self-punishment in Levy's portrait of Sturm was clearly intended to reflect what Levy felt to be Charles's own. When Sturm asks his wife, "Why do you torture me?" she says, "You're torturing yourself." Benn Levy knew what he was up to when he gave Charles the short speech enviously addressed to a visibly embarrassed Cooper: "Must be a happy thing to look as you do. I suppose women love you. It must be a happy thing."

In the late spring of 1932, the Laughtons appeared at sneak previews and openings of the two films Charles had just finished. They went to dinner with James Whale and his friend David Lewis, who later became a gifted producer at MGM and Warners, and Elsa began to feel a little more comfortable in Hollywood. Iris Barry came to stay in the studio apartment over the garage, and aside from her drinking she was a pleasant companion, and a fine conversationalist. Elsa at least felt she had someone to talk to and walk with; they would stroll down Hollywood Boulevard, Elsa taking photographs.

Very early that summer, Cecil B. DeMille, the unbridled potentate director whose flashing eyes, jodhpurs, and boots suggested a turn-of-the-century general, began work on *The Sign of the Cross*, an elaborate version of the old Wilson Barrett play which he had bought from Mary Pickford. This was an overheated melodramatic epic about Nero's martyring of the early Christians, scenes of sticky piety alternated with lip-smacking displays of mass murder in the arena, gladiatorial combats, and orgies accompanied by exotic dancing girls. DeMille had seen Charles in *Payment Deferred* in London, on the first lap of a tour that took him to Russia and Egypt, and he had never forgotten him. He called him in to his huge office at Paramount, the size of a president's or a dictator's, and strode around the room addressing Charles like a schoolboy while a secretary, Gladys Rosson, doggedly wrote down in shorthand every word he himself said, omitting Charles's replies. DeMille made it clear he wanted Charles to play Nero like a Lyceum villain, all cold rage and beetle brows, bringing to the role the icy contemptuous mood he had brought to Sturm in *The Devil and the Deep*. Charles had very different views. He had read Sienkiewicz's *Quo Vadis*, as well as the classic texts, and knew that Nero was a ridiculous, flaunting queen, pampered and self-indulgent, a psychotic baby who would have been an open laughingstock if he had not had the unbridled power of an emperor. There is evidence in DeMille's files to suggest that Charles had in mind the posturings of Mussolini, Nero's successor in Rome in 1932; and evidence, too, to suggest that DeMille was infuriated by Charles's opinion of the method of playing the part. DeMille detested and feared homosexuals and balked at the idea of portraying one, even as a villain.

Nevertheless, he had met his match in Charles. He was vexingly distracted with internal studio problems. He had just returned to Hollywood after a long absence abroad, following the collapse of his own independent company. He had many enemies at court, and he was forced to allow Charles to play the role as Charles wanted to. Charles, daringly for a homosexual, played Nero as one. He supervised his own makeup—plucked eyebrows, rouged cheeks, a touch of lipstick, and a false Roman nose which had a disconcerting tendency to slip during scenes—and he worked out a lisping, Shirley Temple voice that proved richly amusing. The production was dogged by hilarious mishaps. According to his usual custom, DeMille had a bathroom scene which allowed its occupant to show off an amount of flesh just this side of the Legion of Decency. When the Legion complained, DeMille expressed surprise that they objected to cleanliness.

DeMille provided Claudette Colbert, playing Charles's wife Poppaea, with an Olympic-sized marble pool full of genuine asses' milk. Preoccupied with the front office, he neglected to have the animals milked on the third day of shooting, and by nightfall Charles and everyone else in the studio was aware of the disagreeable smell of milk turning into cheese. When Claudette returned to the set after a brief visit to her home, and people told her what had happened, she said, "Well, it's supposed to be a cheesecake shot, isn't it?"

The other great problem took place when Charles was watching the Christians being slaughtered by the lions. Since even DeMille stopped short of having extras nibbled, he arranged for lambs' carcasses obtained from a Los Angeles slaughterhouse to be wrapped in Christian robes. The lions proved to be quite uninterested in eating lamb but stood meekly in line lapping up a seepage of blood. The trainers were forced to crack whips, set up a din, and finally replace the lamb with beef before the doped, toothless, and jaded beasts managed to give a decent display of voracity.

Charles wanted Elsa to play the almost naked young male slave who accompanies the emperor everywhere, but DeMille finally decided it was too risky. If Charles were to play the role as a flaunting homosexual, he might as well go the whole hog and give him a muscular and handsome young man, daringly quite naked in every shot, to sit next to his throne and hand him bunches of grapes.

Charles was only in a handful of scenes, all of them delightfully absurd. At the outset, he is seen plucking his harp, reciting an adaptation of Petronius, and brooding over the destruction of Rome. Later, he is exhausted after a night of excess ("such delicious debauchery"), nursing a hangover, a typical early Thirties touch, while a girl manicures his fingernails. In a brief sequence, he attempts to forgive his favorite Marcus Superbus' dalliance with a Christian slave, only to be overruled by the vengeful Empress; and at the finale he is at his most extravagantly effeminate, presiding over the imperial games, watching lasciviously as an Amazon spears a pigmy, gobbling grapes and vine leaves with equal pleasure.

Simultaneously, an MGM film version of *Payment Deferred* was being cast with Charles repeating his role and Maureen O'Sullivan instead of Elsa in the part of the daughter. For Elsa, losing this role was the last straw. Her homesickness became overwhelming as the long shooting schedule dragged on. She decided to throw up everything for a while and go back to England, where most of her friends were, and where she was a famous name. Charles was sorry to see her go in the middle of a production, but he knew that she would be happier, and he made it easy for her. He was also aware that since she couldn't get work, life was very difficult for her; that she was suffering because people wouldn't say "hello" to both her and Charles; they would ignore her as obscure "Mrs. Laughton," whereas in London she would be called, with great respect, "Miss Lanchester."

Back in London, Elsa found a home for herself and Charles that was to last for seven years. It was a flat in Gordon Square. The basement, ground floor, and first floor were rented to a law firm, and Elsa rented the three top floors, subletting the lower two. Gordon Square was in the heart of Bloomsbury, a beautiful place and an ideal location in view of Elsa's many friendships among the Bloomsbury group. She modernized it with the aid of an architect named Wells Coates. After *The Sign of the Cross*, Charles, very eager to see it, sailed to England and approved it. Several gifted and famous intellectuals lived nearby: Francis and Vera Meynell, Maynard Keynes, Clive Bell and his friend Benita, who later became Elsa's great friend and the wife of the painter and designer John Armstrong. Duncan Grant was living with Clive Bell's wife, Vanessa. Elsa enjoyed this marvelous circle, she also knew the Sitwells—Osbert, Edith, and Sacheverell—and she liked to feel herself part of the group. Elsa acquired Virginia Woolf's cook, Nellie Boxall. Nellie was a Boulestin-trained Cockney, and a treasure.

Charles and Elsa spent happy times at Stapledown as well, walking through the woods and picking flowers. Over the years, Elsa—and Charles when he was in England—made many improvements to Gordon Square. John Armstrong painted Wells Coates's handsome sliding doors between the dining room and the sitting room, and wooden bookshelves with underlit glass tops running through two rooms, while Coates simplified everything, creating a big window at the back which gave a view of plane trees and gardens. Charles and Elsa brought many branches and twigs from Stapledown to Gordon Square, and placed them in pots along the lighted shelves.

Back in Hollywood, Charles was busy making *Payment Deferred* at MGM. Irving Thalberg, the delicate young production genius who ran the studio with Louis B. Mayer, had seen Charles in the stage production, and admired him deeply, but several members of the MGM board felt that he was not a box-office draw and insisted the picture be made on a budget unusually low for that studio. Lothar Mendes, a run-of-the-mill Hungarian director, was engaged for the job; and the script followed the play with few changes. Charles, disappointed that Elsa had not been given the role of his daughter, was listless during the film. His only real interest lay in helping the young actor Ray Milland, who played the murdered nephew, to walk through a door without bumping into it, and to read his lines with a modicum of conviction.

This film version is so feeble, so clumsily managed, that today it holds little or no interest. Charles's performance seems external and unfelt, so that even in the crucial scene when he learns of his wife's death no look of agony crosses his face. His laughter when he realizes he is going to hang unjustly for her death rather than justly for that of his nephew is quite effective, his face shining like a moon, the rest of the room plunged in sudden darkness; and he just rises to the challenge of the final sequence in the cell with his daughter. But clearly the inadequacy of the director and the ineptitude of the cast infected him, and the results were inferior to his best work.

Disappointed with Mendes' approach to the picture, Charles

was really dismayed by Erle C. Kenton, who directed *Island of Lost Souls*, from the novel *The Island of Dr. Moreau* by H. G. Wells. Kenton insisted on acting out scenes dressed up in the evil doctor's white tropical suit and hat, and even offered to teach Charles how to handle a whip—forgetting Charles's knowledge of this—in the scenes in which Dr. Moreau lashes his half-human, half-animal army of slaves on a sinister tropical island. Charles was disgusted by the story. His love of animals welled up; he felt a deep-seated repulsion at what he felt to be a crude exploitation of the theme of vivisection. The journey to Catalina Island—which was partly converted to Wells's island—by steamer was a disagreeable ordeal. The animals used in the picture were in cages, and for a sequence the actors dressed in monkey skins were made to run past them, prodding them. A tiger lashed out and tore one man's arm almost from its socket. The seas were rough; the animals whimpered and vomited, and their fetid odor sickened Charles. During the last part of the journey, the ship became blanketed in heavy fog, a fact which delighted the director and his cameraman, Karl Struss, who were filming the journey, but did nothing to alleviate Charles's feelings of distress.

The completed movie is of great interest. The setting, of a sinister jungle island crawling with creepers and threatening outsize plants, is realized with great imagination by the art department, and photographed in glittering, morbidly fascinating images by Karl Struss. Although the handling of the drama, the arrival of the strangers at the island, the appearance of the half-simian creatures, Moreau's final confrontation with them and vivisection by them, are not as fully realized as one would wish, the mise en scène and the overall atmosphere of suffocating terror are ideally brought off by the director. Charles's acting, despite his dislike of the part, is surprisingly committed. He makes a convincing figure of Moreau, in his white ducks, swaggering or fawning, lasciviously contemplating a new torture or smarmily dwelling on the heroine's charms. The repulsiveness is relieved by a cunning humor, the confidence by a creeping sense of fear that he may have taken on more than he can handle in this remote tropical outpost. Moreau in Charles's hands is much deeper than H. G. Wells could suggest: a perversion of a British Colonial administrator, and at the same time a symbol of Colonial repressiveness.

Charles's playing in the final scene of terror is fiercely controlled: at first brandishing a whip against his simian subjects, he is seized by terror as they turn on him, throwing him on a table, smashing the instrument cases in an alarmingly shot and recorded moment, and carving his flesh apart with his own steel instruments. Above all, Charles suggests, as so often in other films, the loneliness of evil, the fact that it eats on itself. The moments when he is brooding alone at night under a jungle moon, the howls of his captives resounding, really strike fear in the heart. More than any other actor, Charles can involve us in a character. We *become* Moreau; he is no longer a remote and improbable figure. We enter his furtive, indecent, and creepy soul, we know his motives, yet we still feel pity and terror when the game is up, and the victims of his cruelty close in.

After the ordeal of making *Island of Lost Souls*, Charles was consoled to some degree that year by a brief appearance in the omnibus film *If I Had a Million*, in which he played a clerk who, upon receiving an enormous check in an inheritance, walks through a series of offices and blows a raspberry at his boss. The episode was expertly directed by Ernst Lubitsch.

FOUR

While Charles suffered through *Island of Lost Souls*, Elsa met Alexander Korda in London. The gifted, affable, ruthlessly extravagant Hungarian producer-director summoned her to his rather dingy office in Upper Grosvenor Street, striding around and asking her about her own and Charles's plans. He had seen Charles in most of his plays and films, and admired his genius. Actually, he wasn't especially interested in engaging Elsa for anything, but dangled possible offers in front of her nose, simply to ensure that she would encourage Charles to contact him and work for him. His Hungarian compatriot and favorite scenarist Lajoš Birò prepared a screenplay, *Coup de Vent*, as a vehicle for Charles. Elsa was intrigued, and told Korda she would talk to Charles, but she didn't feel confident Charles would accept. Charles really didn't admire English films, and she knew that when he was in London, he much preferred to work on the stage. She was also aware that Charles was only making films in order to afford the less well-paid but far more rewarding work in theatre. Elsa was sufficiently impressed by Korda's suave and high-powered Hungarian manner to write to Charles about their meeting, but

Charles was not interested enough to respond to her, and when he arrived in London he approached Korda with some reserve.

But the two men got along well. Korda had a conquering charm, and a number of possible roles were discussed. *Coup de Vent* was dropped, and amid the cornucopia of ideas which Korda offered, one appealed to Charles: the life of Henry VIII, with Elsa as Anne of Cleves.

The origins of Korda's idea were twofold. He was in a London cab when he heard the driver singing the old music hall song, "I'm 'Ennery the Eighth I am!" and then, while discussing various possibilities for Charles in his suite at the Dorchester with the Honorable Richard Norton and Charles's agent, Lawrence Howard,[1] Norton noticed a statuette of Henry VIII on a table and told Korda, "He looks like Charles." That same night Korda had asked Lajoš Birò to prepare an outline for Charles.

More and more fascinated by Korda, and pleased by the idea of playing Henry—the first film role that really excited his imagination—Charles began a massive research. He conferred with Korda's brother Vincent, who designed the sets, visited Hampton Court, read the existing biographies, and looked at paintings of Henry in the National Portrait Gallery, the National Gallery, and elsewhere. He was particularly drawn to the Holbein portrait, the powerful legs in white stockings stretched far apart, the hands held behind the back, the stomach royally protruding; he grew his beard to the exact length indicated by Holbein; he brushed his hair with meticulous correctness; and he worked closely with John Armstrong on the costumes, ensuring that they worked functionally as well as dramatically.

The moment Korda had achieved his purpose in securing Charles's services, he was no longer particularly pleasant to Elsa. Elsa was hurt, once again, by this neglect of her own ability, realizing that Korda had simply used her as a lever to obtain Charles. Though distressed by this treatment of her, Charles never ceased to find Korda enchanting, and he made arrangements through his agent, Myron Selznick, and his lawyer, Florenz Guedella, to be loaned out by Paramount to Korda when he wanted to be. The fact that Charles remained in England to work for Korda, and kept moving to and fro across the Atlantic, caused major tax prob-

---

[1] London representative of the Myron Selznick Agency in Hollywood.

lems during the 1930s, and pushed his finances to a very low level. There was no double taxation agreement between Great Britain and the United States at the time, and he suffered severely as a result.

Preparations began for *The Private Life of Henry VIII* in the summer of 1933. The flat in Gordon Square wasn't ready until after the picture was finished, so all during the shooting the Laughtons occupied far-from-royal quarters in Jermyn Street. Charles was in an exceptionally good mood during the picture's making—far more sanguine than he had been at any time during his year in Hollywood. Korda was an inspiration, bubbling irrepressibly with ideas; the cameraman, George Périnal, was very gifted; Vincent Korda's sets were authentic enough to satisfy even Charles's meticulous eye; and the Hampton Court locations were ideal.

Work progressed comfortably. Charles and Elsa had a wonderful time in the scene in which Henry is confronted with the disagreeable prospect of bedding Anne of Cleves. Benita Armstrong, who was German-born, an attractive woman with a charming smile, worked with Elsa on her German accent in the dressing room, and the results were entirely authentic. Elsa based her makeup and braided flaxen wig on a small oval cameo of Anne of Cleves in the National Portrait Gallery. Korda's interpretation was that Anne wasn't ugly, but made herself so by pulling faces in the hope that Henry wouldn't want to sleep with her, and Elsa was very funny making those faces.

When Merle Oberon arrived on the set, with her hair severely dressed as Anne Boleyn, she noticed that Wendy Barrie, playing Jane Seymour, had a curly bob in the style of the 1930s. She decided to have her hair re-dressed like Wendy's. Charles heard her muttering about this and said to her, "Listen to me, Miss, if you dare go and change a thing I'll cut off your head, right now."

Binnie Barnes—cast as Catherine Howard—received instructions from Charles behind the set. He insisted on rehearsing her without Korda's knowledge. When she fluffed a line, Charles would say, "Come on my girl, and get on with it!" He liked Binnie, but was infuriated by Wendy Barrie, who, he felt, understood nothing he told her.

Charles often differed with Korda. At one stage the production was delayed for three days because Laughton quarreled with him over which arm he should carry the royal cap. They were both perfectionists and, despite their mutual affection, were prepared to rant and scream to get what they wanted. Charles argued with Korda particularly over the famous scene in which he gobbled capon at a table. Korda wanted him to eat it with a degree of decorum, but Charles insisted he should perform vulgarly, grabbing at the legs, stuffing them in his mouth, throwing them over his shoulder, and belching so violently he gave Binnie Barnes a faceful of saliva, while at the same time talking about "the decline in good manners."

The film was a great success. Lajoš Birò and Arthur Wimperis' script effectively and with an agreeably sardonic wit telescoped the main events of Henry's personal life while virtually ignoring his statesmanship. An opening title insolently dismisses his marriage to Catherine of Aragon as "having no interest for a modern audience" since it was devoid of adulterous intrigue and scandal. This coolly cynical attitude pervades the entire film. The story begins with the execution of Anne Boleyn. The observation is full of black humor: the headsman whistles a cheerful tune as he tests the edge of his blade; ladies in waiting lasciviously feel the royal bed as they prepare it for its new occupant, Jane Seymour, lewd remarks passing to and fro ("I wonder how the king looks in it?" "You'll never know"); a woman spectator of the axing asks the lady in front of her to remove her hat (a touch borrowed from *The Sign of the Cross*) and even Anne Boleyn sardonically comments on her own death ("I shall be known as Anne Sans-Tête"). Charles's entrance as Henry is ideally grandiose. Dressed in an exact copy of the Holbein portrait, he stands in a doorway roaring his displeasure at everyone. His sudden marriage to Jane Seymour is unsentimentally handled ("Always marry a stupid woman") and her death is followed swiftly by the comic scene in which Elsa's Anne of Cleves makes herself look grotesque on the wedding night.

As the film progressed, Charles showed Henry as grandiose, vainglorious, and pathetically dependent on women. The treatment of his relationship with Catherine Howard is most astute. Charles expertly conveys his slavish adoration, and Binnie Barnes, new to films, is ideally deceitful and shifty as Catherine. The best scene in the picture, and Charles's finest moment, is when he breaks down upon hearing of Catherine's adultery with his favorite, Thomas Culpeper. Clasping his beringed fingers to his face, he weeps copious tears, then looks suddenly resolute as we know that he will have both of them sent to the block. In the last scene, he is a fond, foolish man, feebly plucking at a capon which in his youth he would have torn apart with his bare hands, henpecked by a hatchet-faced Catherine Parr, and addressing the audience with a sad, ironical farewell.

Despite his most earnest efforts, Korda was unable to convince distributors to take on the picture once it had been completed. Even though the cast agreed to work on a share of profits basis in lieu of salary, Korda twice ran out of money and had to approach Ludovico Toeplitz, the son of an Italian banker, to obtain new finances. The film sat on the shelves for months as Twentieth Century-Fox, Columbia, Paramount, and MGM turned it down, claiming that the public would not accept Charles as anything but an evil villain. Finally, United Artists agreed to handle the picture, though some members of the English board announced that Korda had no business to have made the film at all as he was a "rank foreigner."

The film opened first in Paris, then in New York, and finally in London, where Charles appeared surrounded, rather to his distaste, with all of his screen wives as a publicity gimmick. Despite everyone's doubts, the reviews were ecstatic, and the picture became an overwhelming international hit, placing Korda in the front rank and making Charles, once and for all, a great star. Elsa's performance as Anne of Cleves was praised for its comic understatement, and Merle Oberon, Wendy Barrie, and Binnie Barnes became overnight successes.

For Charles, this was the moment he had been waiting for: a huge part, and an artistic and commercial hit. He was eternally grateful to Korda for this opportunity, and long regarded Henry as his finest performance. Certainly, no actor could have played it as well. The gusts of laughter, the roars of rage, the moments of husbandly tenderness, the breakdown into cuckold's tears were all beyond praise.

Flushed with his success, Charles was annoyed to learn that Paramount demanded his services immediately for another jungle melodrama, *White Woman*, in Hollywood.

Charles was handed the role of Horace Prin, a Cockney despot of a Malayan river basin, who marries a nightclub singer and suspects her of having an affair with an army deserter, one of his private militia of crooks and dropouts. Faced with a part which was little more than a limp reworking of Sturm in *The Devil and the Deep*, Charles ingeniously enriched the character with many strong personal touches. He insisted on organizing his own wardrobe for Prin: a slack, badly pressed public school blazer, the kind of garment an envious and socially ambitious Cockney would be inclined to wear; an equally pretentious white waistcoat, and baggy tropical ducks; finally—a really witty, ingenious touch—an Oxford boater perched on his head. The entire role was steeped in class hatred. The writers made it clear that Prin despised a world which had looked down on him, that he was obtaining his revenge, and didn't care what the consequences might be. He calls his American bride "Your ladyship" with biting contempt; he sneers at "these bloomin' snobs" referring to the seedy collection of colonials at Baja; he praises his shabby, bamboo-furnished river yacht as a "stinkin' palace"; and he openly despises his overseer as coming from an even more contemptible social environment than he ("Yer an American, are yer—well, I ain't finicky"). Charles's last sequence is so extraordinary one can't help feeling he must have had a hand in it. With hero and heroine in flight, and the natives closing in to murder him, he settles down to a final game of poker with his overseer. The overseer is murdered. Charles looks at his dead face and says: "First time in me life, 'ere I am with a royal flush and yer goes and croaks on me. Blast yer, what are yer grinning at?"

And now, as in certain scenes in *The Devil and the Deep*, Charles goes beyond acting into a personal expression of his anguish. Referring to the escaped lovers, his eyes brim with what seem to be genuine tears as he says: "What did you think they had that I didn't have, eh?" (He corrects himself.) "No! No! Soft! That's what you was! All of you! Mush! Mush! Can you 'ear me now from where you are, Ballister? I'm King of the River, I am, and I always will be!" The painful feeling that he is unattractive, that he does not belong to the romantic world of the goodlooking, and the bolstering pride in his attainment of carving out a place in the jungle—Charles was born to convey these emotions, and the last scene of this otherwise ordinary melodrama was one of his greatest moments on the screen.

Charles did not like the director, Stuart Walker, and often clashed with him on details of his direction of the players. He also disliked Charles Bickford, a hefty, rather crude red-headed character actor. He was not warmly admiring of Carole Lombard, notably awkward as his wife, but he was sympathetic toward a comparative newcomer, Kent Taylor (playing the hero, Van Elst), whom he taught to speak in a subdued voice for the microphones. As always, Charles refused to see the rushes, dreading the thought of looking at himself on the screen. He would call Lombard and Kent Taylor into his dressing room at the lunch break, discussing interpretation of scenes between the three of them without the director's knowledge. Frequently they would rehearse lines and gestures in full. When they reached the set their performances were radically different from those Walker required of them. Charles was as meticulous as always in details of dress, shoes, the use of tiny gestures; as always he used to work himself up to scenes in agonized silent contemplation; and he liked having Ravel's *Bolero* played between sequences to give him the feeling he was living in a jungle filled with recurrent drums. (In one scene, Lombard says, "Those drums out there—Ravel must have heard them.")

After *White Woman*, Charles returned yet again to England, to a more congenial assignment. He was to appear in a season of the Old Vic Company, including productions of *The Cherry Orchard*, *Measure for Measure*, *The Tempest*, *Love for Love*, and *Macbeth*. Elsa joined Charles on the ship at Plymouth and they continued to Paris for the opening of *Henry VIII*. Back in England she managed to find two rooms and a sitting room in Jermyn Street. Gordon Square was still not ready, and Charles was only earning sixty pounds a week, with Elsa at a salary of ten pounds. At weekends they would go to Stapledown, after watching the work on Gordon Square.

The entire Old Vic season was under the supervision of the great Lilian Baylis, with the young and very talented Tyrone Guthrie directing the plays. Guthrie was, Charles and Elsa agreed, like the Butterfly that Stamped, affected and brittle, with suggestions on interpretation that Charles did not find helpful. The two men differed on the reading of the verse. Charles refused to give in to the demands of the pentameter. While other actors counted the beats in a line, Charles preferred to break the lines up into the rhythms of normal speech, extracting the sense from them, believing that following the exact rhythm of the verse suppressed its meaning, rendering it virtually incomprehensible to the audience. Guthrie was all for beat-counting and musicality; Charles wanted the expression of character, Guthrie wanted pure Shakespearean pentameters. It was an uneasy, sometimes painful professional association.

Lilian Baylis was an administrator of genius, but a very ugly woman with a wall eye, a crooked nose, and an unpleasant mouth, a violent battle-axe who ordered everybody rudely about and insulted Charles. She had a disconcerting attitude toward actors. When an understudy took the role of Miranda on one occasion, the girl came off the stage flushing with pleasure at the applause, only to be greeted with Lilian Baylis saying, "Well, you've had your chance, dear, and you've lost it!"

Charles managed to raise the money for the whole season from the Pilgrim Trust on the strength of his name. Miss Baylis, who had tried for years to obtain funds from the Trust without success, was ungrateful and deeply resentful. The season had begun with *Twelfth Night* and continued with Chekhov's *The Cherry Orchard*. Charles played Lopahin on this occasion, and Elsa played Charlotta Ivanovna; Flora Robson was Varya, and others in the cast were Marius Goring, Ursula Jeans, and, in a small role, the very young James Mason. Charles enjoyed renewing his acquaintance with the play, which was directed by Guthrie quite differently from the Barnes Theatre Production of seven years earlier. The earlier presentation had been heavy and lugubrious; Guthrie directed the play with an antic pace, de-emphasizing the Slavic gloom. Paradoxically, as Mme. Ranevsky, Athene Seyler was by all accounts far too self-consciously amusing and stolid to convey the fecklessness which Dorothy Dix had managed at the Barnes. Eyewitnesses asserted that Charles's Lopahin was a fine study, lumpish and loutish, his head cocked to one side as though eternally listening to some unflattering remark, his arms flapping up and down like the fins of a seal. Flora Robson was a touching spinster, and Elsa earned good reviews in her small part.

Lilian Baylis had a passion for opera, and began using the Old Vic alternately for operatic performances. She also spent most of the budget Charles had raised from the Pilgrim Trust on the operas, which infuriated him, and she transferred part of the season to the Sadler's Wells. She made the company perform on certain weekends to a leper colony outside London.

The next production was Shakespeare's *Henry VIII* at Sadler's Wells, Elsa appearing briefly as a Lady in Waiting to sing "Orpheus with His Lute." Many contemporary critics commented, not unfavorably, on Charles's drawing of elements from his performance in Korda's film for this very different portrait. He emphasized the comedy, but with so much skill that only the most severe purists were offended. And everyone agreed that he rose triumphantly to the major dramatic scenes.

Back at the Old Vic, Charles played Angelo to Flora Robson's Isabella in *Measure for Measure*; Elsa appeared as Juliet. The London *Times* said of Charles's performance: "When Mr. Laughton comes to suggest the corruption into which the austere Judge has fallen he does not spare the victim, but he has been equally careful to do justice to the Lord Deputy's determination to put down lust and license with a fine hand. We are given the man of affairs, smiling, precise, and self-confident as well as the sensualist, and Mr. Laughton sees to it that what is horrible in the overwhelming of a formidable talent by the senses is given its full value. But throughout the evening this performance is rich and satisfying, full of subtle penetration and expressive gesture." Elsa remembers that for Charles it was one of the most pleasing performances of his life. Flora Robson, in a part which was perhaps more suitable for Ursula Jeans, was not the beauty that Isabella should have been.

Despite Charles's marvelous acting, *Measure for Measure* failed to draw the same audiences as its predecessors in the season. Many actors and authors rushed to its defense in various publications, urging the public not to overlook it. John Gielgud wrote to the *Times* from his flat in Upper St. Martin's Lane: "(The production) seems to me quite complete and perfect in its way, entirely original, and modern in conception, and yet executed with a sureness and power worthy of the best and oldest traditions of our stage." T. S. Eliot followed Gielgud in writing to the *Times* from his offices at Faber and Faber: "Even those whose principles prevent them from approving either the subject matter or the profoundly Christian spirit of the play might profit seeing it so well performed." Despite these earnest pleas, the production was not greatly successful. By contrast, *The Tempest*, produced at Sadler's Wells in January, was a triumph. Charles was a convincingly weary, jaded, and exhausted Prospero, speaking the lines—despite the fact that he felt he didn't deeply understand the role—with the air of a man who had been dragging chains. Elsa was an exquisitely swift, vital, and weightless Ariel. She learned to fly on a wire for the role, but during rehearsal Lilian Baylis and Tyrone Guthrie decided it would be better for her not to. She managed to give the correct illusion by moving with astonishing speed and dexterity.

The last three productions at the Old Vic were *The Importance of Being Earnest, Love for Love*, and *Macbeth*. If we are to judge by the reviews, the first of these productions was the least satisfactory of the entire season, with Elsa far too young and out of her element as Miss Prism, and Charles too obviously oily and unctuous as Canon Chasuble. *Love for Love* was received more warmly, especially the scenes in which Charles's Tattle instructed Elsa's comically demure Miss Prue in the pleasures of seduction; and *Macbeth* had a generally good press, though many critics complained that Charles sacrificed the music of the verse in order to make his villain convincingly harsh and barbaric. Charles felt very strongly that a declamatory mellifluous approach to the pentameters was particularly wrong in this case. He wanted to expose jealousies and hatred of Macbeth's dark soul in a delivery stripped of all needless affectation.

He was so distressed by rehearsals at which Tyrone Guthrie, a stickler for the correct emphasis in the verse, argued with him on this issue, that his performance on the first night was markedly inferior to the one he had given at dress rehearsal; but he was much more successful and confident at later performances. He never could remember, though, that the pentameter was what might be called the orchestration of Shakespeare; that the speeches have a certain melody which really cannot be altered.[2]

During the run of *The Tempest*, Charles received a telegram

[2] In later years, Charles was converted to the pentameter, and taught his students the necessity of following it.

10. Charles by Elsa, 1940s. (Elsa Lanchester)

11. Charles by Elsa. Asleep after a tooth extraction.
(Elsa Lanchester)

12. The Laughtons at their first Hollywood house, La Brea Terrace,
1932.

13. Charles as Barrett in *The Barretts of Wimpole Street* with Norma Shearer. *(MGM)*

14. Radio rehearsal, *John Brown's Body*—Elsa, left, Burgess
Meredith, center, Charles right—WABC, 1939. *(WABC)*

that he had won the Oscar for *The Private Life of Henry VIII*. Somebody stuck it on the notice board; the cast stood around and exclaimed with pleasure, but neither Charles nor Elsa really understood the significance of the award, which had only been in existence a few years.

In summing up the season in the newspapers, some critics indicated a patronizing attitude—Elsa feels that they resented the fact that a Hollywood actor had come back to appear in Wilde and Shakespeare—but most of the reviews were extremely enthusiastic.

On the last night of *Macbeth*, in which Elsa did not appear, Charles was greeted with cries from the gallery of "Good old Nero!" And someone yelled, "Bring Elsa up!" suggesting Charles invite her to come from the audience to the stage. "Many people have tried to do that, my friend, but none have succeeded," Charles said.

Following on his Oscar for *Henry VIII*, Charles received an offer from Irving Thalberg in Hollywood to appear as Mr. Barrett in *The Barretts of Wimpole Street*. This was the part which Cedric Hardwicke had played superbly on the stage: the tyrannical and unforgiving father of Elizabeth Barrett, who broke with him to marry Robert Browning. Admiring Thalberg, and delighted to learn that Norma Shearer would play Elizabeth, he agreed at once, and Paramount permitted the contract. The Laughtons left on the fastest ship available, the *Berengaria*, then caught a plane in New York.

The flight to California was an ordeal. Charles had told Elsa of a wonderful flight a year earlier, in which he had seen grand American landscapes from the air, but on this occasion they had to change planes six times, there were violent dust storms which tossed the plane around the sky, and at Van Nuys Airport in Los Angeles, a fog forced them to fly around mountains looking for a place to land. As they headed for a dangerous-looking peak, Charles and Elsa held hands, convinced their hour had come.

Charles started work on *The Barretts* in the spring of 1934. The house on La Brea Terrace long since given up, he and Elsa took a suite at the Garden of Allah Hotel for the length of their stay, while Charles continued a task begun in England: losing fifty pounds for the role.

The film's accomplished director, Sidney Franklin, had been

making the picture for several days when Charles arrived from England. He had not agreed with Irving Thalberg's choice of Charles for Barrett. He had seen the play eight times on the stage and was convinced that Charles would not be satisfactory. Later he was forced to eat his words.

In conference, Charles and Franklin decided to indicate the undercurrent of humor in Barrett's melodramatic character to prevent him from being uniformly repellent. The elements of incest had to be sneaked in under the watchful eye of the sanctimonious Louis B. Mayer and the vigilant Hays office. The scene in which Barrett made his intentions known to his daughter, so effective on the stage, was severely cut, but it still carried a potent charge, and shocked some moralistic members of the audience.

According to Fredric March, Franklin was terrified of Laughton, and made this clear during many days on the set. When Franklin asked Charles one day, as Charles strode up and down, deep in thought, how Charles was seeing his role, Charles snapped back, "Like a monkey on a stick!"

Norma Shearer has retained a lifelong affection for Charles. She remembers that when he first arrived on the set he looked as though he had just rowed across the Atlantic from England. He fell at her feet and kissed her hand, while Elsa stood quietly behind him with her mop of tousled brown curls, and a broad smile.

Each afternoon Charles and the rest of the cast would stop work and enjoy eggnogs in Norma's dressing room, prepared by herself. Charles enjoyed these breaks in the shootings; but when he was working, he was totally obsessed. One afternoon, Norma and Maureen O'Sullivan found his muttonchop whiskers irresistibly funny, and giggled irrepressibly, ruining takes. Charles was furious with them, and Franklin finally had to cancel the shooting for the rest of the day.

Though determined to act unselfishly, to give Norma every opportunity in the scenes they played together, Charles unavoidably acted her off the screen. From his first appearance, arguing with her about the need to drink a glass of porter to sustain her failing strength, he was completely in command. While the love scenes with Robert Browning, stiffly played by Fredric March, are preposterous, Charles succeeds in making his own sequences forceful and convincing, his vetoing of Elizabeth's journey to Italy, and his final declaration of incestuous desire, played with startling force.

In the wake of the great success of *The Private Life of Henry VIII*, Charles had become one of the most imitated men in Britain and America. Schoolboys and professional comedians alike could hit off his swaggering walk, his chewing of capon bones, his voice, his humors and despairs. Another actor might have become fatuously vain as a result of this international adulation; but Charles, disliking much of his work on the screen, dreading the sight of his own face and body, and facing each role with terror and uncertainty, obtained little satisfaction from the acclaim. He felt, recurrently, that he had lost some vital element in a part; that he had somehow missed coming to grips with a character's soul. The fact that most critics agreed about his greatness, his ability to feel his way into the blood, bones, the very marrow of the men he played, did little to console him. Just as mirrors threw back the image of a man he thought unattractive, even repellent, so the mirror of his mind threw back a picture of someone who had failed. He sickened of himself, even when the world showered him with praise as one of the greatest actors of his generation.

During 1933 and 1934, Charles was so consumed in his work that, so far as we know, he enjoyed no sexual attachments, not even those depressing, fleeting encounters which had figured in his London days. His agonized struggle with himself before and during each performance, his dissatisfaction with everything he did, the effort it took to endure the ordeal of filming in airless studios under hot lights, of having to provide rich emotional scenes at an hour of day when most civilized people were still asleep—all this exhausted his emotional resources. Behind the portraits of Sturm, Dr. Moreau, Henry VIII, and Barrett lay an emotional void. But, despite long separations, the marriage to Elsa provided a solid backbone for his life, giving it meaning and purpose. Their intense intellectual companionship, the joy they shared in nature —in the woodlands of England, in the deserts and mountains of California—in reading, in collecting furniture and paintings, provided a powerful sustaining force. Three or four times a year the Laughtons attended parties given by Norma Shearer and her husband, Irving Thalberg, both of whom Charles adored. Rogers would motor them to the Thalbergs' Santa Monica beach house from the Garden of Allah. Many of the greatest MGM stars were present in the formal living room with striped sofas facing each other on either side of a fireplace, oval mirror over the mantelpiece, and tables covered in photographs of the Thalbergs. Among the frequent guests were Clark Gable, Jean Harlow, Joan Crawford, and Jeanette MacDonald. Elsa felt nervous and subdued during these evenings, fascinated but still painfully conscious that to the other guests she was not a star, but simply Charles Laughton's wife. The napkins, made of double-sided satin, would slip to the floor from her knee, and she was much too frightened to bend down and pick them up. Fish and chicken were served in patty shells, and strawberries in little pastry boats. As an appetizer, a peach was served with mayonnaise on it. The Thalbergs' chef evidently thought he was being "very French," extremely smart preparing the food in this manner. The Laughtons found Thalberg a delightful personality, very small and fragile, with pretty, exquisitely formed features. Charles felt secure with him, and enjoyed walking along the beach with him, discussing many things.

The Laughtons dined at Kay Francis' house. She served finer food than the Thalbergs, but she was boringly, absurdly hostessy, rapping the table and informing the guests in a haughty voice, "Please be silent. I'm speaking!" She corrected her guests on every possible issue, queening it over them.

Though the Laughtons enjoyed their professional associations, they had no really close friends in Hollywood at the time. Iris Barry was busy at the Museum of Modern Art in New York; Benn W. Levy was back in England, writing plays for the West End stage; James Whale had never been particularly close. Elsa wrote to Benita Armstrong and other friends in London, painfully aware of the fact that her warmest companions were far away. The British colony in Hollywood, which included Sir Cedric Hardwicke, C. Aubrey Smith, Basil Rathbone, and Nigel Bruce, regarded Charles as a flamboyant actor with a sloppy technique and therefore tended to ignore him; the fact that, unlike the others, he didn't play cricket also told against him.

Before he left England to play Barrett, Charles had been offered by Paramount a script based on Henry Leon Wilson's fa-

mous *Saturday Evening Post* serial, *Ruggles of Red Gap*, about a
gentleman's gentleman of 1908, who is won by a crass American
couple from an English nobleman in a poker game in Paris. It is
easy to see what delighted him in the role. With his own growing
fondness for America, his realization that it offered a release from
the stultifying English class system, he rejoiced in this story about
a servant who learns to appreciate the good-heartedness of his vulgar and boisterous hosts, and is able to enter "trade" by opening a
restaurant in Red Gap, Washington. Charles could draw on his
memory of his father, formerly a Ruggles, his experience of tossing
out drunks at Scarborough in the scene in which Ruggles joyfully
throws out a snobbish local socialite by the seat of his pants; and
he had learned much from careful observation of the servants of
the rich. He chose his clothes meticulously, the neat bowler, the
black cutaway, the salt-and-pepper trousers, spats and patent
leather shoes; he knew how valets tended to stand, very still, their
legs pressed tight together, their lips pursed, and their eyes full of
jaded, knowing contempt; and at the end, when the townspeople
sing "For He's a Jolly Good Fellow" to him in the local saloon, he
managed a perfect blending of humility, controlled pleasure, and
dignity melting into grateful tears.

Charles arranged to have Paramount invite his old friend, the
writer Arthur Macrae, to come to Hollywood to keep an experienced eye on the script, checking occasional lapses into
Americanisms in the valet Ruggles' dialogue; and he frequently
advised the director, Leo McCarey, whom he warmly admired, on
the correct behavior of the other characters: the stupid but well-
meaning nouveau-riche couple played by Charles Ruggles and
Mary Boland, the fluttery restaurant helper played by Zasu Pitts.

The film's most famous sequence was that in which Ruggles,
after a couple of drinks, and quite carried away by his hosts' generosity, recited the Gettysburg Address in the local saloon. Although absurd as a dramatic device—if he had done anything of
the sort in a saloon in Washington State in 1908 he would probably have been doused with moonshine whisky—Charles somehow
succeeded in making the scene work. In excellent voice, he spoke
the lines with memorable intensity, though Leo McCarey decided
that it would be more powerful not to show his face during most
of the take, but rather have reaction shots of the awestruck oc-
cupants of the bar. Most actors would have assumed a shining, in-

spirational expression for the delivery; Charles with his customary genius made Ruggles look shamefaced, uneasy, acutely shy, and he deliberately hesitated in certain passages, as a man like Ruggles would.

During the rehearsals for *Ruggles*, Charles fell ill with a rectal abscess, and spent several weeks in a hospital. He looks sick in many scenes, particularly the first sequences; he is visibly in pain, his face drawn. This is one of his most subdued and controlled performances. Even when Ruggles is drunk and cuts up in Paris, Charles's exuberance is in a low key; this was, of course, appropriate to Ruggles, whose upbringing would never have permitted excess. In the scene in which Ruggles ejects the supercilious diner, a fuller expression of a release from inhibition was called for; perhaps because of his sickness, or a need to sustain his interpretation, Charles does not give the scene quite the exultant release the script requires. Nevertheless, Ruggles is among his best performances, alive with sympathy, inspired by contempt for class distinctions, and by a profound love of America. In its wake, Charles became more and more fascinated with Lincoln, reading and memorizing other speeches. This experience may well have been among the early elements which increased his feeling for the American way of life and may have sparked off his later career as a reader of classic texts.

During this period, Elsa accepted an offer from James Whale to play both Mary Shelley and the bride in his Swiftian horror film *The Bride of Frankenstein*. In an amusing sequence, she appears in a thunderstorm as Mary, thinking up her famous romantic horror novel; she is shown at the end of the film as the bride being created in a laboratory, waking up to see her monster husband and screaming with understandable dismay; moments later, she is destroyed as the laboratory blows up. Elsa had to wear yards of bandages, and a strange hair-style like a tall, gray-streaked busby. Her own hair was drawn up over a fine wire cage. Jack Dawn—cool and aloof in a white medical uniform—took three hours to make Elsa up each morning, which meant she had to leave the Garden of Allah at 5 A.M. Dawn gave her long painted eyebrows arched with permanent surprise, then applied false skin with spirit gum; coated in all this material, Elsa had to scream so often for James Whale she almost lost her voice. She managed to improvise a strange hissing sound of terror, which she based on the hissing of swans in Regents Park.

Elsa had appeared earlier in *Naughty Marietta* with Nelson Eddy and Jeanette MacDonald, both of whom she and Charles admired. They spent Christmas of 1934 with the Eddys, enjoying the turkey and plum pudding, while Nelson recorded Charles reciting and singing in the living room.

After *Ruggles*, Irving Thalberg and David O. Selznick asked Charles to play the role of Micawber in *David Copperfield*; Elsa acted a tiny part as the Micawbers' maid Clickett. Charles was not drawn to the part, feeling out of sympathy with Micawber, and convinced he would be miscast; but George Cukor, director of the film, proved very persuasive, and finally Charles gave in. Charles prepared a skillful makeup, based on the original Cruickshank drawings, and worked with Dolly Tree, the costume designer, to make sure his clothes were equally authentic. Cukor remembers that he was astounded when Charles walked on the set the first day: Micawber to the life. But the two men did not agree on the interpretation. Charles suffered agonies between the scenes, and kept fluffing lines, begging for retakes. After three days he asked Cukor to release him, and have W. C. Fields take on the role. Two miserable days later, Cukor agreed.

FIVE

While Charles was making *Ruggles of Red Gap*, Darryl F. Zanuck, the young and peppery head of an independent studio, Twentieth Century Pictures,[1] had offered him the role of Javert, Victor Hugo's implacable police chief, in a new version of *Les Misérables*. Fredric March was cast as Jean Valjean, the galley convict, who rises to become Mayor of Montreuil, only to face a lifetime of terror as Javert pursues him to a final confrontation. The director was Richard Boleslawski, the cameraman the great Gregg Toland, who later became internationally famous as the cinematographer of Orson Welles's *Citizen Kane*.

Playing Javert, Charles simply provided a dark reversal of the character of Ruggles: he played the role with exactly the same stiff-backed, rigid stance, with the minimum of facial expression, and with a rapped-out voice as peremptory as a gavel. He drew elements in both roles from his brother Frank. By fractional differences in delivery and bearing, and the substitution of a 1908 butler's uniform for an early nineteenth-century gendarme's peaked cap, silver-buttoned coat, white breeches and heavy boots, he managed

[1] Later merged with Fox to form Twentieth Century-Fox.

to move from comedy to horrifying menace, from epicene subservience to masculine assertiveness. Like Ruggles, Javert is a man raised strictly within the confines of a system, and it took a genius like Charles to realize the similarities in these very different men. Javert is a servant just as much as Ruggles: a servant of the law. ("Good, bad, or indifferent, the law is no business of mine. *But the law to the letter!*") Javert is like a machine, sexless, bloodless, bent only on carrying out a code; when he fails in the line of duty, he begs for justice. Charles's most extraordinary acting in the picture is his demand for dismissal when he feels he has incorrectly identified Valjean as the Mayor; as so often before Charles's performance goes beyond acting to an expression of an acceptance of punishment. The look of guilt on his face is especially painful to see.

Surprisingly, Victor Hugo's story, adapted by the British writer W. P. Lipscomb, still works: its simple confrontation of pure evil with pure good, its somewhat pious atmosphere, and its mechanized suspense are perfectly realized by Boleslawski, who wisely did not attempt to modernize or smooth out the story. Toland's photography and Richard Day's recreation of Montreuil in the period 1800–1830 are masterly, and Fredric March's stiff, awkward, but deeply felt playing of Valjean has stood the test of time. It is Charles, though, who dominates the film. Though often dropping into an incongruous Yorkshire accent ("Ah moost do mah duty!"), and at times overacting, he nevertheless exerts a hypnotic power, particularly in the scene when he first suspects the Mayor of being a former galley slave. Walking down a row of sycophantic gendarmes, he snaps out a series of instructions: "Where does he come from? How long has he been here? *Who was he?*" the voice steadily gaining emphasis with each question until the last "*Who was he?*" has all the sting of Dr. Moreau's Australian stockwhip, lashing us awake after the slow-moving religiose sequence that preceded it.

In February 1935, with *Les Misérables* completed, Charles and Elsa sailed to Britain to discuss new roles with Korda and to spend a couple of weeks at Gordon Square and Stapledown. They were eager to get home. In New York, Charles gave a brief interview to the New York *Times*, in which he said, "Hollywood is a goofy place. But I like it. It's the perfect mummers' home. If one weren't a little mad one wouldn't be there." Asked what kind of role he preferred—one of those impossible questions journalists always ask—Charles looked nonplussed and irritated; Elsa rushed into the breach with, "He likes comic parts best, and I like him in them!" "Oh yes," Charles said. "Of course—*Ruggles!*"

Elsa whispered: "I screamed so much in *The Bride* my voice is almost out of commission . . . I had a nice time with codeine on our trip by train here to New York. After our last experience, Charles and I never fly."

In England in April, Charles was involved in intense discussions with Korda on two projects: *Cyrano de Bergerac*, which Leonard Woolf was translating, and *Sir Tristram Goes West*, a story intended to cash in on the success of *Ruggles of Red Gap*, about a ghost which travels with a castle when the castle is rebuilt in the West by an eccentric, *nouveau riche* American millionaire.[2]

Lee Garmes, the distinguished American cameraman and co-director of *Crime Without Passion*, sailed to England just after the Laughtons to discuss working on *Cyrano*, and spent many weeks at Gordon Square or at Korda's suite in the Dorchester, going over the production details with Charles, Vincent Korda, and John Armstrong, discussing the script, and helping Charles work out his makeup. But Korda finally began to panic that the American audience would find the verse too hard to follow; and his backers doubted the appeal of a grotesque like Cyrano to the female public. Possibly they were right. When the film was finally done by Stanley Kramer in the early 1950s, with José Ferrer as Cyrano, it was not a success.

With both *Cyrano* and *Sir Tristram* now doubtful prospects, Charles accepted a major role from Thalberg: Captain Bligh in a version of *Mutiny on the Bounty*. Frank Lloyd, the veteran director, had bought Charles Nordhoff and James Norman Hall's bestselling book, and originally a condition of Thalberg's purchase was that Lloyd would direct and even star in it[3] as Bligh, the entire picture to be shot on a replica of the *Bounty* on a new voyage to Tahiti. Thalberg managed to talk Lloyd out of these last two demands, insisting on Laughton. Lloyd finally agreed, provided

[2] Eventually made as *The Ghost Goes West*, with Robert Donat, and Elsa in a small part.
[3] A vainglorious idea if ever there was one. Although he had acted in obscure stage roles, he had never appeared as an actor in a film.

that Charles wore exact replicas of Lloyd's bushy eyebrows as an indication that Lloyd had been promised the role.

In London, Charles began reading everything on Captain Bligh in print. He discovered that Bligh had a tailor named Gieves who had designed his uniforms to be water-resistant. Charles discovered from John Armstrong that the original firm of Gieves still existed in Bond Street. He walked in and told a clerk, "I believe you once made uniforms for Captain Bligh of the *Bounty*."

Without turning a hair, the clerk said, "And what year might that have been, sir?"

"Seventeen eighty-nine," Charles said. The clerk told him, "I'll see, sir," and disappeared into a back room.

Within a few moments the clerk had returned with the original record of Gieves's transactions with Bligh, his measurements, what he had paid, and the exact material. Gieves made the duplicates at Charles's expense, and when Charles cabled the news to Thalberg, the executive was overjoyed.

Charles sailed back to New York with his uniforms in April, leaving Elsa in London to enjoy Gordon Square. In Manhattan, he sat down to yet another long interview with the New York *Times*, this time with the *Times* film critic Frank S. Nugent. Nugent arrived at the Chatham Hotel at ten-fifteen and approached the door of Charles's suite. He heard something that sounded like a porpoise frolicking. The noise of splashing, snorting, and puffing continued to be alarming. Finally, after Nugent had rung the doorbell five times, the door opened and Charles stood inside, his face red, his hair standing up like the bristles of a paintbrush, and a damp towel in his hand. He was wearing a green checked linen dressing gown, left a small puddle of bath water on the floor, and was saying, "Beastly hour of the day. Come on in. Have some breakfast. Don't mind me. I've been on a diet. Bread hasn't touched my lips in five goddamned months."

Charles tackled a breakfast of prunes, ham omelet, and coffee, his guest joining in a much smaller meal. Charles said to Nugent, "Hope this doesn't affect you as it did another writer I met. That story! Excuse me while I eat this prune. This is the way she began. Let me close my eyes so I can remember it exactly: 'Charles Laughton, homely to repulsiveness, sprawled on his couch in his Metro-Goldwyn-Mayer dressing room and stroked the legs of the golden male statuette given him by the Motion Picture Academy.'"

Charles roared with laughter. "I don't care what they say about my appearance. But as for stroking the golden legs! My God! What?"

Charles read the revised screenplay sent to him at the Chatham by Thalberg, on the way to California. Written by Talbot Jennings, Jules Furthman, and Carey Wilson it turned the manly and dedicated Captain Bligh into a raging melodramatic sadist, whose entire life was devoted to flogging, keelhauling, and starving his miserable crew. Fletcher Christian's character is similarly altered. Historically, he was a close friend as well as an officer of Bligh's, who approved his method of running his ship. It was only when the intoxication of the Tahitian islands, and his devotion to his beloved Maimiti, made him turn against the life of the sea that he and Bligh clashed into bitter opposition. In the new version of the facts, Christian was turned into a man who despised Bligh from the outset, a liberal obsessed with the grim life of midshipmen below decks who struck out only because he could no longer endure Bligh's cruelty to the men.

Thalberg devoted more care in preparing an authentic-looking production than he did in preparing an accurate script. His researchers found the *Bounty*'s logbook at the Mitchell Library in Sydney, Australia; they prepared detailed research on costumes and ship's procedure; they had specialists explore details of the breadfruit trees which Bligh collected.

The Art Department under Cedric Gibbons constructed replicas of the *Bounty* and the *Pandora*. The director, Frank Lloyd, and fifty crew members and actors sailed to Tahiti to shoot backgrounds, and recruited the population of the islands for the extensive crowd scenes. Sequences in Portsmouth Harbor and in Tahiti were constructed on the Isthmus of Catalina Island, where the *Bounty* herself was used as a floating set. Each day a special vessel, the *Betty-O*, brought food from Avalon to the actors on board the *Bounty*.

The leeward side of the island was used for the Tahitian sequences of arrival and departure, especially imported coconut palms planted along the shore along with tropical grass and scrub, and a large Tahitian village built of thatched huts. The cast and crew were in Catalina for almost four months, housed in barracks or bungalows, according to their status. Awakened by a bugle at dawn, they were fed in a huge mess hall where loudspeakered assistant directors gave them their instructions for the day's work. They walked by dawn light to the pier area where makeup men were waiting to cover them in cocoa butter so that they would look as though they were sweating severely in the South Seas sun. Equipped with special wigs that were kept overnight in freezing airtight containers, they were taken by water taxi to the *Bounty* several miles out at sea off the western reefs.

Shooting continued in all weathers. Charles entered into the spirit of the show with tremendous energy. He was far less anguished than usual. Inspired by the authentic look of the ship and of his crew, and by the stinging salty winds, he seemed almost to feel he *was* Bligh. But after the first weeks, the weather turned bad, and Charles began to suffer from seasickness. For many days he had to put up with rough seas alternated with fogs; sometimes the ship was in the doldrums, the weather was bleak and damp; and in those first weeks he wasn't very much at ease with Clark Gable, who played Fletcher Christian. Whether because he envied Gable his dashing good looks and superb physique, or because he was living his role of Christian's enemy, isn't clear; but often he refused to speak to Gable off the set. Gable in his turn felt that Charles was stealing all the scenes, and that he was no match for him as an actor. He worked off his frustration by shark hunting in the heavy seas, while Charles brooded miserably in his bungalow. The two men agreed on only one subject: Frank Lloyd. They had little time for him, feeling that he made the ship the star, that he was disinterested in probing deeply into character. Obsessed with details of the ship's rigging and sails, and concerned with sending his unfortunate cameraman, Arthur Edeson, to the tops of the masts to obtain effective shots, Lloyd left the actors virtually to their own devices. Both Charles and Gable complained by telephone to Thalberg, who frequently came out to Catalina by seaplane, screaming at Lloyd that he was unsettling the stars. Lloyd screamed back, and the quarrels, conducted in front of cast and both film and ship's crew on deck out at sea, surpassed those of Bligh and Fletcher Christian in the film.

During the first scene, in which Bligh read the Sunday prayer on the poop deck, the ship's company was fully assembled: ship's doctor, officers, midshipmen, seamen. Everyone doffed their hats. Bligh's clerk handed him the prayer book. Bligh looked at the assembly and said, "Mr. Christian! You got this crew together, how would you describe them?" Christian replied, "In the main, sir, first-class seamen." Charles was under the impression he had played the scene correctly, but the moment it was over, Gable walked up to Lloyd and yelled very loudly, so that everyone could hear, "Laughton's treating me like an extra. He didn't even look at me when he addressed me! The audience won't see me in the sequence! Laughton hogged it!" Charles was furious, and Gable flatly refused to work any further that day. Lloyd canceled work and took Gable to his cabin. The cast could hear angry words through the bulkhead. Every now and again Gable was heard to say, "He's not playing to me, he's ignoring me!" In desperation, Lloyd called Thalberg, who flew over and held a midnight conference on board with Charles, Gable, and Lloyd, using Franchot Tone as an independent witness to give his own views. Thalberg forbade Gable to make any further objections, insisting that Lloyd's instructions must be carried out; but he also cautioned Charles to be sure he looked Gable in the eye when he spoke to him, not glance sideways at the ocean.

During those long weeks on Catalina, Charles was finally broken of his tendency to seasickness. He suffered some muscular tension, brought on by the mental strain of shooting, and engaged a good-looking and muscular young man, Dennis, to massage him and keep him fit with jogging and long walks. At weekends they went climbing in the foothills of the Sierras, flying first to San Pedro by MGM's specially chartered seaplane. Charles and Dennis, according to the actor Ian Wolfe, who played Charles's log-keeper, were intensely devoted. "Charles treated him with the gentleness and consideration of a foster-father. Often in the mornings before the water-taxi trip to the *Bounty*, people who worked on the picture would see Dennis tenderly handing Charles medication and salves in case his back pain would flare up," Wolfe recalls.

Once shooting was finished in the Pacific Ocean, Charles was faced with the grueling ordeal of the sequence of Bligh's thirty-five-hundred-mile journey by longboat to Timor. The opening, with Bligh fiercely condemning Christian from the boat, was actually shot at sea. Despite Charles feeling a little queasy between shots and grazing one knee while descending the Jacob's ladder, he rose magnificently to the challenge of his great speech. The rest of the journey was shot in tanks at MGM.

Jammed into a boat only fifteen feet long, Charles and his fellow crewmen were constantly drenched in water, tossed around by wires which rocked the boat, and made to roast under arc lights of several hundred watts until the makeup ran down their faces. Each day Charles's makeup grew heavier, suggesting the blisters of constant exposure; his lips were made to seem swollen by the application of special waxes which made it almost impossible for him to talk. Then, after over a week of grueling shooting, Lloyd discovered that the young actor Eddie Quillan, playing a shanghaied sailor, should not have been on the longboat at all, since his character was not among those loyal to Bligh, and in fact was hanged for his mutinous behavior. As a result of this oversight, the entire sequence had to be reshot from beginning to end, and the ordeal repeated. Despite this agonizing experience, or perhaps because of it, Charles achieved a thrilling moment at the end of the voyage, in which he cried out, on seeing the coast of Timor, "We have beaten the sea itself!" Several cast and crew members actually wept at the force and beauty of Charles's delivery, and he broke down himself as he finished the final words.

Sometimes, Charles felt he was very bad in a scene and deliberately ruined a take so that Lloyd would be forced to reshoot it. In a studio matching shot on the replica indoor Bounty, he had to pace over the entire deck inspecting the crew. He made this enormous perambulation, finally stopping short to deliver a speech. Lloyd was delighted, and was about to yell, "Cut!" when Charles looked at Lloyd and said, "I wasn't in any of my marks!" The crew roared with laughter.

The toughest phase of the shooting had been saved by Lloyd for the last week: the journey of Bligh and his loyalists to England on the Pandora. A complete replica of the Pandora was built at MGM and swung on huge metal cantilevers which made the Bounty prisoners below decks suffer horribly in authentic period chains. Charles again was doused with scores of gallons of water from special dump tanks, far more violent than those he had experienced during the longboat voyage, and lashed with violent gusts from the wind machines. When the *Pandora* struck a studio reef, the wind and rain were so violent that Charles had to be strapped to the wheel of the ship. Quite a few of the shots involved actual danger, and some cast members fell and broke bones on the slippery decks.

In matching shots of an actual storm up the California coast, a camera boat was upset, and a young cameraman swept away and drowned. The local press picked up the episode and exaggerated it, the headlines reading BOUNTY SUNK. LAUGHTON AND GABLE LOST. The *Evening Standard* called Elsa at Gordon Square with the bad news. Used to newspaper rumors, Elsa reacted in silence, not yet prepared to believe that it was true. Within a few hours the *Standard* called her back to tell her what had really happened, and that Charles was completely safe.

At the end of the picture, Charles had to return to Catalina for some final pickup shots. He assembled everyone on the last day of shooting in the dining hall of the local hotel and recited the Gettysburg Address with all the fire and lyricism he had shown in *Ruggles of Red Gap.*

In New York in the late summer of 1935, Charles called Elsa to tell her that he wanted to make an exciting purchase: Renoir's *The Judgment of Paris,* for $36,000, which virtually absorbed all of his savings. She told him to go ahead. He bought the painting from the New York collector and dealer George Keller. At first he had asked Keller for a small Renoir. But Keller shrewdly produced a very large Renoir, *The Judgment,* knowing Charles would fall in love with it. Charles went back again and again, sometimes lying on the floor for an hour at a time, gazing up at it. He had been hooked.

His passion had started earlier. He already owned a Douanier Rousseau of a hand holding flowers, symbolic of his own love of botany; he owned two Matthew Smiths, and he had installed fine woodcuts in the hotel at Scarborough. Sailing back to London with the Renoir, Charles was, for once, a very happy man.

While Charles was shooting *Mutiny on the Bounty,* Elsa was busy making 8-mm. films with John and Benita Armstrong at Stapledown. The titles were *Mother India, Parlez-Moi d'Amour, The Sleeping Clergyman, Whither Tarzan,* and *The Good Earth.*

Charles came back and roared with laughter over the antic 8-mm. home movies, running the phonograph for background music.

For ten months, during most of 1935, and part of 1936, Charles was working futilely on the script for *Cyrano*. The Laughtons filled their time at Stapledown, picking flowers and walking in the woods, talking by the fire in the evening, cooking field mushrooms, filling pots and bowls with branches. Friends came down for weekends, and twice the Laughtons gave parties in London. One of the parties involved buying bizarre theatrical wigs for the male guests—they bought the straw-colored thatch-topped wigs worn traditionally by village idiots, Shirley Temple moppet wigs, pigtails, and masses of curls. Alexander Korda looked particularly weird in a long flaxen blond wig with pigtails and pink satin bows, while the film executive Sidney Bernstein sported a black Chinese doughnut of hair, like Widow Twankey in the pantomime *Aladdin*.

The Laughtons gave another party for Fredric March and his wife Florence Eldridge, Helen Hayes, and Ruth Gordon. Ruth Gordon had been a specially close friend for several years. Jed Harris and Ruth shared a house and the Laughtons had after-theatre suppers with them night after night during the New York run of *Payment Deferred*. The Laughtons met Ruth later at the Garden of Allah where their cook Jane had served boiled chicken and bread sauce; Charles had wanted Ruth to play the role taken by Zasu Pitts in *Ruggles of Red Gap*, and he had encouraged her to play *The Country Wife*.

When Ruth opened in *The Country Wife*, a great success at the Old Vic under the direction of Tyrone Guthrie, Charles and Elsa stood at the back of the circle so that she wouldn't see them. Later, they drove her to Stapledown, which she always remembered for its outdoor toilet, and for the harsh cold of its rooms under the thatched roof.

In 1935 Korda became obsessed with the idea of making a series of films about famous artists. Determined as always to reconquer the American market in the wake of the triumph of *Henry VIII*, he was further stimulated by the success of Warner Brothers' new cycle of biographical movies, beginning with *The Story of Louis Pasteur*, and was convinced he could beat Warners at their own game. After thinking seriously about casting Charles as Beethoven, he finally decided to prepare the story of Rembrandt for him instead.

Charles was immediately enthused. Irritated by the long and futile months of work on *Cyrano*, and convinced finally that Leonard Woolf's translation would not work for an audience, he was delighted to find a firm offer of work in a part he could believe in.

The part of Rembrandt was a marvelous opportunity for an actor. Korda told Charles he intended to emphasize Rembrandt's hatred of the pompous and stupid aristocracy and bourgeoisie of seventeenth-century Holland which had failed to appreciate Rembrandt's genius, stripped him of his possessions, and reduced him to begging in the streets. With his contempt for class distinctions, Charles was fascinated by Korda's interpretation. In profound discussions with Korda, and based on his own readings of Rembrandt's life, Charles pointed out that Rembrandt felt his artistic gift as a burden, seeing life as a cage, that he was tortured with doubts, and that at times he hated himself as much as he hated the dull and stodgy Dutch public. It must have become increasingly clear to Korda that Charles saw himself in the role, and that this reflection of his own convictions, joys, and despair would help him to play it with compelling force.

Korda daringly cast Gertrude Lawrence, with her large features and threatening, exaggerated voice, as Rembrandt's monstrous housekeeper-mistress. Charles was determined that Elsa should play Hendrikje Stoffels, the sweet-natured and determined maid who, following the birth of her child, marries Rembrandt but dies only a few weeks later. Korda was strongly opposed to the idea, but he was unable to come up with a better suggestion, and finally allowed himself to be overruled.

Charles became obsessed with the painter's character, and he, alone at tulip time, and later with Elsa, traveled to Holland to study all the backgrounds of Rembrandt's life. They looked at paintings for hours in Amsterdam as well as in London, studied the self-portraits most fully, read all of the biographies in print. Elsa gazed at pictures of the aristocratic peasant Hendrikje, Charles grew a moustache to exactly the right length and learned to hold a brush correctly. He had himself made only feeble efforts to draw; now he had Vincent Korda and John Armstrong teach him to give the illusion of painting. Vincent Korda's exquisite sets, and Périnal's lighting, were based on Rembrandtesque principles of rooms illuminated by a north light.

The preparation for *Rembrandt* had been under way for several weeks when Charles left for the South of France with Korda to discuss locations for a possible subsequent life of Van Gogh. At a loose end, Elsa decided to visit Charles's family in Scarborough. She set out with the Armstrongs in a chauffeur-driven car. Seven miles out of York, an automobile swerved into them and Elsa was thrown from the back seat onto the steering wheel. Her left eyebrow badly gashed, she lay in the road bleeding; at last someone picked up the group—the Armstrongs and the chauffeur were not injured—and drove them to York Hospital. Crying and in shock, she went to London with the Armstrongs by train that night, and managed to reach a surgeon, whose careful treatment saved her from being permanently scarred.

Rembrandt began shooting in the late spring of 1936. Charles enjoyed the experience of working with Elsa, and found her presence sustaining in the many scenes they played together. He discovered many points of agreement with Korda; he was able to add a number of highly personal touches to Carl Zuckmayer's script, including Bible readings which years later were among his greatest achievements in live performances.

Gertrude Lawrence was something of a nuisance on the set, constantly telling Korda risqué stories and screaming with laughter at her own punch lines. She proved so distracting that Charles insisted on having screens around him when she was present, to protect himself from her presence and to some extent from her voice. He was aggravated by the fact that she had to have her lines written on her large white Flemish cuffs and on the backs of chairs; she would go from one piece of furniture to another to read her dialogue. Her voice was gratingly harsh, and her manner vulgar and irritating; this was appropriate to the shrewish woman she was playing, but it was hard to put up with her between scenes.

Drenched with white light by Périnal, the sets an abstraction of Flemish interiors, and all of the players made up and dressed to mirror the original portraits, *Rembrandt* was a ravishing production. Charles's performance was among the most deeply felt of his career. His delivery of Rembrandt's great speech at the beginning about his dying wife Saskia, expressing a love of woman of every creed and color, the effect of his words seen on the burghers' faces in a sequence reminiscent of *Ruggles*, provides a resonant overture to the film.

Rembrandt's expulsion of the citizens after they laugh at his new painting, his contemptuous dismissal of his housekeeper-mistress when she complains about his sacrificing everything to art —these are played with all of Charles's genius for dramatic timing and emphasis. He is memorable, too, in the scene in which he broods on the prison cell of life and the body, leaning against a pillar in anguished contemplation; and in the extraordinary episode when he drags a beggar out of the wharves of Amsterdam and dresses him in the tatterdemalion finery of a poor King Solomon. This sequence—more than any other in the film—reveals Rembrandt's intense sympathy for the poor.

All of Charles's sequences with Elsa as Hendrikje Stoffels are movingly played by both of them. Charles's whiskery, heavy face and slow-moving figure is expertly contrasted with Elsa's delicate fragile body and witty, chiseled features. The irreverent iconoclastic humor they shared in life is exquisitely expressed in the sequence in which together they beat off the debt collectors by a clever ruse. Elsa subtly evokes Hendrikje's decline into sickness and death, her eyes growing wider with fear, her skin seemingly becoming almost transparent; and her final moment, when she stands up from her chair as Charles paints her portrait, realizes death is near, stares terrified into space and falls back in her chair, drained of all life, is still very affecting. It says something for Korda's decency that, violently as he had been against her, he acknowledged the force and feeling with which she played this scene.

Although Charles was praised for his performance—most critics agreed that no other actor could have entered so completely into Rembrandt's tragic soul—Charles felt that Korda had missed greatness in the production. He told several interviewers that Korda had not had the courage to reveal the true horror of Rembrandt's existence. As an example, he cited Korda's refusal to include a scene Charles had begged for, in which Rembrandt had sold his first wife's grave to pay for his marriage to a second. This and other aspects of the actual story were, Charles felt, left out to pacify the public; as it turned out, despite excellent reviews the public of the time rejected the film—and Charles in it—as decisively and blindly as the Flemish public had rejected Rembrandt. It was a disagreeable irony which Charles no doubt felt.

Korda was in despair at the commercial results of the film's release, and did not direct again until *The Thief of Bagdad* in 1940. Backed by the Prudential and by the Bank of England, he became a mogul instead, running Denham Studios, which he had built, with great dash, energy, and extravagance.

Charles felt distressed that Korda had ceased to be an artist and had chosen to be an administrator—had, in fact, changed from a Rembrandt to a burgher. He also felt that Korda was beginning to lose interest in him, caught up as he was in the manifold problems of his organization. Determined to create pictures of the caliber of Korda's best, he began to think of leaving Korda, and of taking with him the producer Erich Pommer, who had fled Germany without funds after a long period as head of UFA.

Korda realized Charles was growing restless, and on the spur of the moment bought Robert Graves's very successful novel *I, Claudius*, about Claudius, Emperor of Rome, as a starring vehicle for him. Korda flew to Spain, and took a ship to Graves's home in Majorca, helping Graves to develop a screenplay. In the meantime, Korda engaged Charles, and, in support, Flora Robson as the ancient Olivia, Emlyn Williams as Caligula, and, most importantly, his beloved Merle Oberon as Messalina. Since Oberon had appeared as Anne Boleyn in *Henry VIII*, Korda had been involved with her. His fascination with the exotic no doubt drew him to her dark Eurasian beauty, and she had a fierce, driving intensity and ambition similar to his own.

Korda decided that Oberon must be given a huge star treatment, and that a major Hollywood director of women stars must be hired to bring out all of her mysterious allure. He settled on Josef von Sternberg, whose vehicles for Marlene Dietrich, beginning with *The Blue Angel* and *Morocco*, had made Dietrich's image world-famous. Now that the partnership had broken up, and Von Sternberg appeared to be available, the opportunity had arrived for him to give Miss Oberon the Dietrich treatment.

Von Sternberg spent weeks in London discussing this film with Korda; he had a liking for Hungarians, and for once this icy martinet was considerate and cooperative. Haughty, aloof, and brutal on a set, Von Sternberg was, together with DeMille, one of the two remaining directors from the silent period who dressed up for the part. With his scarf, hunting jacket, breeches, and boots, he had a military air, regarding actors as soldiers in his private army. Yet away from the studio he could often be very human and very kind.

During the discussions, Von Sternberg fell ill with virus pneumonia and lay in the London Clinic. Charles was delighted to learn that Korda had been discussing the job with Von Sternberg, and he visited the director with a gift of grapes in the hospital to convince him he should take it on. He had for many years liked Von Sternberg. When Charles had first come to Hollywood, Von Sternberg had been very helpful, and Charles and Elsa had frequently lunched with him, and with Marlene Dietrich, in the Paramount commissary. Later, when the Laughtons lived at the Garden of Allah, the director had again been most friendly and charming. He had sent Elsa an oversized gift of flowers in a box the size of a coffin on one occasion; the only place to put them was in the bath.

In 1935, when Elsa was in England, Von Sternberg had done Charles an extraordinary act of kindness. Charles had felt ill and had gone to a doctor for a checkup. The test showed that he had syphilis—it had been in his system for years. He was horrified. He couldn't turn to Elsa, calling or cabling her with this dreadful news. Finally, he turned to Von Sternberg and told him. Charles began to break down, feeling a need to kill himself. He wanted to throw himself out of a window. Von Sternberg managed to persuade him not to, and stayed with him for three days and nights at the Garden of Allah without leaving him for an instant. Finally, Charles returned for a second test and discovered that the doctor had mixed up the test tubes and he did not have syphilis after all. The relief was overpowering, and Charles was eternally grateful to Von Sternberg for saving his life.

Charles's visit to Von Sternberg in the hospital could not have been more cordial. But it was the beginning of what proved to be the most disastrous professional association of Charles's career.

The script of *I, Claudius* was the work of several hands. Carl Zuckmayer and Lester Cohen prepared some scenes; Von Sternberg himself and Lajoš Birò did a polish job. Robert Graves's draft was completely discarded. Charles, still immersed in playing Rembrandt, found it difficult to concentrate on the role; he had to move from noble authority and gentleness to stammering, terrified inanity, from artistic force and power to futile subservience. What attracted him to the part was undoubtedly the reversal of character: the fact that Claudius, thrust into power by the death of the infamous Caligula, rose to the occasion and addressed the senate, haltingly but movingly, as a lawgiver. Always delighted by the unexpected, he felt he would be in his element here.

The atmosphere on the set at Denham became very unsettling as the movie began. Von Sternberg, frosty, arrogant, dressed in his breeches and riding boots, ordered everyone about like a general. Birò and Korda were constantly conferring in Hungarian, a habit which Charles found infuriating. Everyone was extremely tense. This picture, following *Henry VIII*, was to ensure Korda's position once and for all as a great filmmaker, and Korda's constant insecurity and overwhelming need for more acclaim made nobody feel easy. The picture was also a test for the director. Von Sternberg's career had waned, and his Paramount contract had been canceled, following the failure of his last two films. With *I, Claudius* he hoped to prove to Paramount that they had dismissed him too hastily, and that he was still capable of making a huge popular success. He too was ill-at-ease, his head on a chopping block. And though he was somewhat respectful of Korda, his master of the occasion, he was by no means gracious to Charles or even to Merle Oberon, whom Korda told him to handle with the utmost care.

Luckily, in the mid-1960s a talented BBC Television director, Bill Duncalf, prepared an admirable documentary, *The Epic That Never Was*, from interviews and sequences of the film itself. In the opening scenes of the picture, Charles is seen as a simpering mooncalf, crouching in a clownish robe, as humble as a victim of a beating, his eyes squinting, or glancing downward in self-pity and self-hatred, his walk loose and shambling. His lips fumble over the simplest sentence; he stammers in an agony of ineptitude; yet he conveys a luminous nobility of character. It is a marvelous, humanist portrait, alive with compassion and kindness, and not for a moment repulsive; when the worm turns, and Claudius addresses the senate, condemning the evil and corrupt government of Rome, calling for sympathy, justice, and decency for the underdog, Charles is unsurpassable:

I, Claudius, will tell you how to frame your laws. Profiteering and bribery must stop. The senate will function only in the name of Roman justice and all of you who have acquired office dishonestly will be replaced by men who love Rome better than their purses.

Here is a goodhearted reversal of Javert: a stickler for the law, not as an excuse for butchery and bloodshed, but as the organ for dispensing goodwill among men. It was ironical in the circumstances that Von Sternberg was a Javert, not a Claudius; certainly, from the beginning their relationship was agonizing. Korda was dismayed by the director's ill-treatment of Charles.

Each day Charles struggled to come to grips with aspects of the role of Claudius, which the various scriptwriters had confused; he battled with the lines; he would be seized by self-consciousness and stop speeches which were perfectly delivered; often he insisted the whole production be canceled, and another actor hired in his stead. Von Sternberg was contemptuous of these demands, not even giving Charles the benefit of a man-to-man discussion. Merle Oberon became flustered and impatient at the interminable delays in shooting. Sometimes Charles would start work on a different set in the hope that something would emerge from his surroundings to spark off his inspiration. Korda was as tolerant of these shifts in schedule as Von Sternberg, used to discipline and obedience, was not. At night, Charles came home and wept to Elsa with heartbreaking intensity. The tears ran through his fingers in anguish, as he clasped his hands over his face.

But at last he found a key to the character. He heard Edward VIII's Abdication Speech on the radio with all of its hesitations, its fundamental nobility; the words of a man who had put love before a crown. He at once saw his way through to a proper interpretation of Claudius.

He played the recording of the speech over and over again, acting all of his subsequent scenes with great intensity, but Von Sternberg was still cold and unappreciative. Much to Charles's relief, an accident completely wrecked the project when it was about two-thirds of the way toward completion. Merle Oberon had acquired an inefficient chauffeur, who smashed into another car while driving through the West End. She was thrown into the street, suffered multiple abrasions, and severe shock, and spent several weeks in the hospital. Korda was so deeply in love with her that he refused to replace her with another actress, and to the horror of the Bank of England, which had put up the money for the picture, he closed down the picture and sent everybody home.

Following the collapse of the picture, Charles held a series of discussions with Erich Pommer, who thereupon resigned from Korda permanently. Charles never worked for Korda or spoke to Von Sternberg again. Paul Tabori records a meeting, in the 1950s, between Charles and Korda on the set of David Lean's film *Hobson's Choice:*

"We're both growing old Charles," Korda said.

"Yes, and I'm glad," the actor replied. "I don't want to go through *that* again. These are the good years, Alex."

"What's good about them?" Korda said, almost savagely, and walked away.

Years later, after a screening of Bill Duncalf's *The Epic That Never Was* in Hollywood, Von Sternberg said coldly to Elsa, "I don't know why Charles couldn't 'find the character.' I was the director, and I was there to tell him exactly what to do."

SIX

In the mid-1930s, Charles was not entirely neglectful of his first love, the stage. Just before *Rembrandt*, he had been given a signal honor: directors of the Comédie Française had invited him to appear as Sganarelle at a midnight gala performance of *Le Médecin malgré lui* by Molière. It was the first time that a British actor had been invited to appear with the company, and Charles was enormously flattered by the offer. He traveled to Paris with Alice Gachet, his teacher at the Royal Academy of Dramatic Art; she aided him in the week of rehearsals.

Charles was terrified by the geometrical precision of the direction at the Comédie, the rigorous discipline from which the players never wavered, the steely adherence to an ancient tradition of performance. He was not only faced with the challenge of speaking in a foreign language, and, given his usual degree of dedication, thinking in it as well, but he was faced with a professional rigor which had never previously been imposed on him. He was unable to wrestle with himself, break off scenes to contemplate, demand changes of schedule, argue with the director, seek out keys to the character by means of music, radio, speeches, reading of books. Every one of the props he needed to support his unhappy psyche was pulled away, and he was left floundering. When Elsa came to be with him, to help him, she found him shaking with terror, praying for a Merle Oberon-like car crash which would put him out of the running, unable to sleep, actually vomiting after the nightmarish rehearsals. Accompanied by the actress Beatrix Lehmann, Elsa watched Charles keenly from their box, concerned that Charles, who had not eaten or slept for twenty-four hours, might collapse on stage. Charles was doubly disturbed because he knew he was last on the bill—a potpourri of scenes—and would not appear until well into the early morning hours. As it turned out, he did not come onto the stage until 4 A.M., after four hours of moaning in an agony of terror in his dressing room.

At last he came on the stage, and the moment the spotlight focused on him, he lost his terror and gave a dazzlingly witty and fastidious performance. But toward the end of his appearance he began to panic again. He realized that his amusing speeches were being greeted by cold silence. Perhaps this distinguished audience found him a failure? He did not realize that audiences at the Comédie, knowing every speech, always receive them in silence in order to appreciate them fully. Just as he concluded the performance, and was ready to make an undignified dash for the wings, Charles was astonished to hear a tremendous thunder of applause coming at him across the footlights. He burst into tears. For years afterward, his acting was mentioned with awe by aficionados of the theatre. The "Laughton interpretation" of Sganarelle was always considered one of the finest in the history of the Comédie.

Press and photographers thrust in on Charles in his dressing room; Alexander Korda arrived full of congratulations; Elsa embraced Charles. Neither Charles nor Elsa felt anything but relief that the performance was over; neither felt that it had worked well at all. Charles, Elsa, Beatrix Lehmann, Korda, and Alice Gachet bundled into a taxi and went back to their hotel. Charles, loaded with gifts from the French company, including a plate painted by Renoir, Sganarelle's green velvet purse containing stage money, paintings, drawings, Coquelin's walking stick, and signed copies of plays in the repertory, took off immediately for Holland with Korda, to work on research for *Rembrandt*.

Charles's second stage performance of the period was as Cap-

AN INTIMATE BIOGRAPHY 79

tain Hook in Sir James Barrie's *Peter Pan,* with Elsa acting the title role. The Laughtons both felt attracted to the play, and were drastically upset when Korda forced them to reject an offer to play the parts in 1935. He did allow them to accept for the Christmas season of 1936, and they appeared very successfully at the London Palladium for the limited run.

Charles was enchanted by the character of Captain Hook, the monstrous pirate with the claw hand and rolling eyes who was a coward at heart. He had seen Gerald du Maurier play the role with lip-smacking relish several years before. Elsa was convinced that Peter Pan, rigorous and overpowering, resembled Adolf Hitler, and decided to play him with the tyrant firmly in mind. But no sooner had they committed themselves firmly to the producers of *Peter Pan,* the Daniel Mayer Company, than they were on the wrong end of a bombshell. The ailing and elderly Barrie wrote to them at Gordon Square telling them quite flatly that he was opposed to their playing the parts, and that they must immediately refuse them.

In a state of shock, the Laughtons wrote back asking for a chance to talk the matter over. They finally decided not to mail the note, and simply arrived at Barrie's flat in Adelphi Terrace carrying it. They handed the note to Barrie's cold, haughty butler, who closed the door sharply in their faces.

Fortunately the Laughtons decided to stay where they were, and in a few moments the butler coolly invited them to come in. Old, sick, and crotchety, Barrie told Charles in a flatly dismissive voice: "I'm very much afraid, Mr. Laughton, that you're going to terrify the children. That's quite impossible, of course. Hook must *never* do that."

"*I'm* not going to frighten the children," Charles replied, looking very nervous, his eyes cast down meekly. Sir James seemed to waver and looked at Elsa, saying, "I think *you* might make a good Peter." At that moment the telephone rang, and the butler announced that Elisabeth Bergner was on the line. Barrie excused himself. He was obsessed with Bergner, for whom he had written his play *The Boy David.*

The Laughtons stood feeling like two naughty school children in a head teacher's room until Barrie returned. He was smiling. "I have been talking to someone," he said, "who says you are both perfect for *Peter Pan*, and that I shall make a great mistake if I don't let you do it."

Rehearsals began in November. Charles perhaps unwisely made his Captain Hook very subdued and quiet, in deference to Barrie's fears. Elsa had a wonderful time learning to fly on a powerful wire which made her seem to be airborne. Other actresses had simply hung on the end of the wire like fish, but she realized that in flight a body would move constantly, and with her supple, flexible body she was able to glide and swoop with miraculous fluidity. She realized the tremendous challenge of the part; looking down at the Palladium stage, with its lifelike scenery of nursery, lagoon, jungle, and galleon at sea, she felt as though she were really a bird in flight.

Barrie came to one of the rehearsals, and was shocked to find that Elsa was not dressed in the traditional Peter Pan costume, but rather like one of the Darling children. She argued with him earnestly, but finally he overruled her, and she realized in time that he was right. The audience would have been so unsettled by her untraditional appearance as she flew through the Darlings' window in Act One that she would have "lost" them for most of the performance.

While Charles was preparing *I, Claudius*, Elsa toured the provinces in *Peter Pan*, with great success, another actor playing Captain Hook.

By the late 1930s, Charles was securely established as one of the most famous of international stars, his reputation safe even among intellectuals who seldom took the cinema very seriously. The public loved him, responding to the humanism and depth of emotion in his playing. When other actors played villains— George Zucco, Lionel Atwill, John Carradine, Victor Jory were among the best-known menaces of the period—they acted them with a Lyceum flourish, concerned only with capturing an external nastiness, leaving the audience uncertain of their motivations and inner feelings. They were simply bristling symbols of contempt for justice and goodness. But Charles, through his worrying over everything he did, his divine artistic discontent with many of his own parts, sought out the human essence of the characters he played. Faced with the fact that writers of his time drew characters in stark blacks or whites, that they failed to show shadings and paradoxes, he struggled with himself to discover the essence of the men he was playing. He forced the audience to share the guilt of these characters by implicating the spectators in his performances, "pointing a finger" at each person watching him, as much as to say, "This might be you, too." Long before Method was a twinkle in Lee Strasberg's eye, Charles was an actor who looked deep into himself for the meaning of scenes. He fought constantly to add touches to scripts which would make his characters come to life, make them three-dimensional. He made Sturm's jealousy in *The Devil and the Deep* more disturbingly painful to watch because of his forced humorous telling of stories, a touch he himself had added to the script. The humor was that of a man trying desperately to keep himself afloat when hatred is about to engulf his spirit. His Nero was made touching and accessible by his very childishness. Charles's petulance was played like that of a spoiled baby demanding its rattle, showing that Nero was infantile as well as psychotic. By revealing that Nero had never had to face adult responsibility, protected and smothered as he was by his henchman Tigellinus and by the Empress Poppaea, Charles made audiences instinctively feel pity and terror instead of the simple hatred DeMille wanted. He also played Nero's homosexual flauntings with witty compassion, making them engagingly rather than unpleasantly ridiculous.

Henry VIII could in other hands have been merely a ravenous monster, using women for political purposes, trampling on his courtiers, obsessed with his imperial power. But Charles turned him into an engaging scoundrel, whose weakness for women was his most human and endearing aspect, and whose grief at treachery was the grief of a man who could still perform acts of trust. Another player might have been all lion's roars and violent alarums and excursions; Charles was compassionate to Henry, seeking out the tender and adoring male, the royal lover, behind the mask of tyranny. He succeeded in humanizing the unnatural monster-father of *The Barretts of Wimpole Street* by showing the sudden moment of agony when Barrett realizes he is going to lose his beloved Elizabeth; and the anguish in Javert when he finally gives up the law, lets his prisoners go, and takes the only logical step: suicide in the swirling waters of the Seine. Both Barrett and

Javert were roles written on one note of ruthless, upright conde-
scension. Charles showed through inventive interpretation that
they were miserable, lonely men whose only hope of survival was
to cling to a line of discipline and order, that once their own
hopelessness showed through to themselves and others, they were
finished.

Audiences loved Charles for these fully realized villains, but
above all they loved him for his portrait of Captain Bligh. He
never really shook off that particular image of a brutal martinet
strutting a quarter deck in white breeches and a three-cornered
hat, rapping out commands for a keel-hauling or muttering lines
like, "I'm going to count the breadfruit." "Listen here, Mr. Christian!" was his most frequently misquoted line, constantly used by
imitative children and music hall comics alike. Yet, whether audiences realized it or not, what had made Bligh one of his
supreme characterizations was Charles's humanizing of a crudely
written part. In his brief look of desperation when his companions
at the dinner table rose in disgust and left him totally alone; his
speech from the longboat, noble and ringing and true; his concern for his men in the voyage to Timor; and the unforgettable
moment of triumph when he says, "We have beaten the sea
itself!"—here we have evidence that Charles managed to em-
bellish scenes with personal actor's touches. He made Bligh noble
as well as cruel, brave as well as vicious, and above all a great sea-
man, deeply in love with the sea. He reasserted the real Bligh, cor-
recting, through his effort alone, the false one the scriptwriters
portrayed.

All great art emerges from a struggle, and Charles's struggle
with himself, his eagerness to find out his own and his characters'
motivations against heavy odds supplied by writers and directors,
made his performances alive and meaningful. Other actors could
rely on looks, natural magnetism, sexual attraction; Charles could
only rely on honesty, rigor, sheer authority, and those manifold
unexpected revelations that made his performances a constant
delight. Nobody could chill as he did: there are moments in all
his performances of evil that are authentically terrifying still. But
deeply as he submerged himself in his rogues' gallery we are always aware that we are looking at people whose evil is not complete and absolute. It is evil rendered understandable and pitiable

because it is portrayed by a man who had a great deal of goodness in him. A complacent actor would have made Sturm, Nero, Barrett, Javert, and Bligh exultantly evil. Charles, constantly exploring and re-exploring his own self with agonized uncertainty and terror, could show us that even in these men a soul, a conscience still existed, and here his Jesuit training clearly asserted itself. His performances are Christian in the best sense: they show compassion through personal suffering; they are at heart forgiving.

During those years just before World War II, Charles's private life was as restricted as ever. Working almost constantly, rising at dawn or earlier and going to bed at nine-thirty at night, allowed him little social life beyond the very occasional parties he and Elsa gave.

He had a masseur, Bob, who replaced the young man who had worked with him on *Mutiny*; Bob was also like a son to him. Charles was tender and kind to the rough young man, and he encouraged him to marry and have children, even though this would mean their eventual separation. This unselfish sweetness was typical of Charles in his relationships with men. He never sought out his intellectual equals, young poets or novelists or composers or even brilliant actors as his personal companions. He was drawn to simple people, whom he could guide and always hope to mold. We may guess that in their flawless faces and physiques he found a temporary escape from his own imprisoning flesh, the round form and heavy features he loathed, but we may also guess that when he returned to a contemplation of his own physical self, the contrast between Caliban and Romeo (as he would unfairly judge that contrast) would be all the more excruciating. He was deeply distressed by his homosexuality. One likes to feel, though, that helping these youths, urging them to a normal way of life, and showing them innumerable acts of loving kindness, gave Charles some of his rare moments of happiness.

Certainly, such happiness as he knew largely came still from his relationship with Elsa. Theirs remained a remarkable marriage, a marriage of intellect, and a marriage of kindred spirits. She, painfully but wisely, accepted his homosexuality. She did not want to lose him, because they had far too much to enjoy together. She had had her own relationships, all with men, and lasting for several months only, and she loved him, as he loved her, constantly and deeply. Their weekends at Stapledown, reading, walking in the woods, picking flowers, of which they knew every Latin name, collecting branches, were marvelous escapes from the pressures of work and of London. They loved to collect good pottery and antiques; they laughed at the same jokes; they liked the same food, good, solid English fare, steak and kidney pudding, Irish stew, boiled meat or fish. They enjoyed satirizing pompous humbugs together; they shared an irreverence for "society" and for the haughtier members of the "cultural" world. Yet they were both deeply cultured, enormously well read. And at Gordon Square they had the pleasure of sharing the environment, elegant and simple and aesthetically flawless, that Wells Coates had designed under Charles's dominating guidance. And the presence of the Bloomsbury group nearby, with all that meant in dazzling conversation, shared interests in painting and music and literature. Above all, *The Judgment of Paris* glowed above the fireplace as a symbol of the permanent beauty that could be earned from the salt mines of picture-making. They began to build up a small collection of paintings in those prewar years.

It is clear that by 1937 Charles was feeling very strongly, in the wake of the fiasco of *I, Claudius*, that he needed to make his own pictures, that he must be able to play parts which he could control at the writing stage, and that he must have a real hand in the direction. He therefore decided to form a partnership with his friend Erich Pommer, who would act as co-producer, and with John Maxwell, head of Associated British Pictures. He would hire writers to prepare scripts, and he would call the new company Mayflower Productions, a symbol of the British need to invade the American market. Pommer, who had come to Britain penniless after Hitler deposed him as head of the giant Berlin studios of UFA, seized the chance of directing a company with great enthusiasm. He turned out to be an irritable, irascible, but gifted partner in the enterprise.

All through the spring of 1937, the political crisis in Europe deepening hourly, Charles and Pommer began to develop scripts which would form the basis of their first three films. Bartlett Cormack, an experienced American scenarist who had worked with

DeMille and written the famous Broadway play *The Racket*, prepared a version of Somerset Maugham's celebrated novel of the South Seas, *The Vessel of Wrath*. The novelist-playwright Clemence Dane wrote a script entitled *St. Martin's Lane*, a story of the London buskers who entertained the London theatre queues, and she adapted Daphne du Maurier's novel *Jamaica Inn*. The partners decided to make *The Vessel of Wrath* first. It provided ideal parts for Elsa and Charles. She would play a bluenose missionary, given to attacking the unrighteous with her umbrella in a Dutch island colony; Charles would be a penniless ne'er-do-well, who gradually becomes drawn to her, and she to him. After many discussions, everyone decided it would be too difficult and expensive to make the picture in the South Seas. Instead, they would shoot it in the South of France.

Throughout May the discussions grew fiercer and more concentrated. Charles relished the idea of being his own producer, no longer having to submit to the whims of various movie moguls with whom he had little or nothing in common. He and Elsa carefully selected the clothes which Ginger Ted and Martha Jones would wear: he a shapeless tropical suit, filthy and drenched in sweat, she brandishing an umbrella, her clothes ill-fitting and prim, hiding her body from the eyes of men. His hair would be tousled, hers drawn back in a tight, officious little bun.

Charles, Elsa, Erich Pommer, and Bartlett Cormack, who was also to direct, chose the supporting cast. Tyrone Guthrie was ideal as the fluttery, hypersensitive, and faintly ridiculous missionary brother of Martha, a character the Laughtons added to Maugham's story; Robert Newton was acceptable as a saturnine local district officer; and various natives recruited from London casting offices were added to the cast. The entire company and the crew left for Ste. Maxime in the late summer of 1937. While Charles, Pommer, and Cormack were looking for suitable locations, Elsa swam and shopped with Benita Armstrong, who came down from England to keep her company. Meanwhile, she read and reread the script, at once drawn to the part of Martha Jones, delighted that at last she had a real opportunity to appear as a major motivating force in a film vehicle, and terrified by the size of the challenge.

Shooting began in August 1937, at the handsome subtropical

garden of the Château Robert between Cannes and Nice. On the first morning the director ordered the Laughtons to be drenched in water and covered in ashes so that they would look as sweaty and dusty as two people in the South Seas would after a long and exhausting walk. Ironically, the sun dried the water, and the whole process of dousing and dusting had to be repeated, Pommer often joining enthusiastically in the job himself, and Charles and Elsa feeling more miserably uncomfortable by the minute.

Making the movie was a grueling experience, not helped by the fact that Bartlett Cormack was totally incapable of directing the picture. He finally had to withdraw, drunk and twitching violently with a nervous tic of the face, and let Pommer take over the direction.

Shooting continued through September on an island off St. Tropez, the players carried to the location each day on a little boat called *Le Loup* (The Wolf, run by a pleasant local couple. In one scene in which Charles had to carry Elsa through rocks to the shore he slipped and she fell into the sea with a splash; in another, she had to fall on a live octopus several times. Most days were spent with the crew thigh deep in water, burned to blisters by the intense sun.

A visitor to the location, Richard Haestier of the London *Star*, reported having an al fresco lunch with the Laughtons on a launch. Both of them wore bathing costumes as Charles carved a chicken with a former hotelier's expertise and passed round pieces of it, saying in broad Cockney, "Excuse me 'ands but it's easier. Just like 'Ennery the Eighth, ain't it?" Suddenly he began quoting G. K. Chesterton:

"The earth is a place on which England is found,
  And you find it however you twirl the globe round;
  For the spots are all red and the rest is all grey,
  And that is the meaning of Empire Day."

Charles was in a rare good humor during much of the shooting, telling funny stories about pukka sahib colonels or regaling Richard Haestier with grotesque jokes. (Sample: "What's the difference between a hairdresser and a sculptor?" "A hairdresser dyes and curls, and a sculptor makes faces and busts.")

At other times, Charles was fretful. Guthrie recorded a troublesome episode in his memoirs: Pommer was shooting a sequence in which Ginger Ted had been misbehaving, the missionary played by Guthrie was furious and slammed out, and District Officer Robert Newton was in a tantrum. The first take went smoothly enough, but Charles decided he had played it inadequately and asked for a retake. Pommer agreed. By eight o'clock that evening Charles still wasn't satisfied.

Next day the agony went on. Charles, a perfectionist as always, was determined to have the scene absolutely correct. He was furious when Pommer stopped shooting, told him he was going to use the first take, and stalked off the set.

Production continued in England, with many scenes expertly dovetailed. The whole final portion of the picture was shot at Elstree Studios. Two sound stages were combined for Tom Morahan's magnificent set of a tropical jungle. Rain machines drenched Charles and Elsa from morning to night for days on end. Crude oil was pumped in to create a look of ground mists, and in the hut where they took shelter, the rain dripped on their heads.

The resulting movie remains very appealing, perfectly hitting off the cool humor of Maugham's story. Charles added many touches to the dialogue. In the scene at the end, when Ted and Martha are waiting for the arrival of natives during the epidemic, he reflects sadly: "I was the fat boy at school . . ." His portrait of Ted is vivid and affectionate. Shapeless, sweating, unshaven, he appears throughout as a drunken nuisance, a beaten ne'er-do-well whose life is a succession of mishaps; but Charles makes him appealing, good-natured, and hedonistic, so that the audience is on his side from the beginning. He has something of the benign ineptitude of Oliver Hardy, whom Charles very much admired. Elsa's performance is equally impressive. She used a special voice for Martha. Overly genteel, suggesting elocution schools, pitched in a high key, it perfectly expressed a peremptory and puritanical mind. Sweeping into barroom or government office, she was Ginger Ted's scourge, condemning him for sleeping with a native girl, denouncing his drinking with a temperance worker's hatred, beating him with her umbrella like a naughty child. In the final sequences, the growing tenderness between this unlikely pair of sparring partners is delicately suggested. From the beginning, the actors had shown that under the prim spinster and the hopeless drunk there dwelt decent and warm spirits so that the final reversal of character seemed surprisingly convincing. Both Charles and Elsa were grateful for parts which offered sufficient contradictions and paradoxes, and they played them with enthusiasm to the hilt.

After *The Vessel of Wrath* was completed, Elsa traveled to New York, where the film was retitled *The Beachcomber*, to promote it with a long succession of newspaper interviews given at Iris Barry's townhouse in Turtle Bay. She also appeared at the première of the picture, talking to the audience from the balcony, since Equity regulations forbade her to appear on the theatre's stage.

Returning to England, she experienced a shock. After reading Clemence Dane's script *St. Martin's Lane*, about London buskers, Charles, Pommer, and Elsa had become convinced that she should play the young Cockney girl who dances with Charles in the picture and becomes a musical comedy star. As a Cockney and a fine dancer herself, and with her intimate knowledge of the buskers on whom the story was based, she was certain she would be perfect in the role. But it was finally decided that Vivien Leigh, who had been a huge hit in the West End play, Ashley Dukes's *The Mask of Virtue*, should play the part instead. The decision was the worst blow for Elsa since her rejection for the part of the daughter in *Payment Deferred*, and she recalls that when Charles told her the news, she went pale and actually felt faint.

The Irish-American Tim Whelan was chosen to direct *St. Martin's Lane*, Jules Kruger and Tom Morahan, the cameraman and art director of *The Vessel of Wrath*, were engaged once more, and Bartlett Cormack was signed to play the role of Strang, an American impresario. In conference much of Clemence Dane's script was discarded. Whelan, Cormack, Charles, and Pommer rewrote a great deal of it, and Miss Dane declined to take credit for the screenplay when the picture appeared. The producing team decided to use London locations as a living background for the story, shooting in the West End, and using queueing theatregoers as extras. The effect was to give the whole production a striking and vivid immediacy, a feeling of London itself as a living ingredient of the drama.

Whelan, working with Jules Kruger, who had shot *The Vessel of Wrath*, used such recognizable locations as Cambridge Circus, Shaftesbury Avenue, Piccadilly Circus, and St. Martin's Lane itself. Tom Morahan, as great an asset to Mayflower as Vincent Korda was to his brother's organization, expertly designed the production, providing equally convincing agents' offices, shabby walkup rooms with peeling flowered wallpaper, and Art Moderne apartments. The busker Charlie Staggers is one of Laughton's most memorable creations. He is first seen entertaining a bored and indifferent Holborn Empire queue with a recitation of "The Green Eye of the Little Yellow God"; he is thrust brutally aside when a swarm of autograph hunters descends on the star of the Empire show. A young girl, Liberty (Vivien Leigh), steals a penny from his beggar's cap. Giving chase, Charlie discovers she is a professional thief who, right in front of his nose at a sandwich stall, slips journalist Rex Harrison's silver cigarette case into her handbag.

Charlie follows her to an empty mansion where, in an exquisite sequence, he sees her dance on the dusty floor in the moonlight. He falls in love, but he is too shy to reveal this to her. In the second half, the film becomes clearly influenced by Pommer: it could have been an Emil Jannings vehicle, this story of an ugly, poverty-stricken little man who is spurned by the object of his affections. There is a cruel, stabbing scene when Liberty tells Charlie after he proposes to her: "Why won't I marry yer? Just look in the frying pan!" and he shakes her in frustrated rage. Later, when she is discovered for stardom, she regrets her hasty unkindness and tries to make amends, but it's too late.

In several sequences—Charlie Staggers' angry defiance as he goes downstairs after losing Liberty to his rival for her hand, talking of the way life has kicked him around, in his halting and confused recitation of Kipling's "If" when Libbie arranges an audition for him, darting ugly glances when the producer calls for a cup of coffee right in the middle of his best lines, and in the scene when he tries to see her after her opening in a West End musical, *Straw Hat in the Rain*, and she is swept away by autograph hunters—Charles is superbly in command. In other scenes he seems uncertain, mugging excessively, but in sum this is a good performance, the character painfully close to Charles's own in its sense of physical inadequacy, its awkward, self-bolstering pride, its agony; pleasantly close, too, in the gentleness and tenderness of the scenes with Libby. Vivien Leigh is unconvincing as a Cockney, frequently slipping into an affected Surbiton accent, and suggesting a cool ambition rather than the tender concern which Clemence Dane gave to the character. She is good in only a few scenes: the dance in the deserted mansion, the theft of the cigarette case, the brutal rejection of Charlie's offer of marriage, when a ruthless streak in the actress really comes out. Only a year later, she was to be Scarlett in *Gone With the Wind*.

St. Martin's Lane proved to be a flop in the United States as *Sidewalks of London*, chiefly because of the extreme feebleness of the musical sequences in the second half, compared with the best Hollywood could offer, and because of the somewhat remote subject matter, the difficulty for many Americans of following Charles's Cockney, Vivien Leigh's weird shifts of accent, and Rex Harrison's haughty pseudo-Mayfair. The persnickety Tyrone Guthrie's performance as a busker, played like an agitated ostrich, brought laughs in the wrong places at the opening in New York; his effeminate portrayal upset the balance of many scenes. The whole picture was simply too specialized, too odd and offbeat, and it seriously lacked a romantic hero. This was a problem too with *The Beachcomber*—though by now it appeared that the earlier film would pay its costs.

Around the time of *St. Martin's Lane*'s completion, in the fall season of 1938, Elsa's reminiscences *Charles Laughton and I* were released to an excellent press. On October 14 the Laughtons were guests of honor at a Foyles Literary Luncheon at the Grosvenor House to celebrate the occasion. Among those who gave speeches honoring them were the French star Mistinguett, Mabel Constanduros, Eric Maschwitz, Mme. Prunier; and other guests included Benn W. Levy and his wife Constance Cummings, Lupino Lane, Roger Livesey, and Ursula Jeans, and the actress Zena Dare. Later the book was published in America, with equal success.

While *St. Martin's Lane* was being finished, Charles managed to bring off a tremendous coup. He succeeded in persuading Alfred Hitchcock, the most famous and successful director in England, to direct Mayflower Productions' story of smuggling in Cornwall, England, *Jamaica Inn*, just before he left for Hollywood on contract to David O. Selznick. Hitchcock had known Charles in the late 1920s, when they had lunched together at l'Étoile and discussed making pictures together. Nothing had come of these plans. They had run into each other on and off during the years; and when Hitchcock's agent suggested he take on a Laughton vehicle to fill his waiting period before he left for Hollywood to prepare the story of the *Titanic*, he happily accepted.

Hitchcock was reasonably sanguine about the project until he read the screenplay. He immediately wanted to back out; but he had already accepted several thousand pounds as an advance and didn't feel sufficiently well-off to return the money. Finally, after much soul-searching, he decided that in order to get out of the picture he would have to sell his house, and he even began to make the necessary arrangements. But Charles managed to persuade him to proceed with the movie.

When the first discussions on the picture began, an immediate problem arose. Pommer hated Hitchcock, and the feeling was mutual. On top of that, Hitchcock became more and more convinced that, if the film was to succeed at all, Charles must not play the central role of Sir Humphrey Pengallan. He felt very strongly that since Charles had played so many villains on the screen nobody would accept his disguise as a simple squire in the story, that they would immediately pick up that he was the smuggler and shipwrecker the Cornish constabulary was looking for.

Finally, Hitchcock went back to Charles and told him, "It's impossible, I still can't make the picture. It won't work." Whereupon Charles replied: "If you don't, it will ruin Erich. You'll be putting a German refugee on the streets." Miserably, Hitchcock felt obliged to proceed. But he insisted Clemence Dane's script be completely rewritten by Sidney Gilliat, who had worked on Hitchcock's *The Lady Vanishes*, and by his own personal assistant, Joan Harrison. Charles would only accept this arrangement if his own part could be created by J. B. Priestley, who had, of course, written the book on which *The Old Dark House* was based. The two scripts—Priestley's and Gilliat and Harrison's —failed to jell, and the whole structure of the film proved to be hopelessly ramshackle.

Everyone began the picture in a spirit of uncertainty. But one element in it pleased Charles. Maureen O'Hara, a beautiful and quite charming young actress, made her debut in the film. Charles and Erich Pommer admired her; they had first thought of putting her under contract to their company as early as 1937, when they were preparing *The Beachcomber,* but she had been too inexperienced and awkward at the first meeting. Later Charles had seen a test that impressed him so deeply he made Erich Pommer look at it. The result was they signed her to a seven-year contract with annual options for renewal.

Finally, *Jamaica Inn* provided her chance. Charles told her as they started work that she must feel her way to the heart of the girl she had to play; that theatrical tricks would never work on the screen. He made her realize that the essence of screen acting was feeling deeply, being completely sincere and straightforward, and having a sense of total conviction at all times. Though she never became a major actress, it was a lesson she never forgot; her performances in the future, though very limited, were often luminous with honesty of spirit, human and alive and touching. All through the shooting, Charles acted as a father to her—much more so than Hitchcock, who treated her rather coolly and seemed to be far more interested in the mechanics of the scenes, or Pommer, who was stern and severe, impatient with her fluffing of lines. At one stage, Charles even told Maureen that, since he had no children of his own, he would like to adopt her. He frequently told her amusing stories, especially one about a clergyman at the Stonyhurst Chapel who used to spit out so much saliva during his sermons that Charles had to put up an umbrella to protect himself.

Maureen told Elsa years later that Charles had said to her she would always be a movie star, but that she must first and foremost be a character woman, that she must never be merely a leading lady. Certainly, she was tested to the limits of endurance by the part. As the tormented heroine, she had to be lashed by spray and high winds, tossed around in a storm-swept sea, cling to a slippery rock, and even wave a burning cloak above a cliff. Hitchcock failed to use a double for these difficult and dangerous scenes. Making the picture was an ordeal for her, and so, too, for Charles.

He had no sooner begun to work on *Jamaica Inn* than he wanted to abandon it. There was a particularly difficult sequence in which he had to tie up Maureen O'Hara, and he couldn't play the scene in the manner Hitchcock wanted. Finally, he was so heartbroken at his failure he sat in a corner of the sound stage and sulked like an angry child. Hitchcock did his best to commiserate with him, but it was useless. Then, suddenly, Charles leaped to his feet. "Now I know how to play the scene!" he shouted. "I'm going to feel like a boy of ten who has just wet his pants!"

Charles needed music, as so often before, to get into the correct mood for scenes. He would play Weber's *Invitation to the Dance*, over and over again, in order to get the correct rhythmical beat in his walk as the squire. Hitchcock felt that these props were unprofessional, that Charles was an inspired amateur, superbly talented but lacking in real technique, discipline, control.

Jamica Inn is among Hitchcock's—and Charles's—least successful works. Set entirely at night, in Tom Morahan's Gothic sets of labyrinthine white stone inn, squire's mansion, or rocky foreshore, it is a somber period barnstormer unrelieved by humor. The opening scene is among the few which really works: Maureen O'Hara arriving in a carriage in the midst of a howling wind, while Squire Pengallan presides over an elaborate dinner party, ecstatically greeting the arrival of his horse as a dinner guest, toasting the beast almost lasciviously as he describes its prowess at the Truro Steeplechase. A moment later, his lovely ward, played by Maureen, appears in the hall, only to be inspected with lip-smacking relish like another horse.

Here, Charles is at his most entertainingly hammy, creating a satirical portrait of a lecherous aristocrat informed with all of his own dislike of pomposity and privilege. With his curled hair, false eyebrows arched permanently in an expression of disdain, Neronian false nose, white waistcoat, massive stomach, white breeches, Javertian boots, and dowager's voice, his Pengallan is a grotesque buffoon, suffering from inherited insanity—the squire's grandfather had died mad—committed to a career of smuggling, wreckage, and bloodshed. Yet Charles evidently influenced the script, providing those odd, unexpected reversals of character which bring it to life. In one sequence, Sir Humphrey is haughtily receiving his tenants on a Sunday. He dismisses a radical from his sight, threatening him with the hangman's noose, but a moment later he shows kindness to an old woman whose roof is leaking, overruling his colleagues in demanding that the entire roof be replaced at his expense. And there is a nice touch in the binding and gagging scene later on, which Maureen O'Hara recalls as Charles's invention. He puts a silk scarf over her wrists to protect them from being severely chafed by the ropes. This hint of fastidiousness and concern makes Pengallan far more interesting, relieving the leering villainy which J. B. Priestley evoked in writing the part, but in much of the playing Charles mugged and overacted outrageously.

Jamaica Inn was a disaster, and by 1939 it became obvious that Mayflower Productions was going to collapse. John Maxwell of Associated British backed out. Charles, burdened with administrative problems as well as the constant anguish of facing up to major starring roles, was almost relieved to see the end of his short-lived venture into executive work. He acepted with pleasure a Hollywood contract from RKO which his Hollywood agent Myron Selznick insisted he take. It called for immediate commencement of work on his second Victor Hugo subject after *Les Misérables:* a new version of *The Hunchback of Notre Dame,* which had been famous as a silent film of Lon Chaney's. Maureen O'Hara was cast as Esmeralda on Charles's suggestion.

SEVEN

Leaving Elsa in London, Charles sailed on the *Queen Mary* for New York in June 1939, accompanied by Maureen O'Hara and her mother. During the past months he had been dogged, not only by the failure of Mayflower Productions, but by major tax problems. As early as June 1937 the Treasury Department had investigated him on the ground that he had set up a British corporation, Motion Picture and Theatrical Industries, Ltd., in London, to which he turned over all his earnings and which paid him $20,000 a year. The Treasury claimed that he had been earning $190,000 a year in 1935 and 1936, that by forming this company he had evaded his responsibility to the American government. Despite the fact that this was a perfectly legal maneuver, Charles was subjected to constant harassment on the matter until, on June 23, the same day he arrived in New York, the Board of Tax Appeals ruled that he was not liable to further taxation, as he had invested whatever sums were earned in excess of $20,000 in Mayflower Productions, the failure of which to earn a profit had wiped out his assets.

In New York, excitement greeted Charles's arrival with

Maureen O'Hara, described by several papers in an excess of enthusiasm as "the lovely fourteen-year-old colleen from Ireland," when she had in fact just turned nineteen. The New York *Times* film critic Bosley Crowther wrote of her, "She is the emerald shower which succeeds the initial explosion of a skyrocket." Crowther boarded the ship from the custom boat, clambering up a Jacob's ladder to find Charles in the midst of "magnificent squalor" in his A-Deck first-class cabin. He wrote: "Six-thirty a.m. is indeed a wretched hour to put anybody on review. But you should have seen that stateroom . . . the long dressing table was littered with an assortment of unrelated objects. At one end was a pile of autograph books, submitted respectfully by members of the crew for Mr. Laughton to sign. (Imagine that—British merchant seamen collecting autographs!) The bed looked as though it had been occupied by a whirling dervish affected with fits. And in the middle of the room stood Mr. Laughton wearing a blue chalk stripe suit which fitted him as though it had been put on inside out, his face blowsy from sleep and his hair impossibly snarled. He was blithely tossing clothes, books, anything within reach into an open suitcase on the floor and pressing the contents down with his foot." Charles told Crowther he had wanted to play the hunchback since 1934, when Thalberg, who had died in 1936, had suggested it to him; that he was still grieving over Thalberg's loss, and that he hoped to see Norma Shearer in Hollywood. He talked of his role in *The Hunchback:* "Naturally, I won't play it as Lon Chaney did. Any actor who understands his stuff always plays to catch the tempo of the moment. As for the spirit of the story, I understand it all right. I know the French cathedrals, Notre Dame and Chartres, quite well. One doesn't have to know much more about it than that." The statement was a deliberate put-on, of course. Charles had spent most of the voyage rereading Hugo's novel for the third or fourth time, and looking over the first-draft screenplay.

Early in July, Charles returned to Hollywood and checked back into the Garden of Allah Hotel. In the meantime, the studio chief, Pandro S. Berman, had hired the autocratic William Dieterle—white-gloved because of his fear of germs, despite the fact that he was a Christian Scientist, and famous for his historical biographies at Warners—to direct the picture.

Although Charles was enthusiastic to begin work, he immediately realized the problem that faced him in playing the role. In that stifling summer of 1939, just before war broke out in Europe, he was confronted with the most devastating ordeal of his career. He had to be turned into a deformed monster, with a hunchback, a walleye, and twisted arms and legs. Lon Chaney had devised his own makeup, but Charles did not trust himself to do more than make suggestions. He insisted on having the celebrated Perc Westmore create his complete disguise. The hump itself weighed four pounds, and was made of foam rubber. Part of Charles's face had to be pulled down, and the other pulled up, to give a lopsided appearance. Special lenses gave one eye a milky consistency. A false eye hung on the other cheek. Charles's clothes were heavily padded and his body covered in rubber to suggest enormous muscular power, and he had to drag heavy chains in many scenes. The heat was so intense that sweat often ran down his forehead, ruining Westmore's work.

Charles's real challenge—a challenge he rose to wonderfully—was to convey Quasimodo's kindness and beauty of character, his tender affection for Esmeralda, and the fact that he was superior as a human being to the handsome diffident worldlings of the court of Louis XI. Another challenge was to convey that he was deaf. His eyes, peering through contact lenses which were so painful they made his eyes run between scenes, had to show no reaction when he heard sudden and violent sounds. To make his part flawlessly realistic, he had special waxes put in his ears which made it impossible for him to hear anything; they had to be removed when Dieterle gave him directions.

Charles did not find Dieterle's personality congenial. Tall, commanding, dictatorial, he was uncomfortably reminiscent of Javert-Sternberg. On the first day of shooting, in a replica of Notre Dame and its surrounding streets, built out in the San Fernando Valley, Charles refused to continue work on the grounds that he simply wasn't fully prepared. Dieterle, with an expensive budget and hundreds of extras milling around, was beside himself. He screamed abuse at Charles in front of everyone, then sent Charles home and began shooting another scene. Charles, before he left, said to Dieterle: "I'm so sorry. I thought I was ready; it just wouldn't come. But I will be good tomorrow, I promise." Dieterle, melting a little at his show of humility, sent him off with a condescending pat on the back. Next day, Charles was letter-perfect, and played the scene flawlessly. Dieterle, who finally came to realize Charles's greatness, wrote to Elsa in 1968 from his home in Triesen, Liechtenstein: "When Laughton acted the scene on the wheel, enduring the terrible torture, he was not the poor, crippled creature, expecting compassion from the mob, but rather oppressed and enslaved mankind, suffering injustice . . ." It was not insignificant that Charles was acutely aware of human oppression during the shooting, because even as he played out the scenes of man's inhumanity to man, Hitler was marching into Poland.

In the meantime, Elsa had arrived safely from England. Apparently prodded by various Universal executives who had just returned from Europe, Charles decided to ask her to come to Hollywood. He sent a telegram, COME AT ONCE, WILL EXPLAIN LATER. She had been enjoying herself sailing with Allen Lane, the managing director of Penguin Books, around the Isle of Wight, and was reluctant to leave; she didn't really believe there would be a war. But she immediately booked passage, and the day after she had been out sailing off the coast of England, she saw it disappearing from the rail of the *Normandie*. She felt deeply sad, saying "Poor little England" to herself, and wondering if she would ever see the White Cliffs again.

When she arrived in Hollywood, she found Charles in a condition of nervous and mental exhaustion. Each night as he came home to her at the Garden of Allah he broke down from the physical agony of five hours of makeup and then day-long shooting schedules in the blazing sun, and the knowledge that Europe was being crushed by Hitler. Dieterle wrote:

> When England and France declared war on the Third Reich the tension on the soundstage was unbearable. The scene in which Quasimodo rings the bell for Esmeralda, high in the bell tower, one of the most important scenes in the story, was supposed to be a kind of love scene between these two, but it developed into something so powerful, that everybody including myself forgot that we were shooting a film. Something super-

dimensional happened at that moment, so that I forgot to call "cut" according to custom, as the scene ended.

Laughton went on ringing the bells after the scene was really over. Finally, completely exhausted, he stopped. Nobody was able to speak, nobody moved. It was an unforgettable thing. Finally, in his dressing room, Charles could only say: "I couldn't think of Esmeralda in that scene at all. I could only think of the poor people out there, going to fight that bloody, bloody war! To arouse the world, to stop that terrible butchery! Awake! Awake! That's what I felt when I was ringing the bells!"

By mid-September, the heat wave had increased in intensity. The heat became so severe that at night the Laughtons had to sleep wrapped in wet sheets. They slept in this fashion for an hour or two, before the sheets dried with their body heat; then they had to get up, soak the sheets again, and return to bed. Often, after a whipping scene, Charles would come home with welts on his arms, hips, and back, groaning, with tears of pain in his eyes. Finally he lost all feeling he might have had for Dieterle. Elsa recalls: "One day, Dieterle went over to him and said, 'Charles, listen to me. We'll do one more take, and I want you—I want you to suffer.' Charles never forgave him for that. Never."

During this dreadful experience, there were very few compensations. Maureen O'Hara, lovely and spirited as Esmeralda, came to live at the Garden of Allah, so the Laughtons saw her at weekends and she would share their misery by discussing the week's work. Then, one memorable day, during a welcome brief break from Dieterle's tyranny, the crew asked Charles to recite the Gettysburg Address as he had done in *Ruggles* and at the end of shooting *Bounty*. He spoke it wonderfully through his grotesque makeup.

As always, Charles was considerate to the young and inexperienced actors in the cast. He was consistently kind to Edmond O'Brien, here playing his first film role as the romantic hero. Terrified of meeting one of the greatest actors of the time, O'Brien was astonished that Charles was sweet and thoughtful to him. He was doubly impressed by Charles's goodness of spirit because of the way that Dieterle handled Charles, screaming at him constantly.

Sometimes, Dieterle's poor knowledge of English provided comic relief on the set. When Charles said that in a scene on Notre Dame Cathedral Quasimodo should resemble one of the gargoyles among which he crawled, Dieterle snapped, "Vast ist diss gargoyle?" One day Dieterle yelled, "I vont two hundred monkeys on ze set tomorrow morning!" When he arrived, baboons, chimpanzees, gorillas, and every other variety were running all over the place, making a terrible din. Dieterle arrived and shouted out, "Mein *Gott!* Vas is diss?"

A prop man said, "The monkeys you ordered!"

"No, I vonted three hundred priests—monks, not monkeys!" the frantic Dieterle screamed.

Far more dated than Charles's previous Victor Hugo subject, *Les Misérables, The Hunchback of Notre Dame* resembles an enormous village pageant, complete with uproariously laughing or raging citizens, stooped old king, sinister chief justice, saintly, ancient archbishop, pretty beleaguered heroine, and dashing liberal-minded hero. The script of Sonya Levien and Bruno Frank—an expatriate German novelist—makes *The Vagabond King* seem sophisticated by comparison. This is an operetta without songs, accompanied by the composer Alfred Newman's crashing chords and celestial choirs suggesting menace or exaltation. In the circumstances, Charles's achievement is nothing short of astonishing. With only a handful of lines of dialogue and a succession of action scenes in which he is crowned king of the grotesques, accused of seducing Esmeralda and whipped on the wheel, seen ringing the bells, and rescuing the unhappy girl from a hangman's noose, he somehow creates a character. At first, all we see is a monstrous presence darting up and down streets or climbing the high belfry; but when he at last has Esmeralda alone and says to her, "I'm neither a man nor a beast—I've about as much shape *as the man in the moon!*" he makes us feel that inside the enormous misshapen form a poet is struggling to be let out. There is a heartbreaking scene when he tries to confess his love for her. As written, the sequence is a cross between *Beauty and the Beast* and *King Kong,* but, aided by the tender and unselfish playing of Maureen O'Hara, he invests it with sweetness and poignancy. Charles added many striking touches of his own. At our very first glimpse of him, he snarls and snaps like a mad dog; when he first talks to Esmeralda, his voice breaks in the middle of a sentence; and at the end, his eyes are filled with affection for a stone gargoyle which he embraces with the words, "If only I had been made of stone, like you!" This is certainly one of his greatest performances. It was as though his hatred of his own physical being had reached its fullest expression, as though we were seeing what he saw in the mirrors of his nightmares. Physically, as well as psychologically, it is a striking achievement. Although a double evidently performed the really dangerous stunts —descending from Notre Dame on a rope to snatch Esmeralda from the gallows and carry her back, all in a single shot, darting along the hundred-foot-high face of the replica of the Cathedral— Charles had to push hundred-pound bells with hands and feet while laden with his rubber coating in the hundred-degree heat, had to perch on rafters without a net below so that Dieterle and his cameraman Joe August could achieve a vertigo-inducing shot, and had to run bent down through a maze of corridors and up and down steps when his face had to be visible. The production was a great success, greater still when it was released in Europe after the war, and aside from a few dissenters, Charles was widely and warmly praised.

After World War II broke out, Charles was conscience-stricken that he had not returned to England. He felt he should have been in London to help the war effort, but his commitment to RKO made it impossible for him to leave America, and after the failure of Mayflower he needed every cent to survive. He was painfully conscious of what war meant in terms of human suffering, since he had never forgotten his experiences in the trenches in World War I, and he still suffered rashes on his back from the after-effects of mustard gas more than twenty years before. He felt powerless. And his feelings were not entirely unmixed. Part of him had rejected England, its stultifying class system at the time; and he felt, more and more deeply, that he could help England and the war effort as a whole more completely by remaining in America, which would, he felt certain, soon enter the war.

His decision not to return caused loud criticism of him in the

English press, but this was tempered a little when it was realized that he would be physically unfit for active duty. In 1940, RKO offered him a script based on the life of Dr. Samuel Johnson, which he instantly turned down because of its gross distortions of the man whom Charles had admired for much of his life. He was quoted widely as saying that "in this version Dr. Johnson did nothing but sit on his fat rump and make cruel remarks about other people." The words "in this version" were dropped in transcripts in England, and in the middle of the blitz the London public was told by its newspapers, "Laughton condemns Johnson."

As a result, Charles unwittingly succeeded in infuriating the Staffordshire Society, which was dedicated to honoring Johnson's memory as a native of Lichfield. The Staffordshire Society met with the Johnson Society at the Lexicographers' Hall in Gough Square, London, and, with bombs falling on every side, solemnly discussed this world-shaking matter. Fred Vernon, secretary of the Johnson Society, delivered a statement to the press which read, in part: "Charles Laughton is, by general agreement, an excellent actor. But he is not fitted to portray [Johnson] in a cinema film, having obviously little sympathy for his personality."

Charles wrote to the Staffordshire and Johnson societies and insisted he intended no offense: "I do beg you to believe that never would I be quite such an idiot as to make any slighting remarks about the great man. One might just as well go about criticizing roast beef and Yorkshire pudding, English bluebells and the Yorkshire moors." The recipients of his earnest letter wrote back graciously forgiving him for his misdemeanor.

On September 18, 1940, Charles was in Chicago for a broadcast when he was told that the flat in Gordon Square had been damaged beyond repair in the Blitz. A Junkers 88 dive bomber had fallen into it after being hit by antiaircraft shells. It had been leased only the week before by Walter Graebner, head of the London office of *Time* and *Life*, who fortunately was not there at the time. Charles was hugely relieved that Elsa had not stayed in London; she might have been killed. He told the New York *Times* just before going on the air: "I should be glad to sacrifice twenty houses if German dive bombers would smash themselves to bits on them. To hell with the cash if they can bring down the

Junkers. It was a glorious end for the house." Fortunately, *The Judgment of Paris* had been brought over, rolled up in a cylinder, on a transatlantic ship several months before, along with the beds and some tables and other items of furniture.

After the ordeal of *Hunchback*, Charles felt the need for a complete change of pace. He was delighted, therefore, that Erich Pommer, who had just signed a contract with RKO-Radio Pictures, had prepared a very interesting new role for him. The idea for the part had apparently come from Garson Kanin, the twenty-seven-year-old writer-director also under contract to RKO. Kanin had overheard Charles talking Italian to a waitress in Lucy's, the famous cafe near the studio. Both Pommer and Kanin wanted Charles to play Tony, the Italian wine-grower who ordered a mail-order bride in *They Knew What They Wanted*, Sidney Howard's Pulitzer Prize-winning play which had already been filmed by Paramount and MGM.

Pommer, with all of the passion for location shooting which had inspired his three Mayflower productions, decided to film the entire picture in the Napa Valley, several hundred miles from Los Angeles, where the great wine-growing dynasties of California lived and flourished. Charles felt uncomfortable about being away from home for over two months, and when he saw the huge house that RKO had rented for him in the Valley he realized he would be quite unable to cope with the housekeeping problems. He shifted to a small comfortable hotel, the Madrones Inn, where he was well looked after by the staff. Garson Kanin expressed snobbish surprise at Charles's modest and practical decision and was still castigating him for it in his book *Hollywood* thirty years later.

For weeks, Charles worked in close consultation with Robert Ardrey on the writing of the screenplay. At the end of the work, Ardrey's script ran into trouble with the Breen office. The problem was that at the end of the picture Tony forgives his adulterous wife. The Breen office was entirely opposed to this: she must be punished according to the Code. Charles, Erich Pommer, Garson Kanin, and Ardrey all went to see Joseph Breen to discuss the problem. Breen raved about Ardrey's work, but finally concluded his paean of praise with the words, *"The sinner must be punished!"* Charles said nothing; Kanin and Ardrey told Breen that there would be no point in making the picture at all unless there was forgiveness. Breen shook his head. At last, out of the depths of the couch, Charles said, very deliberately: "Do I understand, Mr. Breen, that the Code *does not recognize the New Testament?*" Breen recoiled in astonishment, and Kanin and Ardrey shot a gleeful glance at each other. "Christ forgave the adulteress didn't he, Mr. Breen?" Charles asked coldly, pronouncing "Mr. Breen" as though Breen was Fletcher Christian and he was Captain Bligh. Breen sat pale and silent and then said, with considerable difficulty: "Well, Mr. Laughton, you may have a point there." And he let the film's conclusion stand.

Once the Breen office had given the go-ahead, Kanin went into rehearsal with Charles, Carole Lombard, William Gargan, Harry Carey, and the rest of the cast, who sat around the bare sound stage as though they were in a theatre, reading the lines from wooden stools. Once they were letter perfect, Kanin rehearsed them with chalk marks on the floor. Everyone, of course, was in ordinary street clothes. But on the third day, Charles appeared with his complete costume as Tony. Carole Lombard, who had a flat chest, and liked to work in rehearsals without her "falsies," was astounded when she saw Charles. Not to be outdone, she yelled to her maid, Bucket, "Bucket, *bring me my breasts*, will yah?"

Several weeks before shooting began, Charles drove up to the Napa Valley to study the terrain, which he instantly loved. When Kanin drove up to study it also, he was amazed to see Charles walking down the main street of one of the little towns, made up as Tony, his shirt hanging out.

Charles disliked Garson Kanin from the outset. He found the twenty-seven-year-old director to be high-strung, aggressive, and rather pretentious in a way Charles found particularly irritating. Moreover, he must have been annoyed by Kanin's habit of calling him "Chuck" and slapping him on the shoulder or back without warning. Kanin seemed to be unaware of the fact that Charles had not gotten along with Carole Lombard on *White Woman*, and told Charles with an air of triumph that he had acquired Miss Lombard to play opposite him. Charles groaned: he dreaded her bad language, raucous jokes, and habit of breaking up on lines, and he asked Pommer to replace her, without success.

Charles and Kanin continued to be enemies in the two weeks

of rehearsal in Hollywood prior to their departure for the Napa Valley. Charles managed a perfect Italian accent—he spoke fluent Italian—but Kanin dismissed this out of hand. No sooner had he worked, to please Kanin, with an Italian coach—quite unnecessary in the circumstances—than Italy came into the war. Charles immediately decided he could not play a sympathetic Italian, and asked Pommer to change the role to a Spaniard. Pommer refused, and obtained a bizarre statement from the British Embassy in Washington, reassuring Charles that it would be "perfectly acceptable for Mr. Laughton to play an Italian, provided that the period were marked down as the 1930s."

In his book *Hollywood*, Kanin claims that he told Charles, before he worked with the coach, "No Italian on earth sounds like that," and that Charles worked with the coach "at a house on Curson Avenue," which in fact he and Elsa didn't move into until a decade later.

Charles was very happy with the location because of the proximity of so many wineries, and their friendly atmosphere. A member of La Confrérie des Chevaliers du Tastevin, he was able to sample the local vintages with an expert's taste.

In brief breaks in the last-minute rehearsals, overcome by heat in the Valley, he would walk around the dressing room naked, reciting John Donne's Holy Sonnets, unaware that he was being watched by a set visitor, the director Jules Dassin, and several members of the crew.

The night before the production started, Charles drove up to Garson Kanin's hotel to discuss the first scene. He was very depressed. He had been drinking, and he told Kanin, "I don't know how to play this role! I *can't* play it. I'll *never* get it. What can I *do*?" Kanin said, "Why don't we rehearse it now, tonight, out in the Valley?" Charles nodded. Kanin followed him into the vineyards. Finally they reached a peach orchard. After many agonizing attempts, Charles "got the scene." Kanin told him it was marvelous; Charles said that he at last knew how to do it. But the next day he had completely forgotten how to play it.

He insisted that Kanin take him back to the orchard where he could recapture the scene. But now it was blanketed in fog and men were spraying it with insecticide. Charles walked headlong into the chemical spray and the fog, while Kanin stumbled behind him, eyes and nose miserably streaming. At last Charles said, "I've got it now!" He stood in the spray and the fog, almost weeping, and smiling at the same time. "I've got it now. I've *got it!*" he cried out. But it still took ten takes before he was happy.

Another difficult scene was the one in which Tony is waiting for his mail-order bride with a table covered in delectable Italian dishes. Kanin decided it would be a nice local touch to have an open barrel of butter standing on the floor. Charles for no apparent reason sat down on the butter barrel. Kanin thought it might be funny to add this to the script. But Charles refused. He left the set for forty minutes, changed his clothes, and came back. Then he sat in the butter again. Kanin snapped: "You keep sitting in the fucking butter, Chuck. Why don't you just *sit down on the chair?*" Charles near tears, after recovering himself, used the chair.

In one of his rare moments of companionship with Charles, Kanin said: "You know, Chuck, to most of us the idea of death is unthinkable. It's so mysterious. We just know it will happen, but we don't know where it will happen, or what's going to rub us out." Charles looked thoughtful. Kanin continued: "We don't know what's going to kill us, do we? Or at least most of us don't. But you do, Chuck! You're going to die of acting!"

This remark wasn't calculated to please Charles, nor was Kanin's infuriating habit of constantly praising Laurence Olivier. Feeling himself unattractive, Charles knew he could not play many of the great parts open to Olivier and other handsome actors.

Back in Hollywood, the animosity between Charles and Carole grew worse and worse. Robert Ardrey grew worried that she might turn on Charles and physically attack him. He said to Kanin one day, "My God, Gar, if she ever sinks those beautiful teeth in Charles's blubber, it'll be like Captain Ahab attacking Moby Dick."

Finally, Charles did go too far in needling Carole. She turned on him and told him he was "a fucking sonofabitch!" and that she had had it put in her contract she "wouldn't have to kiss his fat lips." Charles was horrified at this outburst, and, according to Ardrey, fell down on the floor and wept with frustration. Kanin had to close down shooting for the rest of the day. That night Kanin told Ardrey, "That S.O.B. He had the whole thing planned. He needed to create a mood where he hated Carole. Tomorrow I'm doing the scene in the picture where he turns on her, she turns on him, and he cries!"

Seen today, *They Knew What They Wanted* discloses all too clearly the problems that afflicted it. Garson Kanin's direction is weak and tentative, showing an urbanite's coolness toward the rural setting and characters, when clearly the lyrical approach of a Ford or a Milestone was necessary. Charles's criticisms of Carole Lombard seem justified. Though she manages the early scenes as a waitress well enough, and her dresses throughout look authentically cheap, she never was very good in serious drama, and her confession and contrition at the end are notably unconvincing. William Gargan was equally miscast. Not handsome enough for the part of the foreman, he played his scenes with Charles angrily, letting his dislike of Charles show all too plainly when he was supposed to be acting his closest friend and exasperated but loving support; Frank Fay as the priest made a cold and disagreeable impression instead of the sanctimonious saintly piety called for by the Breen office, and Charles was well below form. Obviously unsettled by everybody and everything connected with the picture, he acted with little more than an external display of Italianate mannerisms. The scene in which he dictates the letter to his prospective bride, the wedding sequence when he shows off his prowess by dancing on the roof, the scenes in the bedroom after he has fallen and injured his back, the forgiveness scene—all are played without the deep passion and conviction Charles would have undoubtedly managed in happier circumstances. The black shiny suit and high-crowned hat, the walk, the operatic gestures, the voice, the grubby hands and overalls of the scenes in the vineyards —these are hallmarks of a great actor, but, disagreeing with Kanin's direction and irritated by Lombard (whose supposed growth of affection for him is not for a moment suggested by the actress) he apparently settled for visual correctness, and did not give his soul to his work.

In March 1940 the Laughtons moved from the Garden of Allah Hotel to a rented house on North Rockingham Avenue in Brentwood. They stayed there for a year. It was a pleasant house, looking out across a canyon to a mountain, with a small tropical garden and a swimming pool. The interior was, Charles wrote in a letter to the art collector Albert S. Barnes, "an affair of Japanese grass cloth walls, pleasant stone-covered rugs, and draperies at the windows which set off the willow tree and the little tropical garden." He told Barnes "the house does not require heavy paintings —Cézanne and Renoir would make the whole affair look flimsy. But it seems to me about the best setting I've ever seen for Matisse, Gauguin, Dufy, yes, and I guess Utrillo downwards. Hey! I'm not trying to get Matisse and Gauguin out of you, I'm only trying to give you some kind of an impression of the atmosphere and coloring of the house."

Charles told Barnes that he would like to borrow some paintings ("This a pretty blatant letter"). He explained that he could not afford to buy anything because his income tax problems were still pressing and his savings were tied up in England because of the defense of the realm regulations. Barnes responded magnificently, lending the Laughtons twenty paintings and drawings in all, including Utrillo's *Castle in Snow*, a landscape of Soutine, a Vlaminck still-life, and Kisling's *Girl in a Tree*. Charles, who had felt very unhappy without fine art on the walls, was overjoyed when the crates arrived.

In the spring of 1941, Charles and Elsa moved to another house, which they bought, on the cliffs of Pacific Palisades, overlooking Santa Monica Bay. They had never owned a home of their own in America. They felt pleased as they moved in the items of furniture that had come from London, and began buying antiques in Los Angeles. It was a house of great charm, though of no perceptible style; it had Spanish tiles, but it was not Spanish in its design. It had been built by a copper magnate; in the rain and the damp from the sea, all the gutters and external pipes had turned a romantic shade of green. A member of an Indian mystical sect, the magnate had built a massive church organ in the living room, with bells and chimes; when Charles or Elsa played it, pounding away at *Samson and Delilah* or other popular classics, the entire house shook as though in the grip of a minor earthquake. The Laughtons made several attempts to rid themselves of this grandiose contraption; finally, they sold it to a church in San

Fernando Valley, which spent three thousand dollars removing it.

The garden, stretching to the edge of the cliff, was about an acre in size, with orange and olive trees, fuchsias, azaleas, and camellias, all of which flourished in the damp ocean air. Both Charles and Elsa loved to tend it; in the California climate, there was never a month when some part of it was not in colorful bloom.

Nineteen forty-one was not only the year that marked the beginning of eight years of life in a new home, but the year that began Elsa's association with the famous Turnabout Theatre. The writer Helen Deutsch, then working for MGM, had told Elsa over lunch that she knew about three "crazy young men" who were starting an experimental theatre on La Cienega Boulevard, and that she might find this a good venue for singing her collection of songs. The three young men—Brandon, Burnett, and Brown, the Yale Puppeteers—asked her to join the theatre. Elsa opened in the third week with the best songs of her past, A. P. Herbert's "He Didn't Oughter (Come to Bed in Boots)," "The Ratcatcher's Daughter," and "Somebody Broke Lola's Saucepan." Charles brought Deanna Durbin one night and Elsa was so terrified she lost her voice. The principle of the theatre was that the audience saw a performance of puppets; then they turned their seats around and saw live entertainers. Elsa played women all the way up the social scale, from charlady to royal mistress. The gifted Forman Brown wrote sixty songs for her in ten years. She joined Turnabout for two weeks and stayed for a decade; the theatre, and her appearances in it, were a major attraction of Los Angeles in the 1940s.

During 1941, Charles met a young actor called David Roberts, whom he encouraged in his work. Lean and good-looking, with an apparently uncomplicated masculine personality, he fascinated Charles, who was always drawn to men without a trace of effeminacy. Charles, who told David that he was tortured by his own homosexuality, encouraged David to marry and have children; and he was deeply distressed when David's wife was killed in a car crash only four weeks after the wedding. When David needed money, both Charles and Elsa, acting very humanely, agreed that he should be loaned various amounts; and he remained friendly with them for many years; he was among the pallbearers at Charles's funeral. David constantly tried to help Charles by making him feel he was physically attractive, that he should take care of his physical appearance more thoroughly. Charles, in turn, knowing that David had lost both his mother and brother, acted very paternally toward him.

Charles's relationship with David Roberts, at first sexually and then platonically, lasted for more than two decades. It would have wrecked most marriages, even one as extraordinary and binding as that of Charles and Elsa. It was far more serious than Charles's relationships with his two masseurs Dennis and Bob, although it did not involve Charles in the overpowering emotion of falling in love. It says much for the strength of the Laughtons' friendship and marital affection that these survived the crisis; that the freedom each allowed the other was so complete they could accept each other's lives, and take pleasure in the happiness that either partner could find. From shortly after their marriage they had accepted the fact that fidelity was not to be a condition of it.

In their opinions, humors, and responses, Charles and Elsa remained as closely knit as ever. The house was the linchpin of their lives. They were constantly rediscovering, just as they had at Gordon Square and at Stapledown, the shared pleasure of adding beautiful objects to various parts of the house, and the quiet delight of working on their lovely garden. Their similar enthusiasms in painting, food, and wine remained constant. At night, they were separated by Elsa's appearances at the Turnabout. But during the day, when neither was appearing in a film, they could discuss what happened at the theatre, or Charles's experiences visiting friends. It was not until much later that they began to drift apart, their dinners together silent and strained. In the 1940s, their life was solid and secure. For the first time in their lives, they were not constantly traveling, or subject to frequent long separations.

Shortly after the Laughtons moved into the house at Pacific Palisades, Charles signed a contract with Universal to appear in *It Started with Eve*, a Deanna Durbin vehicle in which he would

be an ancient millionaire who plays Cupid for a young couple
from his deathbed. He had admired Deanna Durbin in her earlier
films, finding her presence on the screen wonderfully fresh,
unspoiled, and filled with the spirit of youth, and when he received the script he accepted at once.

The moment Charles was cast, the studio became alive with rumors that there would be trouble on the set; everyone began to
believe that Laughton and Durbin would hate each other. Henry
Koster, the cozy Austrian who had been asked to direct, was nervous about the project; he didn't speak English fluently, and he
was afraid that the great British actor would be impatient with
him. But from the moment they met they had an intense rapport.
Koster, good-natured, witty, and relaxed, appealed very strongly to
Charles, who respected Koster because of his gentle and considerate method of directing. Koster, in turn, was astonished to find
Charles was not villainous or cantankerous, but instead was honest, plain-speaking, and kind.

Deanna Durbin didn't meet Charles until the picture had
started. She wrote to Elsa in 1968: "We were introduced to each
other on the set when I shook hands with a little old man, grey,
wrinkled and stooped, with a shaky voice and a funny little walk.
We worked hard that day and had no time for personal contacts.
So after work I invited 'Mr. Laughton' for a drink. We walked
back from the set and when we got to my bungalow he pulled off
his rubber nose and rubber face and there he was . . . 40 years
younger, straightened out and able to laugh . . . and that's what
we both did and kept on doing through that picture and every
time we got together . . . somehow things clicked between us and
thanks to Charles I found out that making pictures could be fun,
lost all my tenseness and discovered that Hollywood and making
pictures were not the most important things in the world."
Charles loaned Deanna books and paintings, talked to her about
the theatre, and encouraged her to appreciate creative forms of
art. He and Elsa visited Deanna in her Italianate mansion in
Hollywood, and after their marriage she and her husband Vaughn
Paul came over to Pacific Palisades. Making the movie was an
easy, happy, exhilarating experience for Charles; and sometimes
Charles and Deanna enjoyed themselves so much they upset the
balance of serious scenes. In a sequence in which the old man lay

dying in bed, they couldn't stop laughing. They suggested sad events to each other to overcome this mood of hilarity: earthquakes, famines, floods, but nothing worked, and Koster was told by the production office to stop shooting. It was not until next day that Charles and Deanna managed to achieve the correct sentimental mood.

As light and sweet as meringue glâcé, *It Started with Eve* was dreamed up by Hans Kräly, who had been the most gifted of Ernst Lubitsch's comedy writers; but little of his talent is evident in the finished film. It is only Charles's remarkable skill that makes it almost bearable today. He is seen in the first shots lying in bed, in a half-sleep that precedes death, muttering about nothing in particular. When his son, played unctuously by Robert Cummings, brings home Deanna Durbin as a hat check girl, presenting her as his future bride, Charles becomes a capering, grinning old lecher, stealing cigars and Scotch whisky from under his watchful butler's nose, hugely enjoying the near-voyeur role in which his playing Cupid places him, and expressing more than just a pure interest in the young girl himself. Though much of the movie is embarrassing, Charles is fascinating to watch, shuffling along with one foot barely able to step ahead of the other, his voice a hoarse croak, his eyes almost lost in wrinkles, seemingly half-asleep but in fact shrewdly watchful and twinkling with the good cheer of an ancient satyr. The picture was quite well reviewed, Charles was widely praised, and the film's commercial success was of value to him professionally at the outset of the decade.

After *It Started with Eve* was finished, Charles was disturbed by something Henry Koster told him: Koster was forbidden to go out at night because of the curfew affecting resident aliens. Charles drove over to see Henry while Elsa was at the Turnabout, determined to help him with his English, and familiarize him with British classics. He began by reading *Alice in Wonderland*, followed by *A Midsummer Night's Dream* and the Bible.

Charles played a practical joke on Koster when Koster was directing Kay Francis in *Between Us Girls*. Kay was in the middle of a scene when the lights on the set suddenly went out and guns began to go off. Kay, who hated guns, was horrified, screamed, and grabbed Koster's arms saying, "Somebody's shooting." Then the lights went up and Charles came down the stairs in a long nightgown and nightcap he had worn in *It Started with Eve*, singing, "Happy birthday, dear Henry!" accompanied by the entire cast and crew. Koster, who had completely forgotten his own birthday, was astounded, while Kay Francis ran off the set in tears.

EIGHT

During the early 1940s, Charles's contribution to the war effort was unstinting—more so than ever when America came into the war in December 1941. In 1942 he met two young GIs. He learned that they were recuperating at the Birmingham General Hospital in San Fernando Valley; and he read them excerpts from Shakespeare and the Bible. They were delighted, and a few days later Charles appeared at the hospital itself to read to the patients.

The hospital auditorium was filled to overflowing for his performance. Elsa was at Turnabout; he was alone with a huge audience of injured men hanging on his every word, and he was terrified that they would not like or understand the classics. His hair tousled and clothes untidy, he plumped himself down in a wooden chair on the stage, and began to read a few funny limericks. His delivery of Thurber's version of Red Riding Hood was warmly greeted; he followed it with Andrew Marvell's poem *To His Coy Mistress*. He went on to Shakespeare and Dickens, his nervousness gradually overcome. But he began to be afraid that if he concluded his performance with his most famous reading of all, he would bring catcalls. Shakily, he told the audience: "I've recited the Gettysburg Address so many times I've gone stale on it." A blind serviceman called out: "Mr. Laughton, please let us hear it!" Charles obliged, and the applause was overwhelming.

Charles was deeply moved, and as he turned to leave the platform, scores of young men pressed around him. He shook their hands, and left in a rare mood of optimism.

Charles returned to the hospital for almost weekly appearances after that. His readings were consistently powerful and astute. He brought the dusty pages to life, vividly and passionately evoking the atmosphere of the Old and New Testaments.

Not content with giving these readings at the hospital, Charles offered his services to the Treasury for a War Bond tour. Before he left Los Angeles, he and Elsa gave a tremendous party for 150 British RAF men brought to the house by bus. A cellophane tent covered the lawn, and dozens of starlets arrived. Braziers containing charcoal glowed in the night, and a special dance floor was put down; an orchestra played, Deanna Durbin sat on a piano and sang songs from her repertoire, and she danced with many of the men.

Leaving Los Angeles in August 1942, Charles made many bond-selling appearances across the country. Sleeves rolled up, sustained by innumerable cups of coffee, his hair standing on end and his clothes rumpled, he was a dynamic presence, pleading or demanding citizens help their endangered nation. Sometimes he would break up his audience with funny stories about British charladies. Sample: two English chars survey their home after it has been destroyed. One says, "Isn't this a bloody awful war?" and the other replies, "Ooh, I don't know. It's better than no war at all." He said to a reporter in Cincinnati: "This tour is the least I can do. I was in the last war and I know that the soldier and the sailor need encouragement and the feeling that those at home are behind him."

He told a New York *Times* interviewer: "There were some bad moments on tour. In Connecticut I experienced one of the worst things I have ever seen in my life. Eighteen thousand people had come to see me and other motion picture stars, while eight sailors who had been through blood and bullets at the battles of Midway and the Coral Sea remained in the background on the speakers' platform.

"Those fellows would rather go into battle than face an audience. They got up before the microphone all prettied up and they bumbled and fluffed and were miserable. Those men, who went through blood and filth to protect us, had to get up and appear foolish because people were buying war bonds."

On September 1, Charles appeared at a rally of five thousand people in Times Square. Four pallbearers in black frock coats laid coffins marked Hitler, Mussolini, and Hirohito on the triangular island near the junction of Forty-third Street and Broadway. Charles stood before the coffins, saying into the microphones: "Whom of these three men do I hate the most? Why, Hitler of course! He started it, and he bombed my house in London!" Whereupon, Charles took a hammer and drove a nail forcibly into the coffin.

Within forty-five minutes, a long crocodile of people had filed by to drive in the nails. Charles watched approvingly as they bought $4,500 worth of $18.50 bonds. Nobody seemed prepared to drive a nail into Mussolini's coffin, everyone favoring Hitler or Hirohito, until a Greek couple finally tapped two nails into place to indicate their feelings for the Italian dictator. Charles continued to sell war bonds until September 30, when for seventeen hours beginning at 7 A.M. he conducted a one-man bond-selling drive over Radio WEAF in New York; by midnight he had sold $298,000 worth of bonds. He interrupted the programs *Let's Fight, Studio X, You and the War,* and *Parade of Stars* until he was hoarse. One of the first purchasers was Mrs. Myron C. Taylor, wife of President Roosevelt's envoy to the Vatican, who bought a $1,000 bond. Several minutes later Mrs. Edith Earle, an Englishwoman, pledged $5,000.

As the day wore on, Charles grew more and more impassioned. He demanded the purchase of bonds, naming it as "a duty and a privilege" and "the last chance to save the flickering flame of democracy." At the stroke of midnight, hoarse and croaking, he said: "God help you and your children if that flame goes out!"

The Birmingham Hospital readings, the War Bond tour, and the seventeen-hour broadcast were of profound importance to Charles. He obtained more satisfaction from them than from all of his work in motion pictures and the theatre. He could lose his horror of his own being in the challenge of helping the war effort. The genuine admiration of the public seemed at last to have been

won without acting villain or martyr. He had succeeded in striking a responsive chord in a people at war. The popularity he had
known in the 1930s had not, he felt, been fully deserved. At last
he could feel a sense of pride in achievement; at last he could feel
an emotion other than shame when praise was heaped on him.

It is all the more unfortunate, then, that for the most part his
films at the time did not please him. In *Tales of Manhattan*, an
omnibus about the adventures of a tail coat directed by the autocratic Julien Duvivier, he was at his best, though he did not realize
it at the time. He was a composer, reduced to playing the piano in
a seedy New York bar, who at last obtains the opportunity to con-
duct one of his orchestral works when he attracts the attention of
a great conductor, brilliantly acted by Victor Francen. When he
reaches the podium, he discovers that the tail coat is too tight; it
rips across the back. The audience laughs at him. In a splendid
gesture, Francen removes his own coat and the male spectators
follow suit, until every man in the audience watches, coatless, the
embarrassed conductor in his triumph.

Charles's performance was strong. First seen pounding a bar
piano with disgruntled contempt, later he is seen hurriedly and
nervously performing for Francen, hastily trying on the coat with
the aid of a friendly tailor, then stumbling up to the podium, con-
ducting with great authority and attack, only to dissolve into despair when he believes the audience is laughing at his composition. His recovery when he becomes aware of Francen's gesture is
movingly played, embarrassment changing to gleeful excitement,
misery to exaltation. As his wife, Elsa was charming and affectionate, the warmth and sympathy of their relationship mirrored
beautifully in her acting of scenes with Charles.

Charles also performed expertly in Charles Vidor's *The Tuttles
of Tahiti*, based on a *Saturday Evening Post* story by Nordhoff
and Hall—the co-authors of *Mutiny on the Bounty*—about an
old beachcomber, Jonas Tuttle, living in the islands with a ne'er-
do-well family of fisher folk who try to win money on a local
cockfight. Charles's Jonas Tuttle was first cousin to Ginger Ted in
The Vessel of Wrath. Dressed in a virtually identical straw hat—
though this one is decorated with pretty cockle shells—and an
equally shapeless tropical shirt and pants, though these are much
cleaner, and with an equal length of stubble and applied suntan,

Charles looked like Ginger Ted grown to be seventy. But Jonas is a Ginger Ted become soft and sweet with time: he exudes good nature and good cheer, even when he is stealing the gas needed for his nephew's yacht or being cheated by an evil German storekeeper. Expertly directed by Charles Vidor and helped by a fine supporting cast (led by such veterans as Curt Bois, Victor Francen, and Florence Bates) the film was a harmless escapist comedy which got lost in the crisis following Pearl Harbor.

Charles wasn't too comfortable playing in *The Tuttles of Tahiti*, feeling that Charles Vidor, a Hungarian, who had directed Elsa the year before in *Ladies in Retirement*, was something of a mediocrity. Charles's real enjoyment lay in the engaging personality of Florence Bates, who played a native woman in the picture. They held a conversation on the set which went more or less like this:

MISS BATES: Will you tell me, Charles Laughton, when I do badly or well as we make this picture—and be frank?

C. L.: My dear, there is no such thing as good acting or bad acting.

MISS BATES: I don't understand.

C. L.: John Barrymore at times is so bloody awful that he's magnificent. And I know others who are so perfect technically that they're equally awful—if you know what I mean. Furthermore, there are no actors in our business to compare with George Bernard Shaw, Mayor Jimmy Walker, Gertrude Stein, and our old friend Benito Mussolini . . .

MISS BATES: Well, well, I had such great hopes! What do you call yourself for instance? After all these years and so many successes?

C. L.: Oh, as we English say, I've just muddled along, clowning a lot, playing with roles like a cat playing with a mouse. I can't escape it!

MISS BATES: But you wouldn't call your recital of the Gettysburg Address clowning, would you?

c. l.: Come, come, my dear lady. One doesn't come across holy writ like that every week. But don't let's get serious. Where's my cup of tea?

In order to help the war effort during 1942, Charles walked through a routine production, *Stand By for Action*, at MGM. He was cast as a rear admiral. In an important scene, he had to stand on the forward deck and give the crew a speech about their responsibility to the Navy; at the end of his address he had to recite the Declaration of Independence.

The director, Robert Z. Leonard, decided that Charles should be given cue cards in case he fluffed the address. But to everyone's amazement he delivered it without a single mistake, and the entire unit broke into applause and cheers.

Despite good moments in this picture, Charles felt depressed by it, and gained little solace from it, or from appearing as a caricature of Ruggles in a film designed to illustrate British courage under fire, *Forever and a Day*. Fortunately, he at last found, in 1943, a chance to prove himself once again: in Dudley Nichols' and Jean Renoir's movie about patriotism and betrayal in a French village, *This Land Is Mine*.

This Land Is Mine provided Charles's first major opportunity as an actor since *The Hunchback of Notre Dame*: the French schoolteacher, Albert Lorré, is certainly one of the greatest of his portraits.

Unfortunately, Dudley Nichols' script created a somewhat conventional gallery of characters in a French provincial town: a pompous quisling mayor, a railroad boss who is a craven stool pigeon, a coldly "civilized" German gauleiter, a fiercely patriotic young girl, whose lover is shot following a courageous act of sabotage. But Nichols, reacting to numerous suggestions from Charles, created in Albert Lorré a character rich with paradoxes and sudden unexpected shifts of mood. Albert is seen at the outset in his simply furnished house, the victim of a domestic trap: his mother smothers him with affection; terrified of her, he cannot express his feelings for the pretty schoolteacher he loves; during a bombing raid, he quivers with terror in a cellar under the schoolhouse, his mother clinging protectively to him as schoolchildren cruelly mimic his cowardice. But gradually Albert is converted to man-

hood. When he discovers that his mother has betrayed the where-
abouts of a saboteur to an informer, he turns on her in the street
in a startling gesture of defiance and hatred, and from that moment she never recovers her influence over him. Arrested, put on
trial on a false charge of murdering the informer, he at last discovers his masculine nature, defeating the prosecuting counsel in
a magnificently passionate plea for freedom of speech and action
in a defeated France.

Charles had first met Jean Renoir in 1937, when Erich Pommer
brought the French director onto the set of *The Beachcomber* at
Elstree. Renoir thought of him at once when he began work on
the picture. Charles was pleased to learn that Renoir wanted
Maureen O'Hara to play the part of the young schoolteacher who,
at the end, takes over Albert's role in guiding children against
German invaders. Charles also admired Una O'Connor, that famous and gifted graduate of the Abbey Theatre, who played his
mother in the picture. Charles worked most carefully on his
clothes: the baggy suit, the thin shoelace tie, the stiffly starched
collar, all perfect for a Frenchman of Lorré's age, occupation, and
class.

Renoir, in his turn, adored Charles. The ice was broken at the
outset when Charles reminded him of something he had mentioned during the set visit in 1937: the Laughtons' ownership of
Jean's father's *The Judgment of Paris*. Moreover, Charles took an
instant liking to Renoir's famous model, Gabrielle, who lived next
door to the Renoirs on Martel Avenue. He talked to her in fluent
French, unfazed by her rapid speech. She called him "le grand
marseau" or "the great tomcat" which he didn't mind. Charles
also showed a great love for French wines and art, which made
Renoir respond to him at once.

Just as Charles had taught the Austrian Henry Koster to love
Shakespeare, so Charles made Renoir see the spirit of the Bard in
frequent nocturnal readings at Martel Avenue while Elsa was
working at the Turnabout. Renoir and his wife Dido clapped with
joy as Charles took every role in the plays, from cupbearer to the
male and female central figures. Their evenings together were joy-
ful, except for one problem. Charles detested interruptions of any
kind. If a doorbell or a telephone rang he was beside himself. The
Renoirs' chiming clock infuriated him. It would often strike—and

it struck the half hours as well as the hours—very loudly just
when he was reaching the peak of a speech. Worse, the barking of
the Renoirs' dachshunds exasperated him. His concentration was
so charged that the slightest interruption was unbearable, and
those yapping dogs remained in his brain for years afterward.

While making *This Land Is Mine*, Charles grew to know the
talented Walter Slezak, who played the German commandant of
the village. Slezak wrote in his memoirs, *What Time's the Next
Swan?*: "There is an expression in the German theatre which indicates that an actor is especially talented and blessed: 'He has
God's telephone number in his pocket.' Well, Laughton, I'm sure,
has God's unlisted number."

He had met Charles two months earlier in Chicago, where
Charles was changing trains after the bond tour appearance in
New York. He had said: "Good morning."

Charles swung around, astonished. "What do you want?"

"Nothing, sir, nothing! Just wanted to wish you a good morning. I am an actor, my name is Walter Slezak. I'm going to be in
your next picture!"

Charles was even more amazed. "Are you a *good* actor?" he
asked.

"*Brilliant!*" Slezak exclaimed.

"Ah!" Charles said. "A *conceited* actor! Perfect! Let's have
breakfast!"

Discovering a mutual interest in paintings, they had spent
much of the morning walking through the Chicago Art Institute
—a tradition for some travelers between trains. Slezak recalled his
excitement at Charles's knowledge of paintings: Charles would
sweep through whole rooms, dismissing everything in them, only
to stop short at some small and apparently insignificant painting
and say, with an air of finality, "Now THAT is what I call *quality!*"

Looking at the famous Seurat, *Sunday Afternoon on the Island
of La Grande Jatte*, Charles had said, "Light's all wrong!
GUARD! Roll down that door to shut out the glare. Now, Slezak,
sit on the floor with me. It's the best angle, you know!"

A small crowd gathered around them, pointing excitedly at
Laughton. Finally the two men grinned, dusted themselves off,
and made their way to the train.

En route, Charles told Slezak about his life in California, how he rose early in the morning, donned slacks, sandals, a shirt, and a straw hat and wandered down to the wharves to see the fishing boats come in. He astounded Slezak by revealing his knowledge of literature. Slezak wrote to Elsa: "I was fascinated and entranced because I began to realize that here was one of those rare people in whom truth and fiction, reality and imagination had completely fused. Like water colors they had run together with the line of demarcation no longer visible."

Charles was delighted to learn that Slezak had the script with him on the train. He sat up late at night reading it, falling in love with Dudley Nichols' writing, and he woke Slezak up at 1 A.M. to read him every word, playing every part. When the train stopped at Albuquerque, New Mexico, Charles sent a telegram to Charles Koerner, head of RKO Studios, which read: WHAT A TREMENDOUS CHALLENGE FOR A TIRED OLD HAM.

Charles only had one problem with Renoir during the shooting. There was a scene in which Albert's head teacher, played by Philip Merivale, was being led out to be shot. Charles had to stand on his prison cot, shake the bars of his cell with great violence, and scream the head teacher's name. Eugene Lourié's flimsy set couldn't take the force of Charles's hands, and Charles found himself at the end of the scene holding one of the bars and a large piece of plaster wall. Another actor might have laughed, and the crew would have laughed with him; but Charles was appalled. He sat down, thoroughly discouraged, holding his head. After the set was repaired, Renoir told him, very gently, to play the scene again. Charles shook his head. "It's impossible, Jean. It's gone," he said.

"You've got to do it, Charles," Renoir told him. "We're all waiting."

"But I can't believe this is a *real* cell, a *real* prison," Charles moaned. "When Eugene's set came away like that, I lost my belief in the whole picture!"

"Forget the cell," Renoir instructed. "Just think about Philip and the others getting shot out there."

Charles began looking out of the window, and, to help him, Renoir even arranged for Merivale and the other patriots to be "killed" with imitation bullets.

Albert Lorré was a part which Charles seized on with enthusi-

asm. He managed a gradual progression from mother's boy to freedom fighter with all of the skill he showed in the similar transitions of Claudius' character. His great oration in the courtroom is
powerfully reminiscent of the speech before the senate in *I
Claudius*, played with the same beauty and eloquence gradually
emerging from snail-like secretiveness, the shy sidelong blinking
glances focusing gradually into a direct challenging stare, the
shambling movements straightening into an alert stance, the
hunched shoulders squared, the crumbling face shored up, the decent soul shining through mists of evasion and compromise.

Renoir's direction is never technically exciting, but it is serious,
compassionate, and informed by a cool, reasonable humanism.
Like Korda and McCarey before him, he cuts to the faces of the
listeners as Charles delivers his speech, but unlike those directors,
he allows Charles about half the speech's running time to make
his actor's impression on us. The camera focuses on Charles in a
take running just over three minutes, the lighting painstakingly
accurate for the time of day. The extreme simplicity of camera
angle and composition pay off: we see a great actor plain, without
needless decoration.

By the middle of the 1940s, the house on Pacific Palisades had
become the center of the Laughtons' lives. Charles took less pleasure in his MGM contract, finding himself obliged to play parts
which entirely failed to involve his sensibility. It was small consolation to him that he was extremely well paid, at a continuing rate
of $100,000 a film, or that he was patiently and carefully treated
by Louis B. Mayer in view of his friendship with Irving Thalberg
in the 1930s. Anyone who had been close to Thalberg automat-
ically received Mayer's respect, even awe; but that admiration did
not extend to providing the kinds of major acting parts which
Thalberg had guaranteed Charles.

Elsa, appearing in films from time to time, usually in eccentric
character roles, continued to work happily at the Turnabout
Theatre. In the company of the Turnabouters, who frequently
visited the Pacific Palisades house for lunch—walking through
rooms that glowed with paintings, or toward the cliffs above the
shining ocean—she was very much at ease, able to release her
strong sense of the ridiculous, her gift for iconoclastic satire, in

evenings which, if she had spent them at home, might have been lonely and strained. It was fortunate that she enjoyed the fulfillment of the Turnabout, because Charles's relationship with David moved through its highest emotional curve in those days. Whenever Charles was not visiting the homes of Henry Koster, Deanna Durbin, or the Renoirs, or reading at the Birmingham Hospital, he and David were always at the house studying together, talking deeply about the problems of acting, David giving delight because of his youth and health, the straightforwardness and simplicity and practicality of his mind, Charles providing equal pleasure because of his intellect, his profound understanding of the Bible, Shakespeare, and the great English and French playwrights, the warmth and richness of his voice, and the essential kindness and goodness of his tormented spirit. The relationship of these very different men was based on a Socratic concept of pupil and master; it flowed casually in and out of sexual commitment, with each moving toward and retreating from other lovers; it was rooted firmly in mutual respect. Elsa, satisfied with her life, finding her own relationships with men as she had in the 1930s, still continued to feel that she had no wish to break a marriage of complementary minds. She was glad that Charles had found a more or less sustaining sexual and emotional friendship, that he seemed to be gaining a little in a sense of his own worth, that he hated himself just a fraction less.

As well as their lovely house, their garden was a symbol of the comparative happiness Charles and Elsa knew in those years. They went far afield, visiting nurseries, and bought plants and shrubs, and developed the garden richly together. Accepting the subtropical nature of the environment they lived in—though missing the cycle of the seasons in England—they enjoyed the subtle shifts of the California climate, the cool rains of winter, the long dry months of summer, the romantic morning fogs, the sudden unexpected cold of the nights.

During 1943, Charles appeared without much distinction as an Australian war veteran in *The Man from Down Under*. Depressed by this experience, he felt slightly more optimistic when a friend, Clifford Odets, told him he was writing a script for him on the life of Beethoven; but the finished work, heavy and pretentiously overwritten, appealed neither to Charles nor to the studio executives. Charles reluctantly agreed to make *The Canterville Ghost* at MGM, a modernized version of the Oscar Wilde story in which he acted a cowardly and mournful phantom, the spirit of a man walled up alive by his father, who returns to haunt an ancestral mansion during its wartime occupancy by American GIs. A mediocre director, Norman Z. McLeod, began the film, but Charles failed so completely to work with him that McLeod threw up his hands in despair and, after only seven days of shooting, yielded the production to a young studio contractee, Jules Dassin.

Even with the more gifted and sensitive Dassin in charge, Charles felt little or no enthusiasm for the script, which was for the most part a travesty of Wilde. But he was kind and considerate to Dassin, who was quite inexperienced. He helped him with valuable suggestions behind the set when nobody was looking. Even when a scene was going badly, he never corrected Dassin in front of the cast and crew. Sometimes, Charles improvised scenes, performing a grotesque dance among the Canterville family graves or whooping through the great hall of the mansion clanging his chains. He very much admired the six-year-old star Margaret O'Brien, who played the heiress to the Canterville fortune. Already a steely professional, she amazed him with her expert, implacably calculated, crowd-pleasing delivery of lines. She acted one scene, in which she had to address him coolly and tell him to become more manly, with such skill Charles's only retaliation was to swing a long chatelaine with loudly clanging sets of jailer's keys in order to compete with her for the audience's attention.

Though it was not well received at the time, *The Canterville Ghost* today emerges as an accomplished comedy. The opening—a vigorously staged stag hunt, Canterville's disgrace and walling up by his furious father—is directed by Dassin with great spirit and attack; both Charles and Reginald Owen as his father are in good form in these scenes. Throughout the rest of the film, Charles is most engaging. Flying across rooms rattling his chains, screaming or groaning to frighten the GIs, or, in a lyrical sequence, quietly speaking about his need for peace, his yearning to be buried in the rich soil beyond the orchard at the end of the garden, he makes the ghostly Canterville a touching and pleasantly grotesque figure of fun. The performance combines burlesque, melodrama, pathetic farce, the comedy of manners and outright tragedy in a rich range; and at the end, when Canterville calls for his father to release him from his earthly bondage, when he is permitted to sleep at last because he has proved himself a hero, Charles achieves a moving evocation of joy.

Throughout 1944, Charles countinued his series of readings to GIs at the Birmingham and other hospitals in Los Angeles. He appeared on radio shows for Norman Corwin, reading Carl Sandburg, Walt Whitman, and Thomas Wolfe, and he made a picture, *Captain Kidd*, which was certainly among his worst, and quite unworthy of his talent. A preposterous version of the life of the Scottish-born William Kidd, it distorted all the facts of that ncfarious pirate's career, and Charles, working only for the money, acted it in a bizarrely off-color fashion.

In this version Kidd was changed from a Scotsman into a leering, moneygrubbing Cockney whose valet, a kind of Professor Higgins in reverse, has to turn him into a gentleman. Kidd keeps a little book in which the names of his prospective victims are crossed off one by one; he seizes a treasure ship for his own purposes, failing to turn the money over to King William III. The picture fails to convey a sense of the life of the sea, the intrigues of the court of William III, and Kidd's character as a rogue. Charles's only opportunity as an actor comes in the last sequence, when Kidd is hanged at Newgate. Kidd's speech about the rewards brought by corruption and license is filled with Charles's feelings about greed and moneygrubbing. For the first time in the entire production, the actor seems to mean what he is saying. It was an example of the art of the "tirade," or speech of summation, which Charles often uniquely brought to even the worst films, giving them a note of distinction they might not otherwise have had.

Disappointed in this wretched film, Charles was to some extent relieved, later in 1944, when Universal sent him a screenplay by Bertram Millhauser, *The Suspect*, which he rather liked. He was offered the part of Philip Marshall, a tobacconist of the London of 1902, whose home in Laburnum Terrace is a domestic hell. His wife, Cora, is a shrew, capable of complaining about the cost of colored bulbs when Philip tries to improve the sitting room with a Christmas tree. When she threatens the job of the girl he is in love with, he kills her, making it appear that she accidentally fell down the stairs. A cold Scotland Yard inspector uncovers the facts of the crime when Philip murders his blackmailing neighbor.

The director of the picture was Robert Siodmak, a talented owlish German who had begun to establish his name in the field of low-budget melodrama. Siodmak had a shrewd eye for detail, a teutonically somber style, and a gift for handling suspense. He dropped by to see Charles at Pacific Palisades when he heard Charles had been cast. Nobody answered the doorbell, and finding the door open, Siodmak walked into the hallway. He was overpowered by the Renoir, the Sisleys, and the Rousseau which glowed on the walls of the house. Finally, he reached the garden and called out, "Mr. Laughton!"

A voice answered in a clipped English accent, "Yes, sir, here I am!" Siodmak looked about in vain for the voice's origin. Not a soul was in sight. Eventually, on the strength of an inspired guess, he glanced upward. There, perched in the branches of a fruit tree, a pair of pruning shears in his hand, was Charles. With exquisite poise the host hauled himself toward a ladder, and climbed down with the elegance of a ballet dancer. This physical grace, somewhat incongruously combined with rotundity, was one of Charles's most notable features. Later, Siodmak noticed that Charles danced very well, and that he swam around swimming pools with all the agility of a large, pink porpoise.

Siodmak said: "I suggest we discuss the role of Philip as carefully as possible now, until we are mutually agreed on the interpretation. But we won't discuss individual scenes until the night before shooting." Charles smiled and said: "All right, it's amusing. Let's try it!"

Siodmak arranged for Charles to rehearse scenes with the other actors, Henry Daniell, Rosalind Ivan, and Ella Raines, by themselves until each scene was ready. Everything went reasonably smoothly until Charles felt his familiar and overpowering conviction that his interpretation of the role was wrong. Just before a scene was about to start he charged headlong at Siodmak and yelled: "Robert—all we have done so far is RUBBISH! We have muffed the whole part!" Before Charles had time to go further Siodmak played the trump card he had been saving for this moment. He turned on Charles and shouted back, "Are you mad? How dare you insult our intelligence, yours and mine, in this way?" Half in panic, half in genuine anger, Siodmak became increasingly strident as he acted out the scenes as he had discussed them. Charles's anger gradually transformed itself into concern as he tried to placate Siodmak and avert the fatal stroke he insisted Siodmak would suffer if he didn't pull himself together.

Siodmak's only reply was to scream at him: "Are you going to play it the way we discussed it or not? If not, get out. Get out anyway."

Charles looked at Siodmak like a child whose favorite toy has been taken away. But it was a look in which there was something of both shame and relief. He nodded his head in acquiescence, turned and went out of the room, closing the door quietly behind him.

Later, Charles told people that Siodmak was the most hysterical director hc had ever worked with, and that he had "to cope with his fits of temperament every day."

But their friendship survived and grew. Charles read aloud to Siodmak every one of A. E. Housman's thirty-two one-act plays in the evenings, and he tried out on the Siodmaks fine readings of the Bible and of Samuel Pepys's Diary.

The Suspect is a flawed film. The accents of several members of the cast are jarringly American. It is impossible to accept that a coroner's jury would rule accidental death in the case of the wife, since clearly the indentation of the wounds made by Philip's stick would not match those made by a fall from a staircase. It is unlikely that, in a cramped world of prying neighbors, Philip would be able to drag the blackmailer's body to the local canal and throw it in without being observed, or that the body would not be discovered before a period of several weeks had elapsed. Nevertheless, despite its faults, this is a powerfully affecting little study of murder. There are very good scenes: the brief sequence in which the detective imagines the details of the killing, the camera following his gaze subjectively, crawling from the stick in the hatstand up the stairs to a dark cupboard and a closed door; Philip's meeting with the blackmailer in a shabby, genteel cafe, in which their mutual dislike really emerges; Philip's murder of him, the two men's eyes meeting as a feeling of death comes over both of them; and, best of all, the coldly ironical little scene in which Philip has to entertain some unexpected friends of his son's to an impromptu sherry party, while Simmons' body lies under the black leather sofa.

Charles's performance is subtly controlled, much richer than his similar portrayal in *Payment Deferred*. With only a slight widening of the eyes or tightening of the mouth he conveys a lifetime of cramped, penny-pinching near-poverty, the humiliation of a loveless marriage. His hatred for his wife and for his neighbor is conveyed with quiet force, all the more harrowing because it is never melodramatically expressed. It is an especially fine concept of the writer's that Philip should not feel a twinge of conscience over the death of the shrew and the blackmailer, but that he should give himself up when he learns that his neighbor's wife has been falsely accused of her husband's murder. The finest writer's strokes are in the subtle, moving scenes in which Philip is shown falling in love with a girl half his age, his passion for her driving him beyond the bounds of his conventional existence into murder, and bringing about his final destruction. Charles conveyed Philip's feelings for the girl with careful understatement, making them fully acceptable and believable, and at times almost unbearably moving.

In the middle of the war, following the predictable failure of several of the films in which he had appeared, Charles became known in the industry as a commercial liability. He suffered the fate of so many employees of motion pictures: in order to maintain a good standard of living, he was compelled to accept parts which were beneath his level, a method used by studios at the time to unload certain actors. The comparative pleasure of the early 1940s, gained from his income of more than $100,000 a picture, and the power to buy paintings and furniture, gradually crumbled into a sense of despair. Almost symbolically, part of the cliff garden fell away in 1944, burying four lanes of the Roosevelt Highway in Santa Monica and partly covering a car. Another large piece collapsed in 1946, carrying with it a fine pre-Columbian stone figure of a Wind God which he prized dearly. While the figure was being dug out of the landslide, Charles suffered an increased sense of anguish, tossing and moaning in the grip of new nightmares. He was consoled only by visits from a new friend and colleague: the German playwright Bertolt Brecht, who wanted him to act in a play on the life of Galileo.

NINE

Brecht had written *The Life of Galileo* in 1938. He had been concerned, in the midst of the series of crises which ended with World War II, with celebrating the progress of scientific discovery despite the fluctuations in international politics. He foresaw the beginnings of an age of barbarism, in which all human values would be debased; and he felt it his duty to show, through the inspiring example of Galileo, how it might still be possible for the spirit of pure reason to survive and flourish in conditions of adversity. He saw Galileo as a heroic figure, who was compelled by the Church of the Inquisition to confess that the world did not move, but who retained his dignity and nobility despite that futile, agonized admission. In the first draft, Brecht showed Galileo as a man of the people, aware of the lives of craftsmen, responsive to the beauty and honesty of simple people, while hating the authority of the old Catholic ruling class, the hypocritical and corrupt religious society which crushed working men, and which he now linked with the Fascist conquest of Europe.

In the revised drafts, Galileo was shown as a lonely, isolated figure, not so intimately connected with the working class, and bent on a solitary and painful quest for disseminating scientific truth. Brecht wrestled with the play for two years, painfully aware that he could not overcome the major dramatic problem of the recantation: how could he make Galileo's renunciation of his major thesis sympathetic to the modern audience?

At the beginning of the war, Brecht and his wife, the actress Helene Weigel, moved to California. They bought a small, rather uncomfortable house in Santa Monica, and joined a remarkable group of exiles, which included the composer Hanns Eisler, the novelists Lion Feuchtwanger, Leonhard Frank, and Heinrich and Thomas Mann, the directors Fritz Lang, Billy Wilder, and Robert Siodmak, and the actors Fritz Kortner, Peter Lorre, Oscar Homolka, Albert Bassermann, and Curt Bois. They also met several members of the British colony, including Christopher Isherwood, Aldous Huxley, and Gerald Heard.

Charles knew many of these people himself, and ran into Brecht occasionally at the home of Salka Viertel, screenwriter and wife of the director Berthold Viertel, who had a small but brilliant salon in Santa Monica. Charles became intrigued by Brecht, this thin, crop-haired, starved-looking little man in shapeless coveralls like prison fatigues, who always smoked very long and evil-smelling cigars and walked about with loose shambling movements.

Charles recognized Brecht's remarkable talent and showed an early interest in helping the playwright prepare an acting version of *Galileo* in English. Brecht had seen several of Charles's best performances, and appreciated the firmness, realism, and lack of sentimentality he saw in these. While others had found Charles the actor excessively emotional, Brecht thought his work intellectually precise, sensible, and truthful. The two men discovered certain mutual likes and dislikes. They both shared a sympathy and concern for ordinary people, a dislike of pomp and circumstance and the attitude and actions of the European ruling class. They both disliked elaborate artifice in the theatre, as exemplified by the spangles-and-tinsel of Max Reinhardt's stage and film productions of *A Midsummer Night's Dream*.

As early as 1943, and through much of 1944, 1945, and 1946 when Charles was not engaged in making movies, Brecht came to Charles and Elsa's house to work on *Galileo*. Elsa recalls that,

much as she admired his talent, she did not find Brecht very appealing. He smoked his vile cigars and the smell of these weeds
clung to his clothes for days. Elsa had to keep sending out the curtains and the chair and settee covers to be cleaned because they
were impregnated with the stench of smoke. When Brecht
laughed, he showed "piano teeth": some were missing, and some
were black with decay; his mouth opened in a circle like a small
rodent's.

The work on *Galileo* never seemed to end. Charles did not
speak one word of German, and German and English dictionaries
were constantly at the collaborators' elbows when language
proved to be a stumbling block in the discussions. Brecht was constantly bubbling over with ideas; Charles proved to be a master of
construction, of trimming. He understood Brecht's mind deeply,
and Brecht understood his.

After Hiroshima, and the end of the war, two years of work on
Galileo at last began to bear fruit. The play began to change
shape and meaning, and in particular Brecht managed to solve the
dramatic problem of the recantation. In the 1938 version, Galileo
was seen as having confessed in order to make it possible for him
to release his work to the world; in the new play, he admits to his
pupil that the recantation had been a crime, and that there could
be no possible excuse for it.

Undoubtedly influenced by Charles, Brecht revised the character of Galileo in this new draft. Instead of an ascetic, selfless symbol of pure reason, the scientist became a passionate, ruthless ego-
centric, his appetite for life as great as his appetite for discovering
truth. Charles was responsible for humanizing Galileo, making
him touchingly and harshly a real man instead of a saintly martyr.
In preparing this role, he drew from many other parts he had
played. Brecht's biographer, Frederic Ewen, wrote: "How
brilliantly Laughton apprehended the ambiguity of Galileo—that
incomprehensibility, the combination of fortitude and servility,
aggressiveness and vulnerability, sensuality and intellect!" These
human contradictions of character were Charles's major contri-
butions. He thought of Rembrandt and Claudius and Albert
Lorré as he helped to create a character who triumphs over uncer-
tainties and shynesses and interior fears to make a passionate plea

for liberty, for freedom of thought. Just as, for Charles, the burghers of Amsterdam, the senators of Rome, and the collaborators of wartime France became symbols of inhuman oppression and restriction of speech, so the perpetrators of the Inquisition became symbols of everything Charles hated. There can be no underestimating the appeal the part of Galileo had for him, or the importance of his contribution to the final version of the play.

The men worked on: Brecht pinched and shambling and smoking incessantly in his overalls; Charles toiling with him in the library, or walking with him past the fuchsias and azaleas, along the crumbling cliffs above the sea, with his large straw hat, a scarf wrapped over it and tied under his chin, clothes as loose and crumpled as Jonas Tuttle's. At the beginning of the writing, the showman Mike Todd and Orson Welles both felt eager to present what was virtually the 1938 version on Broadway. Unfortunately, neither Charles nor Brecht was able to have a satisfactory working relationship with either Todd or Welles. These baroque individualists gave the impression of wanting to present the play in a highly elaborate and pretentious fashion, with extravagant costumes and designs, whereas Laughton and Brecht wanted an austere, simple, and severely plain production in keeping with the purity and cleanliness of Galileo's intellect. The meetings of all four men proved to be unsatisfactory. Despite many attempts to convince Todd and Welles that they must give the play an ascetic look on stage, the collaborators realized they would never see eye to eye with these men, and when Todd lost a fortune in a ridiculous production of Jules Verne's *Around the World in 80 Days*, the project was postponed.

Both Charles and Brecht began to lose their temper over Todd's—and even more Welles's—procrastinations and displays of irresponsibility. Charles in particular became irritated by Welles's dependence on his own charm and forcefulness of manner. The correspondence between the two men is very revealing: Charles earnestly seeking a production in the fall of 1946 and annoyed that Welles cannot or will not proceed; Welles seeking more and more time, so distracted by his various commitments that he is unable to satisfy Charles on the exact date of his availability. Welles had an infuriating habit of calling Hanns Eisler

"Eichner" both in private conversation and in letters, and he really disliked Brecht, whose somber, quiet simplicity was the precise opposite of his flamboyant neo-romantic self-indulgence.

Finally, in June 1946, Welles made a fatal mistake, which resulted in the cancellation of the entire project. He had his assistant, Richard Wilson, write Charles a long, rambling letter on Mercury Production stationery, expressing annoyance that, during the negotiations for the production, Charles and Brecht wanted to have a hand in it along with Welles. The note begged for one more chance to produce the play, with Mercury exclusively in charge, and Mike Todd ruthlessly eliminated from the arrangements.

Charles was furious. He wrote one of his very rare letters on June 27. It reads:

My dear Orson,

I received a letter from Dick (Wilson) yesterday. I do not appreciate your habit of using a third party to do the calling. I will answer two points only. My contract with Todd is not the same as yours. All the points I protested are eliminated. Second I might have called you up and told you immediately when Brecht and I had decided on Todd if we could get him. I just plain was not going to put up with the inevitable procrastination. Either the play was going on the earliest possible day or I had to do a movie. Time at my age is dear. The rest of Dick's letter seems plain nonsense, including a passage which says "When Orson does a play (I speak from experience) he really does it." I was under the impression we were to collaborate all three on the idea of production and so on, for the new and difficult play, otherwise how could I also function right? You are an extraordinary man of the theatre and therefore I flatly do not believe that you cannot function as a member of a team.

You are the best man in the world to put the Church of Rome on the stage, to mention only one aspect of the play. This appears to me to matter. Cannot this important thing between you and Todd be worked out? Todd

has never spoken ill of you to either of us. The strongest
word he has used is "afraid." That also is nonsense when
there is the play to be told.

Brecht greets you,
Charles

Welles did not reply to the letter. Annoyed that Charles
insisted Todd should be involved in the production, and no
longer talking to Todd by late July, he backed out of *Galileo* once
and for all. In a sense, Charles was relieved: he could tolerate
Welles no longer.

In the wake of this disagreeable experience, it became clear to
both Charles and Brecht that they could not work with either
showmen like Todd or impractical geniuses like Welles. They
needed to become involved with more modestly serious and
dedicated, sensible men of the theatre. Their choice fell on an ac-
tor-manager, Norman Lloyd, a committed and highly skilled man
of intellect who had formed, along with the accomplished John
Houseman, Pelican Productions at the Coronet Theatre in Hollywood and was dedicated to showing plays of finest quality. Lloyd
read *Galileo* and became convinced that the play should be the
Coronet's first presentation. Houseman disagreed, preferring to
open with Thornton Wilder's more commercial *The Skin of Our
Teeth*.

Instead, *Galileo* was scheduled as the second production of the
Coronet. It was to be financed by an "angel," T. Edward Hamble-
ton, who later became President of the Phoenix Theatre in New
York. The Coronet was the perfect theatre for *Galileo:* the play
would not have been suitable in a commercial theatre. John
Houseman remembers that he was immediately excited about the
play, finding Charles's version admirably stark, simple, and severe.
Lloyd selected the young and gifted Joseph Losey to direct.

Rehearsals began with a series of violent disputes. Brecht
screamed at Anya Sakalow, who was engaged to do the choreog-
raphy, "We want none of your tawdry Broadway dances in this
production!" and she promptly resigned. She was replaced by the
mime-dancer Lotte Goslar, who was working with Elsa at the
Turnabout. One of Brecht's friends insisted on taking photo-

graphs from the balcony. Charles screamed, "If she doesn't stop taking pictures I'm leaving the stage!" She left at once.

Charles was extremely nervous during rehearsals, terrified of returning to the theatre for the first time since his appearance at the Comédie Française in 1934. Deeply as he loved and admired Brecht, he was unsettled by the playwright's fits of demoniacal rage, condemning the scenery, his unhappy wife's costumes, and even Charles. Charles was miserable in the summer heat, and at the opening he insisted trucks full of ice blocks be placed around the theatre and ventilators turned on "so that the audience will be able to think."

As the first night approached, an odd, rather comic problem occurred. In the first scene, Charles had to appear in loose trousers and shirt which he was to remove prior to taking a bath. He was so nervous that he unconsciously began scratching himself through his trouser pockets. The preview audience noticed this and began to titter. Brecht was very upset. He felt that this impromptu action was taking away from the proper flavor of the scene. He couldn't bring himself to say anything to Charles, so he asked Lloyd to "do something." Lloyd was uneasy about it; and Losey refused point-blank to speak to Charles. Finally, everyone looked at the wardrobe mistress. She shrugged and next night sewed up the pockets.

The play opened on July 30, 1947, at the peak of a phenomenal summer heatwave. The audience was filled with distinguished émigrés and members of Los Angeles' cultural elite. Charles was prostrated in his outside trailer before the curtain, drinking soda water and trembling. He told Norman Lloyd that he was terrified —perhaps he was doing the wrong thing?—but he had to go ahead, because at last he could overcome his guilt at not having gone back to the English stage at the beginning of the war.

The production as it emerged that night was extremely sparse and devoid of decoration, as its creators had wished. The stage was bare except for wooden platforms and beams, and both backdrops and curtain were based on drawings and engravings by Renaissance artists. The cast of fifty players was dressed by Robert Dawson and Helene Weigel Brecht with equal simplicity. In last-minute revisions, the true nature of Galileo finally emerged, realized without mannerism or self-indulgence by Charles. Due to Charles's influence, the character now contained a number of intriguing paradoxes and contradictions. Galileo was no longer a man of flawless reason and decency. He had become fallible and human. He was shown stealing a Dutch concept of the telescope, selling it to the senate of the Vatican as though he had spent fourteen years developing the special lenses himself. He was shown naming the planets after the names of the Medicis in order to curry favor at court. His recantation of the moving earth theory was played by Charles with trembling terror, so as to convey that Galileo was capable of extreme human weakness. Because of the realism of the writing and the portrayal, Charles's final speech to his beloved student, indicating the necessity for courage in pursuit of truth, was all the more affecting.

The reviews by Virginia Wright in the Los Angeles *Daily News* and by Edwin Schallert in the Los Angeles *Times* were enthusiastic. Miss Wright singled out several members of the fine supporting cast for praise, including Hugo Haas as the sympathetic Cardinal Barberini, Frances Heflin as Galileo's daughter, and Peter Brocco as an angry old Cardinal. She gave special mention to Joseph Losey's use of a gauze curtain pulled by a tiny pageboy to indicate the passage of the scenes, and the thirteen chants or recitations sung to music composed by Hanns Eisler, which provided the introductions to these scenes, exquisitely delivered by three boy sopranos.

During the rehearsals and both during and after the first night, the political atmosphere surrounding the production was dark and threatening. J. Parnell Thomas and the House Un-American Activities Committee had begun their inquisitorial hearings in May. They were scarcely unaware of Brecht's political leanings, the Marxist, anti-inquisitorial tone of the play, and the strong possibility that Pelican Productions might have left-wing leanings. Brecht was, in fact, questioned by the committee in the last weeks of rehearsal, and Charles's attorney, Loyd Wright, by no means happy that Charles was involved in the production at all, had occasion more than once to warn him that despite his total lack of commitment to any political party, he might well be investigated himself. In view of his association with Brecht, the attorney warned, Charles must be scrupulously careful not to make any public statement which might be open to question, not to attend any political meeting whatsoever, and not to accept any pamphlet, book, or other document through the mail. The problem was aggravated by the fact that Joseph Losey was being accused of being a communist sympathizer, and in fact subsequently was compelled to leave for Europe.

There is no doubt that Charles acted with all the courage of Galileo himself in persevering with the production in the circumstances, and in pressing for its production in New York. He was fully aware of what he was doing and fully aware that the play's meaning increased in significance throughout each day of its performance, each day it lay under the shadow of the inquisition.

The run continued for a month. Plans were finalized for the Broadway production. But the financier T. Edward Hambleton, among others, felt that it was a mistake to open in New York before drastic improvements had been made. Though he liked the simplicity and beauty of the production, he felt that it lacked passion, excitement, color, that it was too restrained and cerebral to appeal to Broadway audiences. Another play about Galileo, A Lamp at Midnight, had just opened and had been warmly reviewed by Brooks Atkinson in the New York Times. Moreover, despite good local reviews, the national reviews of Galileo were not enthusiastic. The New York Times' West Coast correspondent, Gladwin Hill, wrote that the production lacked energy, drive, dash and color; that Charles, in his effort to avoid the castigation of critics who had in recent years accused him of hamming and mugging, played in far too subdued and monochromatic a fashion, and that the episodic nature of the play diffused the dramatic force and vitality inherent in the subject. Variety, so often excessively kind, simply denounced the production as drab and boring.

T. Edward Hambleton and his partners delayed production in New York until December. It turned out to be a fatal decision. On October 30, with many revisions still to be done, Brecht appeared before the House Un-American Activities Committee in Washington. The committee consisted of J. Parnell Thomas, John McDowell, Richard B. Vail, and one Richard Nixon. Robert E. Stripling, official investigator for the committee, cross-examined Brecht with the aid of a translator whose English, if anything, was worse than Brecht's. The committee, reluctant to admit it was in error at any time, realized while Stripling was still bullying Brecht that the entire investigation of him was somewhat pointless (they also hated the smell of his cigars). They had bigger fish to fry. He was, after all, an obscure figure so far as the American public was concerned, his verse, his plays, and even his songs not very widely known. He was allowed to go; and, very wisely, he left for Europe at once.

Galileo opened without Brecht at the Maxine Elliott Theatre in New York on December 7, 1947. Brooks Atkinson's review was devastating. He seized on the loose and episodic nature of the play, described the presentation as less than profoundly revealing, and, while praising Charles for playing for only ten dollars a performance wrote: "He is casual and contemptuous: he is ponderous and condescending, and there is a great deal of old-fashioned fiddle-faddle in his buffeting of the books and his giving of orders to underlings . . . both as play and performance, *Galileo* is fingertips playmaking. And the production is stuffed to the ears with hokum. Nothing the play says justifies Mr. Brecht's humble and fearful prayer for science in the brief epilogue."

Despite this and other bad reviews, the play was a moderate success. Its limited two-week run was extended to three. John Mason Brown praised the production in the New York *Post*. Audiences were large and enthusiastic, and many performances played to standing room only. Unfortunately, the Maxine Elliott was already committed to another play, and no other theatre could be found. Losey tried for years to present the play in England, and later to make it into a film; as recently as 1975, his American Film Theatre production was seen, produced by Ely Landau, with Topol indifferently playing Galileo.

During the interval between the West Coast and New York productions of *Galileo*, Charles appeared in a character part as the hanging judge Lord Horfield in David O. Selznick and Alfred Hitchcock's *The Paradine Case*. Robert Hichens' original novel had been a heavily dated story of adultery and murder: a distinguished counsel falls in love with his client, a murderess who has killed her blind husband in order to free herself to sleep with a groom. Hitchcock was evidently intrigued by the theme of an exquisite woman's degradation, a recurrent concern of his work. But Selznick rewrote the original script by James Bridie, changing Mrs. Paradine from a working-class Swede into a distinguished, elegant Italian whose background as a prostitute was rendered inexplicable by the casting of the frostily assured Alida Valli; and the coarse, foul-smelling groom was changed to an equally elegant valet, played by Louis Jourdan. Bored by both these performers, and annoyed that Selznick insisted on casting them, Hitchcock devoted most of his directorial skill to handling Charles—and Ethel Barrymore, who was cast as Lady Horfield, his browbeaten and unhappy wife.

The role of Lord Horfield was easily the best written in the film. The learned judge is first seen presiding over a dinner party, rather like Sir Humphrey Pengallan in *Jamaica Inn*, reminiscing with jaded contempt about an incident at Deauville: "I managed to persuade Lady Millicent to go swimming at seventy. I watched her frolicking in the surf and had sad thoughts about the impermanence of beauty." Later, Lord Horfield lecherously holds the hand of the wife of Mrs. Paradine's defense counsel, his eyes swooping on her bare shoulder, while her husband is temporarily out of sight. At the Old Bailey, petulant, sleepy, his hand half-hiding his scowling face as he sinks back in his chair, Horfield dismisses the defense counsel's emotionalism, sternly warns a witness, or more gently corrects the prosecution; calling a recess, he trots round-shouldered and potbellied out of the courtroom, drawing his robe around him like a dressing gown.

The best scene in the picture shows Lord Horfield finishing a quiet dinner with his wife just before the guilty verdict comes in against Mrs. Paradine. Sulking, he comments unfavorably on his wife's coughing in court, which has caused him several irritated sidelong glances. He remarks on the resemblance between the convolutions of a walnut and those of the human brain, as he dismisses Lady Horfield's sympathy for the murderess. "You silly woman . . . the Paradine woman will be hanged after three clear Sundays." Charles, excellently cast, made a real figure of the judge, at once somnolent, spoilt, and ruthless—and Selznick's elaborate sub-Wildean dialogue rolled smoothly off his tongue.

Charles's gift for making even the most repellent figures accessible and sympathetic is shown in many small touches. The edge of humor he gives to his instructions and corrections in court is revealed in numerous tiny petulant gestures, and in the scene in which he addresses Lady Horfield as "you silly woman" he says the words not with cold contempt, but with the affection a man might have for a slightly gaga old spaniel. The monster becomes human, though still as horrible.

The rest of this elegantly made film is flawed by the fact that the defense attorney Geoffrey Keene's passion for Mrs. Paradine is, despite her beauty, quite inexplicable, given her cold and contemptuous attitude toward him from the start. Gregory Peck is miscast as Keene, not only in terms of accent and bearing—the part would have been perfect for Laurence Olivier—but in terms of character; he is far too well-adjusted and bland to play a man in the grip of a neurotic obsession. *Pace* Hitchcock, both Alida Valli and Louis Jourdan are admirable, conveying a mutual erotic feeling despite the cold and detached direction; Miss Valli in particular gives an impressive portrait of destructive viciousness, a cobra about to strike.

In *The Paradine Case* Charles was merely a featured player, but in John Farrow's *The Big Clock*, made just after the production of *Galileo*, he received second star billing under Ray Milland, whom he had helped as an awkward young supporting actor in the film of *Payment Deferred* fifteen years earlier. *The Big Clock*, based by Jonathan Latimer on a scrappy and confused novel by Kenneth Fearing, remains one of the most entertaining movies of Charles's career. Charles played Earl Janoth, a heavy, obvious, and vulgar tycoon who rules over a Luce-like magazine empire in New York. When Janoth murders his mistress with a sundial clock wrapped in green ribbon, he is forced to engage the resources of his organization to track down the one witness to his guilt: a man glimpsed in a corridor at the top of a flight of stairs. Ironically, the *Crimeways Magazine* editor (Milland) sent to head the investigation is himself the witness. The giant clock which dominates the proceedings—nerve center of the Janoth organization—is magnificently created by the art department. With its ticking dials, pulsing dynamo, and gliding levers, it reminds one of the heart of Fritz Lang's *Metropolis*, and its impersonal energy is meaningfully shown pulsing through the mutual hatreds, the tensions of office life. As we are taken along the endless shadowy corridors, penetrate the publisher's office where tycoon and evil familiar quarrel, invade a conference room at the height of a tense exchange, we are brought very close to the feeling of commercial power.

Like *The Paradine Case* before it, *The Big Clock* is a mechanical film, as cold and intricate as the clicking mechanism which forms the center of its action. Charles's Earle Janoth is in every way a memorable creation. Janoth first makes an entrance in the midst of an editorial conference of *Crimeways Magazine*. Circulation has been falling, various promotional gimmicks have failed to pay off, and Janoth demands an immediate solution. In about thirty seconds, aided by Latimer's excellent dialogue, Charles establishes Janoth's character. Dressed in an immaculate gray-flannel pinstripe suit, with a carnation in his buttonhole, he strides into the room like a bull elephant, a tycoon used to trampling everyone and everything in his path. His pinkie finger, wet with saliva, keeps pressing a recalcitrant moustache into place. He raps out instructions to his employees, tosses off figures—he has three thousand employees, the organization is worth thirty-seven millions dollars; he shouts for action like a baby screaming for food; he quickly dismisses one absurd circulation building idea after another until he finds one he likes and condescendingly pats the approved editor on the back.

Charles's acting never falters. One second after telling the editor Ray Milland that he will dismiss him and blacklist him forever in the magazine business, Janoth asks a secretary how her baby is getting on. Charles gives the inquiry just the right note of unctuous phoniness. When he kills his mistress, Janoth's rage at her description of his flabby appearance is wonderfully conveyed by a convulsively twitching upper lip; his murderer's lunge forward is superbly managed. Gradually, as though fitting together the pieces of a mosaic, Charles builds up a multifaced portrait of bullying, cowardly arrogance and assertiveness. There is a fine moment when the big timepiece in the building stops without warning. It turns out that it controls every electric clock in the place. "First time this has happened in twelve years," Janoth says, as he impatiently shakes a clock in his office. Charles invests the line with the impatience of someone who cannot believe anything in the world he controls can possibly go wrong; and he rises to the effective last scene, when he tries to make his henchman George Macready take the rap for him. Like Javert, Barrett, or Squire Pengallan, Earle Janoth is a highly individual Laughtonian image of power, informed with a satirical humor that at once criticizes and illuminates the part. Elsa also appeared in the film, as a painter, Louise Patterson, who has created a bizarre sub-Daliesque painting of a pair of hands; with her four daughters, long silver double-stranded necklace and flowered shawl, she is a funny and delightfully absurd creation, especially when she confronts an art critic who had panned her last exhibition in 1941: "I've been wanting to strangle you ever since!"

It was unfortunate that, after this fascinating and enjoyable movie, Charles should have become embroiled with the mediocre films *Arch of Triumph* and *The Girl from Manhattan*, both of which are best forgotten.

In 1948, Charles became involved in a new and interesting venture: teaching students in a classroom. Kate Drain Lawson, wife of the left-wing writer John Howard Lawson, and an accomplished theatrical designer of sets and costumes, had begun the classes with two actors, William Cottrell and the plump and irascible Thomas Gomez. The classes were held, with the blessing of Norman Lloyd and John Houseman, at the art gallery of the Coronet Theatre. Charles dropped by one day and was appalled at the ham-fisted techniques Gomez was using in class. Cottrell and Mrs. Lawson asked him to replace Gomez, who was dislodged and, red-faced and furious, threatened to punch "that filthy dirty actor Laughton" in the nose should he happen to cross his path. At one stage, Charles had to dodge around a potted palm to escape Gomez's unbridled fury.

The classroom shifted to Pacific Palisades, and later to the house on Curson Avenue where Charles and Elsa moved in late 1949. Among the students were Jane Wyatt, Shelley Winters, Robert Ryan, Denver Pyle, and Arthur O'Connell. From the beginning, Charles established an atmosphere of mutual discovery, discarding the traditional condescending approach of so many drama teachers. He made it clear that in order to succeed an actor must have a total aesthetic awareness, that he must be fully conscious of all of the arts, and particularly of music, since a strong musical sense was vital in the reading of lines. He wanted the actors to remove all pretentiousness from their minds, to approach the plays simply, freshly, and nakedly, as though they had never read them or even heard of them before. His purpose was to obtain "fast readers," students who could seize on the meaning of a line at a glance and deliver it with every word felt instantly, responded to without inhibitions.

In dealing with the pentameter, Charles reversed the argumentative position he had held against Tyrone Guthrie in the Old Vic season of fifteen years earlier. He insisted that the pentameter be followed. But he also insisted that his original precept at the Old Vic should be maintained: a scrupulous adherence to the meaning of the texts, and a refusal to be simply "musical," sacrificing meaning to mellifluous delivery. He had discovered over the years that the music of the pentameter did not conceal the meaning Shakespeare intended, but made it more readily absorbable by the ear. He taught his students to approach the verse without restraints, but not to deny the necessary restraint the author had imposed on himself.

Sometimes, Charles would seize on a line and ask the class what they thought of it, what their interpretation was of its meaning, and whether it had authentic musicality. Charles would give his own interpretation when he had listened to everyone else, but never with an air of finality; he was always, as he put it, "discovering among friends."

Sometimes, Charles would break off from Shakespeare and have the class read Hans Andersen's fairy tales, chiefly to show that readings need not be confined to plays. On other occasions, he taught the class that screen acting was acting with the eyes, that sincerity was essential in movie acting, that the actor must "be" the part, not "perform" it. When young actors were accepted for the class from the many hundreds of applicants, they often began by imitating major stars. Charles always corrected them, telling them that unless they were prepared to be simply themselves, he would rather they went home.

The class offered much for very little financial outlay, but Charles was strict about the rules: punctuality and regular attendance, and a single-minded devotion to the work in hand. This was not merely an imposition of his own will expressed in a show of discipline; it was intended to help concentration, a necessary capacity in any artist. Charles taught moral and humanistic integrity, and methods of bringing out of the memory recalled experiences which could help in acting emotional scenes.

At first, Charles envisioned the class as forming the nucleus of a theatrical repertory company, rather like the Old Vic, with the members alternating seasons of plays with work in movies and in television. But gradually he began to see the impossibility of this scheme, preferring to plan for a more modest production of a play, a scheme that came to fruition with his student production of *The Cherry Orchard* in 1950.

In that period of the late 1940s, Charles and Elsa discovered a new sanctuary away from the world. Their cabin at Idyllwild, retained since 1941, had become too remote in view of their schedules; they sold it and bought instead a two-room shack on the Palos Verdes peninsula. The shack stood in a decayed tropical orchard, which had once been the country's largest bird sanctuary, with the shack a former bird hospital. Despite their pleasure in this haven from the world, they began to drift apart by 1949. Charles was increasingly gloomy and silent, while Elsa became increasingly overbright and humorous and flippant in order to conceal the fact that she felt alienated from him. She realized that many people in their lives had been "dividers," pushing them apart instead of encouraging them to cement their relationship, to rediscover the sexual links they had known at the beginning. Korda, Pommer, Charles's masseurs, and employees had come between them instead of helping their marriage. The Turnabout Theatre, keeping them apart six out of seven evenings a week, had also proved divisive. They were, like so many couples in their position, the victims of confidantes, who listened and reported to each of them separately with an evil "concern for their welfare."

Yet the Laughtons were not constantly estranged. They still, as they had long ago in England, loved to pick and arrange flowers together, break off branches and put them in pots—pots of exquisite design by Hamada and by Bernard Leech. Elsa wrote in an essay:

It was always interesting, even exciting, to see Charles choosing a branch from a tree in the country to put in a particular pot. Usually choosing one that would sit in the pot in the precise position that it was originally growing in. If it was growing horizontally he would counterbalance it with a rock, allowing the stalk to reach the water in perhaps a flat dish.

Charles felt intense pleasure, amounting almost to ecstasy, in the wild flowers of California. At the end of their country or desert days together, Charles and Elsa would often drive home, tired but happy, to, in Elsa's words,

> put California poppies in aluminum saucepans, placed in a casual mass undisturbed, as we had picked them, as we had strolled and bent to gather them, lupins thrust in a kitchen bucket straightening up like ranks of soldiers in the sunlight next morning.

Yet, amid this shared pleasure, Charles was constantly haunted by anxiety. He never felt totally at ease; he lived with fears. The escape to the country and to the wild flowers was only a temporary vacation from his private suffering.

During 1949, Charles began a serious professional association with the accomplished and mercurial actor Burgess Meredith, who had, Charles always felt, one of the finest speaking voices in America. They had met in 1939 when Meredith had been the narrator of Norman Corwin-CBS radio's *The Pursuit of Happiness*, and Charles and Elsa had made an appearance on the program; again with the Renoirs in 1946 (when Meredith appeared as an ancient eccentric who ate roses in Renoir's film *The Diary of a Chambermaid*) and in 1947, when Charles appeared in a tiny bit role as a minister, in a film which Meredith conceived and produced, *On Our Merry Way*.[1] Charles and Elsa sometimes traveled to Palm Springs, to join Burgess and wallow in the very muddy undeveloped hot springs, where Charles enjoyed reciting to the old people sitting in the warm pools.

During late 1948, Meredith received a call from Franchot

---

[1] The scene was cut by Paramount, whereupon David O. Selznick offered to buy the film and release Charles's scene as a short, destroying the rest. The offer was refused.

Tone, saying that Tone was interested in making a film version of one of Georges Simenon's Maigret novels, A *Battle of Nerves*, with Charles as Maigret. Although Charles was reluctant to leave his students, he could not refuse any offer of work. His financial prospects were far from encouraging, taxes had swallowed up much of his income, and he had already begun to think sadly of giving up the house at Pacific Palisades.

Once he had accepted the contract, Charles threw himself into preparing the role of Maigret with his customary intensity, driving over to Western Costumes and selecting a bowler hat and dark suit, not unlike the outfit he wore in *This Land Is Mine*, to convey the temperament and meticulous nature of Simenon's famous detective. Untidy himself, preferring to wear shapeless trousers held around his waist by ancient frayed neckties, Charles as always proved able to sink himself into a character, and the Maigre-tesque suit he took to Paris was brushed and spotlessly clean. However, knowing that Maigret was apt to be absent-minded, he always made sure that the suit was badly pressed and a little baggy. He read and reread the Simenon stories to work himself into the right mood.

Charles, with Robert Hutton and other members of the cast, flew to New York and sailed on the *Mauretania* on August 29, 1948. The producer-director Irving Allen, Franchot Tone, and the actress Jean Wallace had already begun work at the Villancourt Studios when Charles arrived. In the meantime the film had been retitled *The Man on the Eiffel Tower*, and had been given a three-month shooting schedule.

After three days, Charles found it impossible to work with Irving Allen as director. He insisted that Burgess Meredith take over. Allen was furious, but when Charles threatened to return to England, he was forced to give in, staying on as producer only. There were many problems during the shooting. The AnscoColor process was weird, creating bizarre distortions. Autumn rain delayed the shooting for days. Irving Allen, resenting Charles, quarreled with him constantly. Local electricity shortages caused a series of power failures, plunging the set in darkness.

Depressed by the badly written script and by his friend Burgess Meredith's inexperience, Charles took refuge in the company of David Roberts, who stayed with him at the Prince Des Galles

Hotel, and in a new friendship, with Belita, the ice skater, who was appearing at Les Ambassadeurs and whom he cast in the film. Charles was enchanted by Belita's show, and went backstage after it to offer her the greatest compliment of her life: "Watching you gives me the feeling I'm flying."

Belita wrote to Elsa in 1968:

> I adored Charles . . . I was, it seemed, the first person who skated that he had ever met, and owing to his great curiosity he asked endless questions about boots, skates, quality of ice . . . it ended in our making a date the next day to meet at the Prince des Galles skating rink!

Belita managed to lure Charles to her favorite restaurant. On the fifth floor of a private house, it could only be reached by climbing five flights of stairs, and boasted a mere fifteen tables occupied mainly by clerks and prostitutes. Despite the climb for a man of his bulk, Charles loved it, adored the simple couple who ran it, and went back many times, saying to Belita, "Don't let's tell any of the others about this. Then we can eat in peace!" Belita begged to be allowed to come to Hollywood and join his group, but he dismissed the idea with uproarious laughter: "My God, Belita, YOU need teaching? Oh no!" and he laughed again. But Belita added:

> In his own way Charles was teaching me all the time. He gave me so much, not only professionally, but by opening doors to broaden my mind and vision, what he called "letting in fresh air." He used to take me with him when he wandered about the streets looking for books and prints. I had not had much time to read and I think Charles knew this instinctively, and he deliberately set out to show me the wonderful world of words.

Charles frequently attended performances of the Jean-Louis Barrault–Madeleine Renaud Company at the Théâtre Marigny, marveling at the classical precision and control of the stars and their devoted supporting players, and he was often seen at the Comédie Française also; he saw Beaumarchais' *The Marriage of*

Figaro four times. When in New York on his way home, he dropped in to see *Death of a Salesman,* and went backstage to congratulate Lee J. Cobb on his magnificent starring performance. He told Cobb, with tears in his eyes, "This is a great American play, and you are the greatest American actor. You *must* play King Lear."

Unfortunately *The Man on the Eiffel Tower* turned out to be a great disappointment to its makers, although Georges Simenon, then living in Arizona, said he liked it. Most of the picture consisted of a complicated series of chases across Paris, with a clumsy if hair-raising final sequence on the Eiffel Tower itself, for which the courageous Franchot Tone actually walked around struts on narrow girders eight hundred feet above ground without a net. The only good sequence in the picture was directed by Charles himself, who handled most of Burgess Meredith's scenes. Charles's directorial opening was masterly: an eccentric, gnome-like knife grinder, typical of Meredith's well-known gallery of oddities, enters a house in Paris, and stumbles over the blood-drenched corpses of a rich American widow and her maid. The slow, loping knife-grinder's walk, the stealthy climb upstairs to burgle a room, the shocking touch of a corpse, bloodstained hands spread out as the horrified man races down the stairs—the sequence had a macabre power that looked forward to Charles's major directorial achievement, *The Night of the Hunter,* five years later.

Back in Hollywood at the end of 1948, Charles began to take stock of his career. It was obvious by now that *The Man on the Eiffel Tower* would not be a success. Crude and overemphatic, it was a futile effort, doomed to both critical and popular failure. Charles, despite the disappointment he had experienced over *Galileo,* felt an urgent need to return to the stage. But at the moment no opportunity presented itself.

In the meantime, he continued with his acting class, and late in 1949, following a blank spot in his career, he and Elsa finally moved from Pacific Palisades to a more modest house on Curson Avenue in Hollywood. They took with them a new and welcome member of the household, Heidel, whom they both admired. She was a cook-housekeeper, a good, strong, and kind woman, very stubborn and capable.

The Laughtons were helped in the move by a Captain Walters who had dropped by one afternoon while visiting a neighbor. He helped them find a buyer for the house at Pacific Palisades because, with his long experience as a captain of passenger liners, he could scent money very easily. He made all of the arrangements for a sale, and he helped Elsa find the house on Curson while Charles was working on a film—now forgotten—called *The Bribe*. With his knowledge of marine engineering, Captain Walters made a series of magnificent improvements at Curson. He created a circulating ventilation system which insured that the house was always airy, he built floodlights at the four corners of the house, he put in a buzzer system, and made other improvements based on the same principles used in shipbuilding. Charles, standing on the doorstep on the day of the move, ordered every piece of furniture to its allotted place in his precise plan, issuing instructions, like Captain Bligh. Everyone worked ferociously, but when the task was finished, it was worth it. The house looked attractive and spacious, full of unexpected nooks and crannies, and a room, ideal for the purpose, was set aside as the schoolroom, where Charles's classes continued.

Six months after they moved into Curson Avenue, on April 29, 1950, Charles and Elsa became United States citizens in a ceremony before Federal Judge Jacob A. Weinberger in Los Angeles. He asked them if they had been in any trouble. Elsa became very nervous and said, "I've had a speeding ticket!" Everyone present broke up laughing. Photographers and reporters were there, and Elsa told them as she hugged Charles, "We are very proud and happy, both of us." Charles added: "The oath of allegiance is beautiful. It has a wonderful rhythm and a marvelous use of words. I would like to include it among my readings." On May 29, Charles received a bronze plaque from the California Association of School Administrators for appearing at schools and colleges without payment for his readings. That same week, he and Elsa celebrated their citizenship at the Los Angeles *Examiner*'s "I Am an American Day" celebration.

The outset of the 1940s had been marked by a new career in Hollywood, a firm decision to settle in California, and the purchase of a new home. Now the outset of the 1950s brought the assumption of citizenship and the beginning of life in a new house. And another event made 1950 a significant year: the acquisition of a partner who was to help propel Charles to the most extraordinary achievements of his career: the shrewd and handsome thirty-year-old theatrical impresario Paul Gregory.

TEN

In the late 1940s, Paul Gregory was an employee of the talent agency MCA—still in operation before it was forced to abandon its activities in the agency business. He was at the Chambord in New York one Sunday evening, waiting for the actor-singer Dennis Morgan and Morgan's wife to join him for dinner, when he started watching the Ed Sullivan Show on the television set at the bar. He was only mildly interested, until suddenly Charles appeared and read "The Burning Fiery Furnace" from the book of Daniel. Impassioned, marvelous, the reading fascinated him. He seized on the idea of promoting Charles in one-night stands across the country. He was already handling one-night stands of singers and orchestral groups and felt this might be an entirely new form of entertainment. When the Morgans called to say they had been delayed, Gregory immediately hailed a cab and rushed over to the Ed Sullivan Show theatre on Broadway. He ran into Charles and Charles's agent—Frances Head, of the John Gibbs office—as they came down the alleyway.

"Oh, Mr. Laughton," Gregory said, all in a rush, "I'm Paul

Gregory. I loved your reading and I want to book you into one-man shows all across the country."

Charles swept him aside and disappeared down the street. Crestfallen, Gregory returned to his dinner date with the Morgans. But next morning the telephone rang at his office. It was Frances Head, who knew him slightly. She told him: "You know, it struck me, what you said in the alley outside the theatre—I think if you'd like I could make an arrangement for you to meet Mr. Laughton."

Gregory replied, "Well, I'd like that." Next day at four o'clock in the afternoon, Gregory went over to the Algonquin Hotel to have afternoon tea with Charles.

Charles listened patiently. Gregory was very personable, intelligent, and astute. But Charles did not respond warmly to his proposal. He dreaded the thought of one-night stands—the months away from his new home, the loneliness, the constant uncomfortable traveling. Only one aspect of Gregory's argument was totally unanswerable: money. Gregory rashly said that Charles could earn two thousand dollars an engagement, and Charles, who was very worried financially, sat up. With his movie career at a low ebb, he was prepared to snatch at any straw. The conversation ended in Charles grudgingly saying he was "quite interested." As a result, MCA booked him for several months of readings across the country.

Untidy as always, his hair in a tangle, huffing and puffing theatrically, Charles appeared on the stages of numerous colleges and in small town theaters, carrying a small pile of books which he set down deliberately on a lectern. If a lectern was not available, he would find crates and pile them up to the exact height he needed. His appearance of reading from these books was only a disguise, because he knew the passages by heart. He wanted a light to shine in his face if possible. He had obtained the idea from descriptions of Charles Dickens' famous British and American reading tours, in which the novelist had insisted on a light to illuminate his eyes.

Charles had an irresistible technique of fixing individual people in the audience with his gaze throughout a performance, rather than giving the entire group of onlookers general sweeping glances. One old man said that listening to him was "like seeing the Bible in Technicolor." Several ladies of various ages proposed marriage to him, forgetting that he was already married. He was not entirely at ease on the long tour, despite its success. He missed Elsa and the house on Curson Avenue; he longed for David Roberts, who was unable to join him except very briefly because of acting commitments in Hollywood films; and his only personal consolation was that he was able to talk to Elsa frequently by long distance telephone. When he finally returned home, he was visibly tired, but flushed with the joy of an actor who had achieved a great personal success. Elsa told him: "You look exhausted—and ten years younger."

In 1950 Gregory decided to leave MCA and manage Charles on his own. They shared the profits of the first tour, with Charles earning between one thousand and fifteen hundred a performance instead of the two thousand that Paul Gregory had hoped for. Charles felt that Gregory would be able to promote his tour dates in advance more effectively than MCA. In some areas, attendances had been mortifyingly small, and Gregory should be able to correct that.

A promoter of great toughness and flair, aided by his exceptional looks and his smooth, persuasive manner, Gregory managed to increase the appearance fees for many engagements to four thousand dollars a performance.

Under Gregory's adroit guidance, Charles made several shorter tours in late 1950. In each case, Gregory went ahead to individual towns or cities, laying the groundwork, making churches and social clubs buy tickets in bulk, sometimes by the hundred, convincing schools they should send every one of their pupils to the performance. This promotional skill paid off handsomely.

In the late fall of 1950, Charles made one of his most remarkable tours—to Canada, beginning with Montreal. While he and Paul were driving across the border, Gregory said, "Why don't we develop a drama quartet with three other actors?"

Charles almost leaped out of his seat. "What do you mean, old boy? Tell me about that. Sounds very interesting."

Paul said, "I've been reading Shaw's Prefaces. What about the Preface of *Back to Methuselah?*"

Charles said: "No, that would never do for four readers. But I have a better idea. What about *Man and Superman?* The part of it nobody ever performs. The colloquy between the Devil, Don Juan, you know."

As soon as the two men reached Montreal they called a friend in New York and had him mail the fourth act to them. It was perfect. At first, Charles wanted to have four players dressed in cloaks—scarlet for the Devil, orange for Don Juan, white for the Statue, and mauve for Doña Ana. Gregory disagreed.

Don Juan in Hell is a dream sequence, occurring in Act III of *Man and Superman.* Omitted from many acting versions, it was first performed at the Court Theater in London in 1907, the star Robert Loraine playing Don Juan with a Shavian red wig and beard. Most performances were presented as a masque, in a fashion which Shaw himself had laid down: the actors dressed as though appearing in a commedia dell'arte, the stage surrounded by multicolored bulbs. Charles and Paul Gregory decided to dispense with this form of presentation, using instead a classic form, with a bare stage, the actors on stools with lecterns and texts, and dressed in sober evening clothes.

The play-within-a-play is a passionate outcry of Shaw's spirit. In it, he is represented by Don Juan himself. Sickened by his lifetime of sensual indulgence, by the meaningless gratification of the appetites, Juan finds in hell a mere continuation of a life of selfish pleasure. With an eternity in which to contemplate, he has discovered that the purpose of the force of life is to develop self-awareness: that man's destiny must be to perceive his own mind, to be conscious of the depth of his own ability to reason. Without this he must remain in a hell of frustration, of constantly seeking sensual fulfillment, of the agonizing awareness that declining health, impotence, and decay will swallow up his imaginary happiness. In the play, the Devil becomes the voice of lazy, heavy, overpowering self-indulgence, and the enemy of reason. Doña Ana, who once loved Juan, is the voice of propriety, of rectitude; her father, the Statue, is an old military commander, the voice of earthy common sense, stuffy, middle-class complacency, and Philistine contempt for aesthetics. He is the only one of the four who has not been condemned to hell. He is visiting his daughter from heaven, a place which Shaw reveals to be peopled by the dull, the gray, the saintly, and the unattractive. Hell, on the other hand, is filled with joy, love, happiness, and physical beauty. But Shaw makes clear that these are all illusions, that life on earth or in hell is simply vanity, nothing but vanity.

The play contains a number of intriguing contradictions and paradoxes. On the one hand, Shaw condemns marriage and child-bearing through Don Juan's mouth, yet at the end we see that in order for the life force to be expressed in self-awareness, supermen must be born. In order to further their species of supermen they must still sleep with women, who must raise their children; and they must endure the earthiness and restrictiveness of women which Don Juan/Shaw constantly complains of. Shaw, terrified of sex and marriage in his own life, never solves this problem. He would, it seems, prefer some system whereby supermen were born through parthenogenesis. At the end of the dream-play, Doña Ana exits with the exultant cry: "A Father for the Superman!" indicating that she will find a human of superior intellect to couple with her and thereby create a superchild. But Shaw cannot mean us to take this literally, since Doña Ana is a dead woman of seventy-seven. He means us to feel that Woman's destiny is to bear a superman, that through this she can be fulfilled; he nowhere suggests that Woman herself could achieve a divine self-consciousness, and thereby fulfill the purpose of the life force in her own being.

The danger in Shaw's argument—stemming in part from Nietzsche, it found its evil flowering in a Hitlerian concept of divine physical and mental power—is reflected in the many arguments which the play contains. Significantly, Charles and Paul Gregory cut a passage toward the end in which the Devil discloses that "Nietzsche has gone to heaven, and good riddance, too." The reference to Nietzsche as one who has infuriated the Devil is a typical ploy of Shaw's to drag in a reference to a favorite philosopher. Charles must have warmed much more to another passage which awakened memories of earlier work:

> THE DEVIL (commenting on Don Juan's departure to heaven): I cannot keep these Life Worshippers. They

all go. This is the greatest loss I have had since that
Dutch painter . . . who would paint a hag of seventy
with as much enjoyment as a Venus of twenty.

THE STATUE: I remember. He came to heaven.
Rembrandt.

This is the weak side of Shaw's argument. That the artist who
seeks the truth can achieve celestial release is a fine concept, but
Shaw forgets that Rembrandt was not the embodiment of bloodless reason; that he was, as Charles's own portrait of him on film
so clearly demonstrated, a man deeply rooted in the body, in sensual experience. If Shaw had followed his own line of reasoning to
its conclusion, Rembrandt would have gone to hell, like Don
Juan, and found there, in the deprivation of all except the illusion
of physical fulfillment, a leaning toward pure reason.

Nevertheless, despite the many holes in Shaw's arguments and
dramatic presentation, and the streak of fascism and misogyny
which today might make the dream-play open to criticism, its central theme of the search for bodiless, pure self-conscious reason
must have had a profound appeal for Charles. Since his own physical being displeased him, since he found the gratifying of the
senses largely dissatisfying, since he still carried his Jesuit training
with him like Quasimodo's iron ball and chain, he must have
been drawn to a vision in which his brilliant mind could be seen
as the life force's emergence in him.

During discussions in Montreal, Gregory asked Charles what
part he would like to play. Charles said at once, "Don Juan—and
I should direct."

Gregory told him, "You'd be perfect as the Devil."

"No! *Don Juan!* He's *got* to be an Englishman."

"I don't think so, Charles."

"What do you mean?"

"Don Juan wasn't English. And American audiences won't be
able to listen to four British actors. They'll never understand it."

"Who do you think should do it?"

"A romantic figure—Charles Boyer."

"Never! He can't speak English! How can he read Shaw?" But
Gregory finally convinced Charles that Boyer would be perfect.

When the tour reached Boston, Gregory called Boyer in Hollywood. Boyer told him he could not play the part because he had an insufficient command of English. In New York, the telephone conversation continued. But it was not until Charles and Paul Gregory actually talked face to face with Boyer in Hollywood that the actor agreed.

In November, Charles met Elsa in New York. He performed his reading at the Brooklyn Academy of Music, and she appeared at the new Persian Room at the Plaza, on leave from Turnabout, causing a sensation. Paul Gregory also handled her act, touring her from Montreal to Boston just behind Charles. But he had neglected to note that Charles's appearance in New York would coincide with hers. When Charles reached the Plaza, where Elsa was staying, a clerk called her suite and spoke to her piano accompanist, Ray Henderson, saying, "There's someone down here saying he's Charles Laughton. What shall I do?" Since the hotel was completely booked, the hotel had to supply Charles with a truckle bed, which he occupied miserably in the living room of Elsa's suite.

Charles came to her performances, commenting unkindly on them, and hurting her deeply. Fortunately, her confidence was restored by her dress designer, Valentina, who called her "a genius," and by the maître d'hôtel, who said he liked hers "better than any act at the Persian Room to date." She played to full houses every night.

Charles's appearance at the Brooklyn Academy of Music was a triumph. His two-hour reading was greeted by a standing ovation. He won his audience over immediately with one of Harry Graham's Ruthless Rhymes:

> Billy, in one of his nice, new sashes,
> Fell in the fire and was burned to ashes.
> Now, although the room grows chilly,
> I haven't the heart to poke poor Billy.

He continued with Thurber's version of *Little Red Riding-Hood*, an excerpt from Thomas Wolfe's *Of Time and the River*, Charles Dickens' *Pickwick Papers*, the first political speech by Lincoln, the Gettysburg Address, and selections from the Book of Daniel and from Shakespeare.

This performance in New York was the culmination of Charles's achievement of twenty-five years of acting. What had made him supreme among performers was his mastery of the tirade, the speech which, in a film, suddenly emerged and summed up an entire theme. No other actor had made this his trademark, and Charles at the Academy of Music provided a tirade to his own career up to that time. His performance provided an experience nobody who saw it would ever forget, and the reviews were almost uniformly good.

Preparing *Don Juan in Hell* for public presentation, the actors made a number of changes. Further alterations were made later. Among the passages cut were the Statue's "The saints, the fathers, the elect of long ago are the cranks, the faddists, the outsiders of today," Ana's "Is there nothing in heaven but contemplation, Juan?" Don Juan's speech about beauty and imagination, his "I made curious observations of the strange odors of the chemistry of the nerves" and his observations on the decline of population in the twentieth century, clearly unacceptable by 1951; the Devil's cry to the statue, "Have you forgotten the hideous dullness from which I am offering a rescue here?" and Don Juan's speech about the marriage ritual of the Church. Individual words were altered: among them, "thither" became "there," "thrice" became "three times," "Maxim gun" became "machine gun," the word "sixpenny" was cut, "workhouse" was changed to "poorhouse," "gull" was changed to "dupe," "ay" to "Oh, yes," and "at your service" became "entirely at your service." The actors made a rather startling number of additions to the text, and some slighting references to religion were toned down or removed altogether—possibly in deference to local religious bodies who might be represented in the audience. Typical of these changes was a passage in which Don Juan says: "I spent an evening lately in a certain celebrated legislature, and heard the pot lecturing the kettle for its blackness, and ministers answering questions." In this new acting version, "ministers" is changed to "politicians," a change not calculated to soothe Shaw's soul, whether in heaven or hell.

While *Don Juan in Hell* was being prepared, Charles produced with his students a new version of *The Cherry Orchard* which he had appeared in for Komisarjevsky and for Tyrone Guthrie at the Old Vic. For this new presentation, he combined forces with the Russian actress, Eugénie Leontovich, whose Stage Theatre was attracting a great deal of attention in Los Angeles. Leontovich would play Mme. Ranevsky, with Charles as her brother, Gaev, and Belita as Varya, the adopted daughter. Richard Lupino played Charles's old role of Lopahin, while the rest of the crew was made up of Charles's other students.

Harry Horner, an outstanding artist, designed the production. By all accounts, Charles directed *The Cherry Orchard* with immense flair. Preparations began in May 1950, with Kate Drain Lawson providing accomplished help with sets, costumes, and lights. Nobody earned more than ten dollars a week, the minimum permitted by Equity in those days; profits would be shared by all at the end of the month.

There were frequent quarrels between Charles and Kate Drain Lawson before the play opened. Kate told Charles he was speaking too quietly and that he couldn't be heard at the back of the orchestra, a statement he found infuriating. Her constant checking up on tiny points of detail irritated him beyond endurance. She walked out just before opening curtain, only to be lured back by Paul Gregory.

The whole rehearsal period was an ordeal for Charles because his relationship with David Roberts was, after nine years, beginning to break up. Another problem was that he felt an inner conflict: he was being pulled toward his career with Paul Gregory and away from his beloved class. The rest of the cast sensed Charles's devastation, the depths of his sheer misery, and they were unsettled also by his frequent outbursts of temper, his harrowing conflicts with Kate Drain Lawson. Finally, David left Charles and went to New York. For both, this was a horrifying decision, which caused them an equally acute sense of despair.

The production of *The Cherry Orchard* opened in June. Despite all the anguish that had existed during its fashioning, it was a quiet, composed, and subdued production with a warm autumnal feeling. The reviews were excellent, many critics expressing astonishment at Belita's fine acting under Charles's guidance.

In late May 1950, during last rehearsals for *The Cherry Or-*

chard, Charles wrote to Bernard Shaw in London seeking permission to perform *Don Juan in Hell.* After outlining the details of his plans, and of his previous reading tour, Charles added:

> This kind of theatre has advantages to offer the actor. He knows that he will be in employment for the four months of the concert season, and he is able to plan. He is not out on the street in 48 hours as he would be if he struck a flop in either the West End or Broadway, and he is not tied for two years if there is a success. As far as the actor is concerned, the tour would be repeated with the same actors, if available, if not, with others, for several years. It takes five years to cover all the colleges and universities which would be interested in such a project in this country alone.

George Bernard Shaw replied that he felt the hell scene was such a strange piece of theatre that he advised against experimentation. He did hope that Laughton would try to do the normally omitted scene which he had not written to be played. [The Maurice Evans revival of *Man and Superman* on Broadway did not include the hell scene.] Shaw reminded Laughton that he himself had performed it a few times with Robert Loraine. [Court Theatre, London. *The Man of Destiny* made up the balance of the evening.] Shaw luxuriated in the decor and lighting; blazing Spanish costumes, black background achieved by covering everything on stage and lighting from the front. He was high in his praise of Lillian McCarthy in the Infanta role, and of the Devil in red covered with hearts.

Shaw went on to say that years later Esmé Percy, while doing theatricals for the troops in World War I, gave the soldiers the whole work including the hell scene. Later still, he did the whole business for one evening to a packed house in Glasgow. As a result he played it for a week.

Shaw urged Laughton to try it but to give careful attention to stage and scenery to avoid a costume reading performance and for certain to have front lighting.

He closed with a memory of seeing Laughton in a Gower Street performance where all the others paled against him. On the basis of that evening he saw a great future, at the time, for Laughton.

Charles was overjoyed by the letter, which arrived just before the first night of *The Cherry Orchard*. He knew at once the meaning of Shaw's reference to Gower Street: Shaw was talking about Charles's performance as Professor Higgins in *Pygmalion* at RADA. He told Shaw in his reply that Shaw would not receive royalties until the following February, when the play would be performed, and thanked him profusely for his note.

When Charles told him of this reference to royalties, Paul Gregory was annoyed. He told Charles the play was in the public domain, since Shaw had neglected to renew the 1901 copyright. When Gregory was in England later in 1950 to arrange the British tour with Lew and Leslie Grade, he called Shaw at Shaw's house at Ayot St. Lawrence and told him: "Mr. Shaw your piece is in the public domain—and whether you give me the rights to it or not I'm going to do it—but I would rather pay you a commission, pay you a royalty and be correct about it." Shaw replied, "It's not in the public domain." And Gregory told him, "It *is!*" Finally, Shaw agreed to accept 5 per cent of the profits instead of his usual 10 per cent, the first time in his life he had agreed to such an arrangement. As it turned out, Shaw died before the production was put on.

During *The Cherry Orchard* rehearsals, and before and after the correspondence with Shaw, Paul Gregory and Charles finally settled on the cast for *Don Juan in Hell*. The nervous and hypersensitive Charles Boyer backed out, returned to his commitment, backed out again, and at last agreed to play Don Juan, despite the gravest misgivings and a painful feeling that the long tour would exhaust him and separate him too long from his wife and his son. After seriously mentioning Florence Eldridge as Dona Ana, with her husband Fredric March as Don Juan (in case, at the very last minute, Boyer should back out once more), the partners settled on Agnes Moorehead. No sooner had they made this choice than they discovered she was in the South of France working on a picture. She replied with great enthusiasm from the Hotel Negresco in Nice, saying she would love to appear in *Don Juan in Hell*, but she would not be free until January.

Because of this, the plans were postponed until the beginning of 1951: both Charles and Paul Gregory felt that nobody else would be quite right. For a while they toyed with the idea of

Beulah Bondi. She was ruled out because, although she might be acceptable as the crone Doña Ana at the beginning of the dream-play, she would be absurd as the twenty-seven-year-old Doña Ana whom the Devil evokes in later passages.

Rehearsals began at Charles's house in January 1951, further discussions taking place with each actor individually at his Palos Verdes cottage. The players all appreciated Charles permitting them a great degree of freedom in interpretation. Charles was a marvelously adroit and cynical Devil. Boyer, despite his poor command of the more complicated passages, turned out to be an ideal Don Juan, a passionate spokesman of Shaw's ideal. Agnes Moorehead expertly used a skittish, rather hysterical laugh which expressed the girlish evasive hypocritical spirit of Doña Ana. Cedric Hardwicke was fine as the Statue: at once stuffy and jovial, upright and cynical. The rapport between these four great actors was a marvel. They embarked with the greatest élan on the tour at Claremont College near Los Angeles, on January 27, 1951. Just before the performance began, Charles became overpowered by his usual sense of terror. He told a handsome new young friend, Steve Martin: "I've destroyed these actors, I've mucked up their careers." Steve told him he was wrong, but Charles was so petrified with guilt and fear that he almost failed to deliver his opening speech.

The auditorium at Claremont College held only forty people, but the response from the tiny audience was warm and heartening. A later tryout there was equally pleasing. The tour continued in San Francisco and Oakland.

Gregory had reserved a bus, which normally traveled eighty people, for himself, the four actors, two members of the staff, and Steve Martin, whom Charles had met after David left for New York. Charles Boyer was extremely nervous, sitting just behind the driver, jumping up and complaining loudly every time the bus traveled at more than forty miles an hour. Laughton and Moorehead used to sit on either side of the aisle and exchange wisecracks about Boyer's terror of speed. Finally, Charles told the driver: "Disconnect the speedometer." He did. Whenever Boyer asked what exact speed the bus was traveling at, the driver would say, "Forty," or "Thirty-five." Boyer settled back, feeling perfectly comfortable, even though the bus was rushing along at sixty miles an hour.

Often, the passengers suffered from tension, snapping at each other in the long journeys between towns. At other times, they played jokes. In one place, when Charles had to judge a beauty contest, Agnes appeared at the end of the line, vamping away in a swimming costume. Charles promptly floored her by giving her the prize.

The tour continued through California, Arizona, Utah, and Canada, and in July left for England, where the presentation was a complete disaster. Originally, the plan had been for Lew and Leslie Grade to present the production in the West End as part of the Festival of Britain, but unfortunately John Clements put on special performances of *Don Juan in Hell* in the West End, alternating with the rest of *Man and Superman*, which was already running. Instead, the Gregory-Laughton company embarked on a provincial tour which was a flop. For once Gregory miscalculated, booking the Quartette into huge theatres (with special ticket prices) where they were completely lost.

Feeling expansive despite this disastrous tour, Charles bought a Cadillac on his return in August, and began to make preparations for a swimming pool by Lloyd (son of Frank Lloyd) Wright at Curson Avenue. In the meantime, Paul Gregory booked Elsa on a successful nation-wide tour of her one-woman show with an appearance at the Café de Paris in London. Saddled with some inferior American songs, she felt uncomfortable, and some of the notices were vicious partly because, like Charles before her, she was felt to have stayed misguidedly in America during the war. When the management asked her to replace one particularly successful song, she refused, and left. Charles's brother, Tom Laughton, came down and drove her to Scarborough for a brief stay, asking her about Charles's companion, Steve. She told him of Charles's homosexuality, and he proved to be warm and understanding.

While Elsa was in Europe, Charles opened with the Drama Quartette at Carnegie Hall late in October 1951. After a one-night appearance there, the company moved on to the Brooklyn Academy of Music, made some out-of-town appearances, and then returned for a four-week run at the Century Theatre on November 29. Brooks Atkinson led the chorus of praise, commenting enthusiastically on Hardwicke's perfect command of the amiable, stuffy character of the Statue, on Agnes Moorehead's combination of sparkle and sententiousness, on Charles's gusto as the cynical and devious Devil, and above all on Charles Boyer's performance as Don Juan, which today emerges on records as the greatest of the four acting tours-de-force.

The run continued until January 1952, when Paul Gregory felt that every conceivable city had been exhausted. Plans for an Australian tour fell through when the Australian production company, J. C. Williamson's, proved unable to come up with satisfactory business arrangements. Instead, Gregory and Charles between them decided to begin a new production, also without costumes or scenery, of Stephen Vincent Benét's famous verse drama, *John Brown's Body*.

Stephen Vincent Benét wrote *John Brown's Body* in Paris in 1926 and 1927, basing his great work on a reading of Villard's life of Brown, on the lives of Abraham Lincoln by Lord Charnwood and others, and above all on newspapers of the Civil War period. Working for months at the American Library on the Rue d'Élysée, casting and recasting whole passages, and adding a little each day, he intended to provide images of the landscapes, the people, the feelings of a whole nation in a tragic time. The work was fluid and rhythmical, at times incantatory, at others ruminative. It was divided into several sections, each powerfully complementing the other. By the fall of 1927, Doubleday, Doran had received the manuscript and the editors there felt they were in possession of a masterpiece. Throughout early 1928, letters of praise from writers flowed in. Book Club selections were followed by an avalanche of praise and the greatest sales for any poetic work since Whitman's *Leaves of Grass*. Benét received hundreds of letters from descendants of both the Union and the Confederate armies. Dudley Fitts compared the descriptions of Bull Run and Gettysburg with Virgil's *Aeneid*. Edna St. Vincent Millay and Harriet Monroe were respectively "impressed" and "quite bowled over." Sinclair Lewis mentioned the poem in his 1930 Nobel Prize speech as evidence of the rebirth of American letters at the outset of a new decade. The book was a big success—the greatest seller on Doubleday, Doran's list in almost ten years—in 1928 and 1929 it sold 130,000 copies a year. The poem became a staple of countless American schools, it was performed constantly on the radio, and by the time Charles and Paul Gregory produced it, it was a noble peak of American literature.

While Charles was discussing the new venture with Paul, he performed briefly in O. Henry's Full House, an omnibus picture in which he was an old tramp in "The Cop and the Anthem," a performance reminiscent of both Ginger Ted and Jonas Tuttle. Soapy is a gentlemanly deadbeat who constantly tries to get himself arrested so he can pass the winter in a nice, warm, hospitable jail. His efforts are hugely amusing: he tosses a brick casually through a shop window, eats the most expensive dishes in a high-priced restaurant, and even kicks a cop on the shins, but he still remains left out on the street. With his shabby bowler, once expensive but beaten-up clothes and ill-fitting shoes, Soapy is almost a Chaplinesque character, and Charles is at his wittiest in the performance.

His next picture, Abbot and Costello Meet Captain Kidd, made in order—he was never above this—to earn enough money to buy another painting, is certainly best ignored.

Charles was very busy in early 1952 working on John Brown's Body. He felt that on this occasion he must not appear in the production, he must only direct it. At Palos Verdes he began editing the poem, cutting it to actable form. Gregory often went down to the house there and Charles read him long passages, acting all the parts with great flair. Sometimes, Gregory would be so tired, or bored in the longer passages, he nodded off to sleep, and Charles, infuriated, would slam the book shut, making Paul sit up with a start.

Discussions on casting proceeded all through the early spring of 1952. Raymond Massey was obviously an ideal choice for Abraham Lincoln, since he had played the part on stage and screen; he could also play John Brown. Paul wrote to him in London, and he replied with qualified enthusiasm; but from his home in Connecticut later, he said he had firmly decided to proceed.

Early that summer, with the other parts still not cast, Charles made a brief trip to England to see his family. He returned to make a picture, Salome, which was among the worst of his career.

William Dieterle, the dictatorial director of *The Hunchback of Notre Dame*, wanted Charles to play Herod in this version of the Bible story. Harry Cohn, the crude and violent head of the studio, was only interested in making a multistar epic to rival Cecil B. DeMille's *Samson and Delilah*, and was convinced that "Laughton's no star." Dieterle managed to make Cohn change his mind after reminding him of the one picture of Charles's that Cohn had seen, *Mutiny on the Bounty*, and of the huge success of Charles's Bible readings.

Dieterle wrote to Elsa in 1968:

> Working with Charles in this picture was very different from the work on *Hunchback*. Quasimodo was deaf and dumb. Herod had many long dialog scenes and there was the rub. When it came to dialogue, the gap between Laughton and the rest of the actors was unbridgeable. I knew but few actors who could handle dialogue like Laughton, and none of them was in the cast of *Salome*. I used every trick of the trade to bring the rest of the cast up to Laughton's level, but to no avail. He too rehearsed with his partners, hoping to improve his scenes, but a "fencing master cannot fence with amateurs" was his private remark to me. He played Herod, this Quisling, with uncanny slick softness, a man trying to please both sides, the Romans and the people. But Cohn had a different idea of the King of Judea. Being himself a little tyrant who bullied his people in the filthiest tongue, he asked me again and again to make Laughton tougher. When I told Laughton about Cohn's idea, he raised his shoulders and snarled with almost closed eyes: "Tell that son of a bitch up there that he must stick to his business and leave the acting to me. Or else!" I did not have to bring this answer to Cohn, he got it quickly from his stool pigeons, who were always around—the fact that he heard this resulted in his leaving us alone.

During the picture, Charles became friendly with Judith Anderson, who played Herod's consort, Herodias, and decided to cast her in *John Brown's Body*. She was excited at once. Hating

15. Charles and Elsa—New York opening, *The Spiral Staircase*.

16 & 17. Brecht collage, using a Japanese reproduction (front and back). *(Brecht)*

18. Portrait of cast and crew, *The Night of the Hunter*. (*United Artists*)

19. Charles directing Billy Chapin in *The Night of the Hunter*.

making pictures, she longed for a distinguished opportunity on the stage. She often dropped over to Curson Avenue, talking over the poem, sitting in the shade as Charles splashed around the pool. She drank champagne while he drank martinis.

The final addition to the cast was Tyrone Power, who, like Massey and Anderson, would play several parts. Both Gregory and Charles felt that a young and handsome man was needed, not simply to play the more youthful characters, but to give visual appeal and variety to the production. Gregory located Power in Mexico, and flew down to Mexico City in August to talk to him and his wife, Linda Christian. Power read the script Charles had edited and said: "I don't understand a word of this, but if you want me to work for Charles Laughton, I will."

The rest of the summer was taken up with constant wranglings between producer, actors, and agents until the contracts finally were ironed out, and the tour could begin. The stars made extraordinary sacrifices to appear in the season. Tyrone Power was asked to appear in the first CinemaScope picture, *The Robe*; he turned it down. Raymond Massey rejected two offers and Judith Anderson declined an invitation to take her famous production of *Medea* on the road.

The fall of 1952 presented Charles with an almost incredibly complicated work schedule. All three of the stars of *John Brown's Body* had to be brought in from widely spaced locations for last-minute rehearsals and discussions at Curson Avenue and Palos Verdes. Lloyd Wright began designing the sets for the production, and the script changed from day to day. Charles was busy completing the swimming pool Lloyd Wright had designed at Curson. To make matters even more difficult, Charles and the other members of the Quartette went on a final tour of *Don Juan* through California, concluding with an appearance at Los Angeles. In the midst of this crushing workload, Steve, Charles's lover, proved to be unreliable and the two men drifted apart. Charles longed for David to return from New York, but it was to be another year before he came back.

At last, after seemingly endless delays, *John Brown's Body* began its long and difficult tour in the fall of 1952. Because of the compressed schedule, it proved impossible to follow the leisurely bus route of *Don Juan in Hell*. Gregory put the very large supporting cast and chorus in the bus instead, and sent his stars with Charles through heavy weather in planes, cars, and trains, an exhausting and even shattering ordeal.

The stage presentation of *John Brown's Body* was beautifully worked out by Charles. As in *Don Juan in Hell*, the actors were dressed in contemporary evening clothes. But this time the eye was relieved: there was a brown balustrade with a red bench top that the actors rested on, and red velvet chairs spread out in the darkness for the chorus. On this occasion, the actors did not sit still, but moved about freely, sometimes actually leaving the stage while one or other of them gave a long speech, sometimes sitting while another stood. As the poem moved on through the history of the Civil War, the mood of the actors became more intense, Judith Anderson in particular rising to a great force of feeling.

Today, we must judge the performance of *John Brown's Body* by records, and it is fortunate that Columbia Masterworks has preserved it permanently on disc. Although the pace is occasionally too fast, apparently because of a need to compress a great deal of material on two records, the presentation gives a very clear picture of Charles's authoritative direction of the three main voices and of the supporting chorus. It was a daring idea to match the free-moving and fluid structure of the work with an equally free-flowing use of the actors. No single narrator is used, but instead the players take up the narrative in turn, never arbitrarily but always unexpectedly. At times, Charles arranged it so that an actor would not only play a particular role but narrate the thoughts of the character, a device that at once renders a historical figure subjectively alive and enables him to be objectively observed. At times the actors even play the same role. Tyrone Power is John Brown before his execution, and Raymond Massey plays the part of Brown when he is dead. Both actors narrate the details of Brown's life, and Judith Anderson is given the great line which indicates the continuance of slavery after the great man's death: "Nothing has changed, John Brown!"

The most remarkable passages in this acting version are those in which the Southerner John Ellyat meets the wilderness girl Melora in the forest. Here, Benét's passion for nature evidently met its match in Charles's own, and the results in the reading are electrifying. All three players convey the pastoral magnificence of

Benét's lines, the stillness and purity of the forest during a temporary lull in the fighting.

Like Tolstoy, Benét moves between the general and the particular, from the roar of battle to the stillness of woods, from the agony of the slaves to the joy a man has in a woman's arms, from the marching troops of Bull Run to the quiet lonely death of John Brown on the scaffold. In order to mirror this conception, Charles interspersed long, subdued soliloquies with Walter Schumann's score, which used massed chorales based on Civil War anthems and folk tunes. By removing many extraneous elements in the text, cutting it from over 350 pages to about 100, he further emphasized the contrast between the individual agonies of the Northerner and the Southerner who were Benét's protagonists, and the agony of the country as a whole. And through a skillful rearranging and telescoping of the scenes he achieved a performance astonishing in its range and depth, conceived essentially like a musical work, a form somewhere between the cantata and the opera.

There can be no question that aside from his technical mastery of the elements of the work, Charles responded to it on a deeply personal level. Once again, his sympathy for the oppressed, his hatred of rule by force, and his passion for justice, for the root causes of democracy in America, were excited and released in the work. Tyrone Power, Judith Anderson, and Raymond Massey had all been flawed at some time in other performances: Power by a degree of blandness and emptiness, Anderson by an excessive emotionalism, and Massey by physical awkwardness and clumsiness. But on this one occasion, all three were inspired by a director who could sweep aside their weaknesses and allow them to discover themselves. Another director might have allowed them to indulge in theatrics, but Charles made them echo the simplicity and lack of sentimentality of the text in the direct and unforced power of their delivery. The result was, and happily remains, a masterpiece of direction and performance as well as of editing—an American triumph.

In ten weeks, the tour proceeded through sixty-eight cities. In Washington State the company ran into a blizzard. In Salt Lake City and Cleveland, Raymond Massey fell ill with a feverish cold and Charles took over his part; and in several cities, Judith Anderson was seriously ill with pleurisy, and barely able to proceed with her performances. The constant changes of transportation, late nights, early mornings, the lack of sleep, and the adjustments to different water and to different meal schedules took their heavy toll, but Charles's robust constitution and Tyrone Power's youthful vigor withstood the ordeal.

They opened at the Century Theatre in New York in January 1953. Brooks Atkinson wrote: "*John Brown's Body* was not stage literature until Judith Anderson, Raymond Massey, and Tyrone Power took hold of it. But it is stage literature now. It brings into the theatre the brooding beauty of a literary masterpiece."

Atkinson called Charles "the good genie of the literary readings" and talked of "acting with conviction" by "remarkable players." He said Charles was "artist as well as showman," and spoke of "a somber (directorial) style that becomes a tragic epic." Praising all three performances, Atkinson concluded with: "Out of nothing but words, three inspired actors re-create a sorrowful interlude in our history. And the words are the music, sad and homely, that Stephen Benét consecrated in the service of America." As a result of this and other good reviews, the production enjoyed a very successful limited run in New York.

During this period, Charles continued to work on and off in motion pictures. In August 1952 he had returned to MGM to appear in George Sidney's film, *Young Bess*, about the childhood and adolescence of Elizabeth I of England, in his familiar role of Henry VIII. The film was made to coincide with the world-wide publicity attaching to the coronation of Elizabeth II in England. Charles found himself uncomfortable with the director, who had made his name directing musicals. He felt he was simply playing a caricature of the king he had acted so perceptively for Korda; but he was consoled to a degree by a brief friendship with Jean Simmons and her husband Stewart Granger, who visited Curson Avenue and marveled at the Matthew Smiths, the Cézanne, the Rouault, and the Renoir.

Seen today, *Young Bess* emerges as a handsomely photographed, staged, and costumed historical romance devoid of any real vitality. The stately, solemn script and direction entirely lack the cynical wit and flair of Lajoš Birò and Alexander Korda's treatment of twenty years earlier.

Charles appears only in the first third of the film. We see Henry VIII picking up his infant daugher Elizabeth from her bed, presenting her in pride to his courtiers, roaring with laughter at a table, stabbing a piece of pork with the end of a jeweled dagger, and then, in the only sequence in which Charles had a real opportunity to act, on a ship at sea, trouncing Archbishop Cranmer for having arranged the translation of the Bible during his absence abroad. He furiously discovers that his sixth wife Catherine Parr was responsible for this, and clashes with his daughter, who, with all the spirit of the future Elizabeth, saves Catherine Parr's life by distracting her father's attention. She points to a vessel on the horizon. He denies it is there: "It is over the horizon, we have not seen it yet, daughter, and the world is round." She replies, "I say that the world is flat!" He shouts at her, "You dare reshape the world?" And she says, "Didn't you?" Henry roars with laughter at her royal spirit, only to collapse in a paroxysm of coughing. Charles's last scene is Henry's dying, addressing all of the family and hangers-on clustered around the foot of his great bed.

It was a strong performance, at once comical and horrible, impish and heavily menacing. It was played entirely without tricks: no blinking sidelong glances, no mugging or pouting, no vocal mannerisms—simply a gusty, vital, and totally royal figure brought to life with little help from the writers.

On September 25, 1952, Charles's last day of working on *Young Bess*, Paul Gregory received a telegram from Sir Alexander Korda in London asking if Laughton would like to do a picture in London. He said that David Lean would direct it and that the picture would be based on an old Lancashire play called *Hobson's Choice*. He was offering Laughton the role of Hobson. The production would start in February and run about ten weeks.

Charles, who had not seen Korda since the 1930s, was delighted. He had acted the part of Hobson in Harold Brighouse's famous farce as a young man at the Scarborough Amateur Theatre. By February 1953, Korda had made the necessary arrangements to make the film. While Charles was appearing in San Jose, California, on an individual reading tour, following the opening of *John Brown's Body*, he received a telegram from the brilliant director of *Hobson's Choice*, David Lean, saying that he was delighted that Laughton would play Hobson and that he had written the script with Laughton in mind. He thought it was a marvelous part and was sending a copy of the script via Gregory. It was a generally exuberant message.

Charles wrote to Korda from Colorado, telling him that he was well aware of the crush of the Coronation crowds expected in London that summer, and asking for "a house as near to the studio as reasonable, and—though all these conditions I know cannot be satisfied—a pleasant garden if possible, and quiet and countrified." He asked for two servants, indicated that Steve would be along as his companion—he knew Korda would understand —and added, referring to Korda's address, "You really got what you wanted, didn't you? Living in a penthouse at Claridge's must be Korda Heaven—God how I would hate it!! . . . I do want to be in an English garden again and have some elbow room to work—and I loathe London! I do not even know where your studios are now."

On March 14, while Charles was in Cedar Rapids on his tour, Tom telegramed him with sad news: MOTHER PASSED PEACEFULLY AWAY 10:30 THIS MORNING ALL MY LOVE TOM. Charles was deeply shocked and destroyed. One of his main reasons for going to England had been in order to see his mother once more.

Korda wrote on March 16 that he and his company would put Charles up at a hotel on the studio grounds.

Gregory answered the note for Charles: "Mr. Laughton would like least of all living at the studio." Despite this fact, and Charles's hatred of hotels, Korda went ahead and booked him at the Great Fosters Hotel, Egham, in the Tapestry Suite, which, Korda's secretary Hilda Sloane announced, "was occupied by Jennifer Jones when she was in London." To Charles's annoyance, Korda had his secretary write to the effect that his friend Steve would not be paid for.

It was an exhausting early spring. Charles combined his reading tours with flying in and out of various cities to supervise the continuing road tour of *John Brown's Body* (with Anne Baxter replacing a still ailing Judith Anderson). *Hobson's Choice* was held up five months for his arrival. Reading the script David Lean sent him while traveling on successive plane journeys, he began to lose his enthusiasm. Too many drunk scenes had been emphasized in the writing, and Charles had not overcome his hatred of drunks from the old Scarborough Hotel days. But he realized he would have to go ahead with the commitment.

ELEVEN

Making *Hobson's Choice* in England was a very unhappy experience. The problem was that neither David Lean nor Alexander Korda was suited to the task of turning this timeworn regional farce into a satisfactory film. Lean's chilly, academic, and formalized approach, and Korda's tendency to opulence and exaggeration combined to create a highly artificial, lush, and overripe version of a story which should have been treated with warmth, simplicity, and austerity if it were to work at all. Given the unfortunate fact that the script as it stood consisted of little more than a series of family and marital squabbles in small rooms and on narrow stairs, a director had to bring out the harsh decency and kindness of Northern people in order to make a modern audience identify with the characters. Lean was emphatically not the man for the job. He was far more at home with the frosty upper middle-class confrontations of his films *Madeleine* or *The Passionate Friends*, the tight-lipped ironical asides and glittering indifferences of the movies' idea of the *haut monde*.

Alexander Korda, having hired Charles, barely extended to him the courtesy of an old friend and colleague. Korda was preoccupied with a new venture—the story of the Taj Mahal and its builder, Shah Jehan, to be made in India in collaboration with the Bengali Bishu Sen, a project which never materialized despite scripts by John Masters, Michael Powell and Emeric Pressburger, and Charles Higham and Bishu Sen. Korda was busy at his offices in Piccadilly, and rarely saw Charles. His assistant, the Baroness Budberg, was also neglectful. Charles was uncomfortable at his hotel in Egham, and he was aggravated by Korda's behavior. He was also nagged by the popular press, particularly *The People*, for having "deserted England in her hour of need." He did not care for Brenda de Banzie, who played his daughter, and was annoyed that Robert Donat had been replaced in the part of young Mossop. He was aggravated also by having to run around in several scenes dressed in long woolen underwear.

Although Charles liked David Lean, he hated making the picture more every day. It emerges today as a highly contrived technical exercise—most adroit in the scene in which Charles chases the moon drunkenly through the puddles of a street—in which Charles's excessive overacting was clearly a disguise for a great inner discomfort. Quarreling with Gregory, isolated from Korda, hating Brenda de Banzie, and convinced that his marriage to Elsa had finally come adrift, he was never more miserable.

Back in Hollywood that fall, Charles became involved in an entirely new and much more interesting project: *The Caine Mutiny Court-Martial*. Herman Wouk, author of the novel *The Caine Mutiny*, had obtained the idea of turning the book into a dramatic reading by seeing *Don Juan in Hell* in New York. He first suggested the idea to Leland Hayward, who told him to write a play instead. He then submitted it to Paul Gregory and Charles, who concurred. He had to rush out the acting version because it had to be performed ahead of Edward Dmytryk's film, which was already being planned.

The Caine Mutiny Court-Martial was predicated on a powerful dramatic thesis, virtually a contemporary reworking of *Mutiny on the Bounty*, although in this instance the story was wholly, instead of partially, imaginary. Aboard the U.S.S. *Caine*, the atmosphere has been charged with acute tension and stress. Captain Queeg, commander of the vessel, is an old-fashioned martinet whose rigid dictatorial methods have aggravated his men beyond endurance. When it becomes clear that Queeg is no longer simply a disciplinarian, but a psychotic and cowardly sadist, a novelist who has enlisted as an officer takes it upon himself to provoke a mutiny. The subsequent trial of the mutineers forms the substance of the play.

Unlike Nordhoff and Hall, authors of *Mutiny on the Bounty*, and Talbot Jennings and his confrères who adapted it to the screen, Herman Wouk did not present the play as a simple conflict between good and evil. He showed that on both sides there were various arguments for or against an aggressive position, so that the trial became threaded through with humorous and intriguing ambiguities.

Charles, Herman Wouk, and Paul Gregory all agreed that the production should be done on a bare stage. They also agreed that the best man to play the defending counsel for the mutineers, Barney Greenwald, should be Henry Fonda, an actor who represented honor, uprightness, and decency to the American public. Fonda, attracted to the part, and aware of the huge success of the book, accepted at once.

While Charles was in England, Paul had begun to look around for someone to direct the play. He asked Daniel Mann, who wasn't interested, and Harold Clurman also turned him down. Finally, he approached Dick Powell, who was just embarking on a directorial career in films. Powell accepted, not knowing he was the last choice of anybody who might be available, and, although his wife June Allyson complained and wept because he would have to leave on a long tour, he took over. With Lloyd Nolan cast as Captain Queeg, the vicious and psychotic master of the *Caine*, and John Hodiak as the leader of the mutiny, rehearsals began in Los Angeles in August. The actors were against Dick Powell, feeling that he was hopelessly incompetent; Gregory decided to fire him after two disastrous weeks of work.

Charles returned to America from *Hobson's Choice* to find Gregory very distraught. Paul begged Charles to assume the job. Herman Wouk flew in from New York, and Charles, working with him for two exhausting weeks, managed to edit the four-

hour-long show into a lean, muscular play of two and a half hours.
Wouk trusted Charles's editorial judgments completely. He wrote
to Elsa:

> I recognized the editorial art he was wielding and went
> along with it. We had a hell of a good time. Charles was
> a charmer and I got to admire the man for his gifts, his
> energy, his humor and his high spirits.

Charles took over the show's direction before the first performance in Santa Barbara. Henry Fonda was enraged. Many of
his scenes had been cut and he felt that Charles had reduced his
part much too radically. Several actors, their parts equally reduced, wanted to leave the show immediately. Finally, Charles
walked on the stage at rehearsal and said: "Gentlemen, we have
one week. We have almost no time in which to save this play. If I
step on someone's toes, if I am brusque, if I am rude, please understand that there just isn't time to be kind. If I have cut a favorite speech, or eliminated one of your favorite bits of 'business,' my
dear friends, it's because of necessity. I have no other choice."
The effect of his words was electrifying, even on Fonda. Every
actor on the stage called back with a chorus of "Yes, yes! Anything you say!" From that moment he was firmly assured of the
loyalty of everyone.

Throughout rehearsals Charles did in fact make radical further
cuts, and did tread on many toes, especially Henry Fonda's.
Often, the company would meet at Curson Avenue to iron out arguments over the interpretation; Herman Wouk would arrive and
make additions and line switches.

Under Charles's strict guidance, the performances finally took
shape: Lloyd Nolan as Queeg, assured at first but gradually crack-
ing under the strain of cross-examination until the infantile
narcissism and weakness of character emerge, gave a performance
full of rich textures and shadings. Fonda made a quiet, stern, and
thrusting Greenwald, his subdued playing ideally contrasted by
Charles with Queeg's growing hysteria and final breakdown.[1] John
Hodiak, Robert Gist, and other players responded vibrantly to
Charles's sympathetic and searching work with them, and the

[1] This performance was apparently less satisfactory in New York.

openings in Santa Barbara, and then in eleven cities before Chicago, were uniformly successful.

There were many troubles when the play opened in Chicago. These, Herman Wouk feels, stemmed from Fonda's intuitive sense that the opening of the play was underwritten, and needed a solid expository scene. Charles was equally aware of the problem, and tried to have Wouk write one. Wouk drafted and redrafted several, none of which quite worked. Henry Fonda felt more and more strongly the need of a preamble; and even with standing-room-only performances in Chicago, he insisted it be added before New York. Charles and Paul asked Wouk to make an emergency trip to Chicago; he talked the whole thing out with them again, and he inserted some fresh early passages which in part met Fonda's requirements, corrected later passages, and gradually but surely strengthened the structure of the drama.

Another problem emerged from the climactic scene, insisted on by Fonda, and drawn from the novel, in which Greenwald tosses a glass of wine in the face of Keefer, the novelist who has provoked mutiny. A theatrically effective dramatic stroke, this scene broke the visual pattern of the play, since it was staged in a hotel during a naval banquet. Wouk observes:

> The ending of the play will be controversial as long as the work lasts. I might have managed the theatrics better, if I could have contrived to keep it all in the court-room. But to me, the novel's scene at the hotel was vivid, and certainly the substance of the scene is utterly crucial to the story. The entire play, and the entire novel, build to the splash of wine in Keefer's face. I'm not sorry I did it that way. Hank Fonda, who added it later, said it was "no scene" and "unplayable" and got ovations with it night after night. That was his way. I think he always knew how he could play it, and God knows he did. Charles said that with the epilogue any actor worth his salt ought to be able to play Queeg off the stage. I'll stand on that judgment.

Paul Gregory was entirely opposed to the banquet scene, feeling that it wrecked the play's classical balance and Wouk's observ-

ance of the unities of space and time. He preferred the finale of
the very first acting version, in which Greenwald, putting his
papers together, indicated his uncertainty about the outcome of
the case, as well as his fundamental attitude toward law and order
and human decency. Gregory told Elsa years later:

> That was a marvelous speech but Henry Fonda wasn't
> able to play it. He couldn't find the right sniff in his
> armpit to get him into the air . . . He was too much of a
> Method actor, he never had the lung power for that
> enormous plunge that certain actors are able to make—
> simply lifting the audience out of its seats. Out of the
> fear of his own inadequacy, and out of his weakness, he
> insisted on another device which destroyed the play's
> ending.

As if the tensions with Fonda were not bad enough, Fonda
kept redirecting the actors, making them rework bits of business
and various movements when Charles was absent. Charles sent
Fonda icy notes asking him to desist. Fonda would not. This
problem continued at the Plymouth Theatre in New York during
last-minute rehearsals for the Broadway opening. Simultaneously
with changing everybody else's, Fonda refused to vary his own
performance by so much as a hair, even picking up a pencil with
identical speed and deliberation each night.

The production opened on January 21, 1954. Brooks Atkinson
wrote: "In his velvety style of staging, Charles Laughton has
given the play the perfect performance . . . having had some very
basic experience with concert style drama, Mr. Laughton is not
loading it down with inessentials."

Richard Watts, Jr., said in the New York *Post:* "Pungently and
powerfully written, superbly acted, brilliantly staged and possess-
ing that aura of showmanship which makes everything in it seem
to go right, (this) represents the contemporary American theatre
at the peak of its excellence."

Heard today in the recording, the play is a very affecting experience, except for the final speech in which Greenwald becomes the
mouthpiece of Wouk's plea for discipline in the Navy. The sudden reversal of the play's point, which was that Queegs of the
world must be destroyed, representing as they do the evil and

repressive forces in society, is exasperating, since it forces the audience to go back on its own judgment. By using the specious argument that any mutiny is wrong, that Queeg should never have been deposed, Wouk comes to the edge of Fascism.

Another disturbing aspect of the play is that the novelist Keefer is turned into the butt of the audience's hatred at the end. He is made to seem misguided and hateful for allowing his intellectual's sense of justice to provoke the mutiny; the audience invariably cheers when Greenwald throws the wine in his face. By making Keefer a target, Wouk discloses a complicity with military hatred and mistrust of intellectuals. Again, one can understand why Paul Gregory so urgently wanted to cut the scene. The military attitude was particularly dangerous, because of the McCarthy hearings, the public image, as Arthur Schlesinger, Jr., described it, of "the cynical college professor, misleading and betraying his students; the suave writer, palming off subversive views to his gullible audience; the smooth liberal intellectual, inducing good-hearted politicians to front for his wicked ideas."

John Mason Brown was equally bothered by the finale, and George Jean Nathan talked of the conclusion as "sheer hokum." He earnestly called for deletion of the scene, complaining that it came near to wrecking the fine impression of all that had preceded it.

Henry Fonda's public ensured him several standing ovations during the run which helped the play to be the greatest commercial hit of Charles's directorial career. The play ran for just under a year, with Barry Sullivan finally replacing Fonda in New York and later in Los Angeles. Meanwhile, Charles, inexhaustible as ever, flew back to California and organized a second touring company with Paul Douglas as Queeg and Wendell Corey as Greenwald.

In the spring of 1954, after a brief reading tour of Canada accompanied by his young companion, Steve, Charles embarked on an entirely new and equally exciting venture. A year earlier, he and Paul Gregory had come across a novel, *The Night of the Hunter*, by Davis Grubb, which fascinated them so much they took an option on it.

Davis Grubb's novel has not worn well; it can now be seen to belong to that odd, hybrid "lyrical" genre that included works like

Dark of the Moon and *Finian's Rainbow* on the stage. The author aimed at a kind of folksy poetic approach which never quite
comes off: a cross between Thomas Wolfe and Sherwood Anderson, the dialogue printed pretentiously like that in a French
novel, without quotation marks. The descriptive passages are
rather heavily lyrical: "Something in the wind's dark voice caused
him to open one eye . . . John's tongue grew thick as a mitten at
the growing dread within him" . . . "The air was unbelievably
rich and sweet with the temper of the season: the river smell like
the incense of some primal pagan fertility." The application of
this overripe sub-Wolfian style to a simple story is never very satisfactory, creating an impression of purple prosiness, rather than the
fully realized bravura literary mode so strenuously aimed for.
What drew an immense public to the book at the time was
clearly a combination of two things: first, the critics fell for its
elaborate surface, mistaking Davis Grubb for a major new American talent; second, the story, dressed up though it was in its quasi-
poetic wrappings, was still a good and a powerful one.

It was the story of a murderous Preacher, who hates women
and kills them for their money. With the words LOVE and
HATE tattooed on his fingers, he drives through the depressed
back country of the Ohio River basin in the early 1930s, pursuing
two children, whose father has been hanged, in order to obtain a
buried cache of several hundred dollars. Preacher is a terrifying
figure, an evil distortion of a religious devotee. The children are
immediately sympathetic to the mass audience. Millions of parents could share with them their anguished plight as they jour-
neyed down the river.

Charles warmed to the tale, and with his liking of Grubb's literary progenitors, Wolfe and Anderson, he probably respected at
least some of the writing as well.

The Night of the Hunter was on the national best seller lists
for sixteen weeks in April and May 1954; after Paul Gregory
bought the book, and widely publicized its purchase, it stayed on
the lists for twelve weeks more. Gregory and Charles decided that
a major star would have to play the part of the Preacher. United
Artists, which was to distribute the picture, arranged for James

Agee, the celebrated film critic and essayist, to be added to the package as writer. When Charles suggested to the United Artists executives that Robert Mitchum should play the Preacher, they enthusiastically agreed.

Charles sent the book over to Mitchum, who immediately read it and called Paul Gregory to say he would start working as soon as he was needed. The partners decided to co-star Shelley Winters with Mitchum in the part of Willa, the murdered mother of the two children. Mitchum was horrified, feeling she was quite hopeless for the part. He remembers saying: "All she could manage, in acting this, is to float around convincingly with her throat cut." Charles ignored Mitchum's remarks and cabled Shelley in London, where she was playing in Henry Cornelius' *I Am a Camera*, offering the part. She accepted at once.

Once Shelley Winters was signed up, Charles traveled to New York, and ran all of D. W. Griffith's films at the Museum of Modern Art through the good auspices of his and Elsa's old friend Iris Barry. He was overwhelmed by the experience. He had instinctively felt that Griffith would provide him with the visual inspiration he needed to direct a film with an American pastoral setting, and now he knew he had been right. Griffith's exquisitely sensitive and poetic response to landscape, which he invested with almost mystical properties, his disposition of figures in the frame, his miraculously fluid cutting, all were marvelous and enthralling. But most of all Charles learned from his direction of the players, who at their best acted with extreme sensitivity, as though they were living their parts, fulfilling in their every movement the precepts of screen acting Charles had taught his students in the schoolroom on Curson Avenue.

Charles felt that the greatest of the Griffith actresses was Lillian Gish. Her vibrant responsiveness to the demands of scenes was so complete that nothing, no trick or artifice or use of gesture, no single member of her body or even pore of her skin, held her apart from a totally instinctive sense of what her part meant. Her purity and the innocent directness of her approach left him astounded. Tiny and seemingly fashioned of finest steel, she used her narrow face, huge fluttering liquid eyes, and pursed butterfly mouth with the formal precision of a Kabuki actor. Her control of bodily expression was indeed almost Japanese. Given Charles's love of Japanese art, one can see the appeal she would have for him—the appeal of a great artist in miniature.

At tea at the Algonquin Hotel, Charles told Miss Gish of his warm devotion to her work, and the reason for that devotion. James Agee joined them, but refused the tea and sullenly drank alcohol instead, barely saying a word. Finally, he drifted away, while Charles offered Lillian the part of the spinster in the story. She promised him she would read the script. She liked it and agreed to appear in the film.

Back in Hollywood, Charles began developing the screenplay with James Agee. While Charles splashed naked in the pool, or paced around the house like a caged bear, Agee worked away in the heat, sweating profusely, for weeks, drinking himself into a stupor every night. Neither Charles nor Elsa particularly warmed to Agee, who was tense, swarthy, dark, and nervously introspective. When Agee finally delivered the script, it was alarmingly large—and Charles was horrified to find that Agee had eliminated the few good poetic passages of the book, underplayed the drama, and introduced a whole new social background which reflected his neo-Marxist concerns as a critic. He had scenes of the WPA, the wobblies, the breadlines and soup kitchens of the Depression which were his obsession.

Charles and Paul Gregory sent Agee back to New York, and Charles began working desperately hard to edit the script, to bring it back to the novel. He constantly called Davis Grubb, seeking his advice, and received immensely long letters, typed from end to end of the pages without paragraphs, giving exhaustive advice on the correct way to handle the treatment. Finally, Charles, with all of the editorial skill he had shown in his stage presentations, managed to edit and rewrite Agee's pages until at last the script was a fluent, lyrical, delicately somber reflection of the novel itself.

James Agee was horrified by Charles's wholesale changing of his work. Paul Gregory told Elsa:

> He lay on the floor of my house in Santa Monica dying, saying that Laughton had killed him. Was killing him. And he was there for fourteen days drunk in my guest room. So drunk you couldn't believe it. Then we finally

moved him to a hotel. And Charles wouldn't come near him. Charles wouldn't see him—and because of that Jim drank even more. And then he turns this thing, this script like a telephone book in to Charles. We paid him $30,000 for it. Next spring, he died.

Subsequently, Charles engaged Stanley Cortez, brother of the silent star Ricardo Cortez, to photograph the picture. Cortez had shot *The Man on the Eiffel Tower*, and Charles had always deeply admired his work on Orson Welles's *The Magnificent Ambersons*. That film had exactly the right period quality, of nineteenth-century daguerreotypes, which Charles wanted for the new work. For several weeks, Cortez went over to Curson Avenue to point out technicalities of cameras: how much a camera could and could not do to capture reality. Charles amazed Cortez with his knowledge of lighting and composition. Cortez recalls that

Charles was a poet. He grasped everything instinctively. The master became the pupil.

Charles also engaged the talented brothers Terry and Dennis Sanders to handle the second unit direction in Ohio: a few shots of the countryside from a helicopter. The rest of the picture would be made in the Pathé studio, the wizardry of cameraman and special effects men creating an illusion of a countryside indoors.

The Night of the Hunter began shooting on September 14, 1954. Though he was drinking heavily, Robert Mitchum listened to everything Charles told him with the deepest respect. But Mitchum hated Paul Gregory, and when Gregory accidentally ran into his car in a parking lot, he retaliated violently. Charles called Mitchum about the incident, saying:

My boy, there are skeletons in all our closets. And most of us try to cover up these skeletons. Or certainly try to keep the door closed. If someone passes by we even try to divert the attention of the passerby from the closet. We want them to look in another direction and we purposely design our actions to distract them. My dear Bob.

You not only do not distract the passerby you open the door, you drag forth the skeletons, you swing them in the air, in fact, you brandish your skeletons. Now, Bob, you must stop brandishing your skeletons!

Mitchum maintains that Charles hated the little girl in the picture, Sally Bruce:

I'll never forget when her grandparents—show biz grandparents—asked her to sing a little French song one day on the set she began piping Rodgers and Hammerstein: "Dites-Moi," from *South Pacific*. Charles almost threw up.

Lillian Gish enjoyed working with Charles as intensely as Mitchum did. She told a story to the New York *Times* years later (June 8, 1969):

He wanted me to do a dozen takes of one scene. I kept pitching my acting higher and higher and then I said, "Is that what you want?" Laughton answered, "No, the first take was fine. I just wanted to see how many different ways you could do it."

Before each scene, Charles took the actors aside, asked them quietly how they would interpret it, and then made small and modest suggestions on improvements. He never bullied, overrode, or harried an actor. He knew that once an actor was ideally cast, there was no need to tell him how to act a part; it was a question only of leading an actor deeper and deeper into his own resources as a human being until the emotional truth of a sequence was fully understood. If any falsehood then seemed to exist in the lines, Charles instantly and powerfully changed those lines for the better. Peter Graves, who played a small part, says:

I was working with John Ford in a picture. One day I started to say: "About this scene. This part I'm playing. I think that—" Ford snapped me shut. "Don't think in my picture," he growled. Moving from Ford to Charles was like walking from hell to heaven.

Charles's mastery of the art of film was so complete that when he began to work he was able to embark on some of the most extraordinary sequences since the beginning of cinema. It was necessary to create a dreamlike effect for the sequence in which the dead Willa is trapped in an automobile under water, and Charles, Stanley Cortez, and the special effects department combined their talents with remarkable results. First, they tested a special tank at 20th Century-Fox Studios; but the paint came off the sides, coloring the water, and ruining the photographic look. Instead, the team commandeered a tank at Republic which had been used for the film *Wake of the Red Witch*. They employed a large crane, from which they suspended a platform, and on the platform set up special arc lights which penetrated the water to create an ethereal, eerie atmosphere. The special effects crew devised an underwater current of air which made the hair on the dummy of Shelley Winters stream out as Charles wanted. An underwater cameraman was dressed in a scuba diving outfit, and a camera had to be held by him on a hook, drawn up slowly on a length of twine like a fishing line, to photograph the imitation corpse.

The scene in the bedroom in which the Preacher murders Willa was planned with equal care. Shelley Winters was lying in the foreground and Mitchum in the background. Silently, Mitchum had to make a series of strange, unsettling movements to reflect a murderer's disordered thoughts. An A-shaped composition was prepared by Cortez under Charles's meticulous guidance, using the conical ceiling of the room as the topmost point of a unilateral triangle, to suggest the quasi-religious nature of the Preacher symbolically through the indicated shape of the nave of a church. The entire sequence was prepared to match the movements of Sibelius' *Valse Triste* in images, a kinesthetic effect of startling brilliance.

Cortez says:

> In the scene when the two children are on top of the hayloft and in the distance you see the mother by the light of the moon, we used some very elaborate tricks. But better still was the scene of the children in the loft, looking down and seeing the preacher in the distance; we built the whole set in perspective, between the hayloft and the fence, which was about five hundred feet away.

The figure moving against the horizon wasn't Mitchum
at all. It was a midget on a little pony.

Directing the two children proved to be more difficult for
Charles than directing Mitchum and Shelley Winters. According
to Mitchum, he hated directing them, and would frequently
throw up his hands in despair at their misbehavior.

Mitchum recalls:

> We had a woman from the Welfare Department who
> used to hang around in a white hat and constantly threat-
> ened to report to the Welfare Department about the
> drinking and cursing on the set. Charles did not drink
> but Shelley and I always did, and so did the crew, when
> Charles wasn't looking. One day we caught the Welfare
> woman drinking beer behind a bush at Rowland V. Lee's
> ranch when we were shooting there. She gave up all
> thought of reporting us after that.

Once the picture was finished, Walter Schumann, the inspired
composer who had prepared the music for *John Brown's Body*, developed some fine imitation folk songs with lyrics by Davis
Grubb. He also adapted, in sinister incantatory or lyrical fashion,
various hymns to indicate the murderous nature of the Preacher.
In a picnic scene, he used "Bringing in the Sheaves," which becomes a terrifying recurrent theme as the children are hunted.
The results were striking, and Charles was exceedingly pleased
with them. Terry and Dennis Sanders did an excellent job of the
Ohio location sequences, their helicopter shots of the river country beautifully linked to pastoral sequences photographed at Row-
land V. Lee's ranch.

Charles's experience with readings of the Bible and of fairy
tales stood him in good stead in directing the film. The sound
track is alive with the sounds of the Bible, whether recited by the
Preacher in his psychotic rages or pious pretenses, or uttered by
the spinster Miss Rachel who befriends the children. Alive, too,
with the sounds of hymns: the Preacher's entrances announced by
his singing of the timeworn phrases, or disembodied voices
ironically or quasi-sentimentally commenting on the action. And

the imagistic framework is conceived purely in terms of fairy tale. The opening, with Miss Rachel reading to a group of children whose faces are isolated against the stars, suggests Mother Goose addressing her captive flock; and the next sequences, apparently realistic in style, in fact have the underlying tension, the sudden shifts of scene and mood, of a dream. Swiftly, electrically, the drama is built up: a shot of a girl in a gingham dress, stretched dead on a staircase leading to a cellar; a flurry of townsfolk, threatening vengeance on the killer; the Preacher, obviously insane, thanking God from his convertible roadster as he drives along a country lane.

The prison scenes have a jagged, unsettling quality, the Preacher's madness suggested by a shot of his head upside down, as he leans over the upper bunk in the cell to talk to the occupant of the lower, the man who has hidden the cache of dollar bills. Black shadows and deathly white slashes of light suggest German films and woodcuts of the 1920s. The Preacher's arrival in the small community where the treasure is buried has a sharp sense of the strange: the people are in their way as manic and dislocated as the Preacher himself, gripped by religious hysteria. They are symbolized by a vindictive old woman, played by Evelyn Varden in a style almost too theatrical for the film; and their evil is seen as the perfect setting for the Preacher to operate in. His easy, effortless seduction of Willa is conveyed in an economical series of short scenes, counterpointed with the townspeople's mingled suspicion of him and delight in Willa's capturing of him. This series of stabbing sequences culminates in two extraordinary episodes. Willa's wedding is conducted in a revivalist tent, the flaring torches and flickering shadows suggesting a ritual sacrifice. The wedding night is directed with icy concentration: we first see Willa in the bathroom, ritually cleansing herself for copulation, at once aroused, terrified, and humiliated, then standing by the bed, while the Preacher spells out the fact that he has no intention of consummating the marriage, using his religious beliefs to disguise the fact that he is using her to obtain the money. Willa sinks to the bed with a sob of disappointment, but a moment later she stands at the mirror, ready to purge herself of desire, praying that her body will be holy, a flawless vessel should the Preacher deign to plant his seed in her.

Charles directed all of these scenes with great intensity, relent-lessly conveying Willa's sexual frustration in the face of a preda-tory male's indifference. In all of these episodes, despite the bold compositions, the heavy contrasts of light and shadow, the impres-sionistic use of sound, the mood has been quite close to realism. But halfway through the film, Charles begins to change it into a mood of fable suggested by the opening. He brilliantly alters the feeling the moment the children are introduced. Up to now, we have seen the world from the director's point of view: the point of view of an accurate, jaded, and cruelly honest man who sees through the phoniness of the townspeople, and unhesitatingly comes to grips with the Preacher's madness. Subsequently, the di-rection reflects the dislocated oversized world of the children, magically re-creating the terrors and delights of infancy. While the children sleep together under a checkered counterpane, Willa's murder seems to be their evil dream. The Preacher moves to his *Valse Triste* against the beams of the nave-like room, mak-ing a strange incantatory gesture at the window like a sacrificial priest before he swoops on Willa. The cutting of her throat is not actually seen, but matched instead to a vertical wipe in which the device itself becomes symbolic of a life being wiped out. When Willa is in the river, seen by a half-witted old boatman, she again seems close to being a figment of his nightmares. Long, drifting fronds of a strangely outsize submarine plant quiver across the image, their slow, tentacle-like movement accompanied by the delicate floatings of Willa's hair. Willa sits in a suspended state of death, behind the cold metal and glass of the windshield, which provides an immobile counterpoint to her Ophelia-like watery sleep.

The children's voyage along the river also has the pure and pas-toral feeling of legend. Charles's love of nature emerges in the shots of reeds like black swords against the icy silver of the water, a white screech-owl shivering against a patch of dark leaves, a rab-bit crouching, its eyes like stars, a frog with its throat bulging like a goiter victim's, unwitting creatures observing the journey, not knowing the terror that inspired it. Places seen on the voyage as-sume a poetic density: a birdcage hanging in the window of a nearby house, a fluttering chaffinch symbolizing the terror of imprisonment; barns rising against a flat, washed-out sky; dawn

20. Mixed casts, *The Caine Mutiny Court-Martial* and *John Brown's Body.* Left to right, Lloyd Nolan, Charles, Tyrone Power, Raymond Massey, Anne Baxter, John Hodiak, Dick Powell, Henry Fonda.

21. *John Brown's Body* reading. Left to right, Raymond Massey, Tyrone Power, Charles.

22. Charles in beard grown for *King Lear*, Rollright Stones, Oxford-shire. *(Elsa Lanchester)*

23. The house at Pacific Palisades.

24. The house in Hollywood. *(Elsa Lanchester)*

25. Charles. *(MGM)*

lighting a hayloft, as we hear the distorted singing of the old hymn "Bringing in the Sheaves," peering up through the straw and the creeping sunlight to see the Preacher on the horizon like a cut-out paper silhouette, his horse moving lazily against a mackerel sky.

The chase after the children is handled like another dream. The movements of the horse are slow and suspended, as though it were floating in water, while planes of dark barns trisect the images, a symphonic effect of black triangles, faintly stirring figures, increasing light, terrified faces, and at last the complacent moonlike face of the Preacher under his clerical hat.

The mood shifts yet again when the children, sleeping, drift into reeds and are wakened at the break of dawn by Miss Rachel, briskly marshaling her Mother Goose's flock. She becomes a symbol of protectiveness, peace, and security, a Virgin Mother, challenging the fake Christ which the Preacher has become. The last third of the film does not quite sustain the perfect balance between the realistic and the poetic achieved in the rest. The Preacher's arrival, Miss Rachel beating him off, his discovery that the money is hidden in the little girl's doll, his capture and the subsequent attempted lynching are directed in a mood that wavers between the children's subjective, exaggerated, and fantastic view of the events and the more harsh and down-to-earth approach of the earlier scenes. The Preacher's bundling off to the hangman is almost perfect. Snatched from the mob by the sheriff, he passes the hangman's house on the way to a refuge, and the sheriff coldly says to the hangman, "We've been saving him up for yer!" The Preacher withdraws, shuddering almost imperceptibly, into the shadows of the car: he is dead already, his madman's assumption of power stripped, the townsfolk's revenge just as intense as its previous worship. This is marvelous; but the subsequent scene—Miss Rachel at her kitchen sink, talking about the endurance of the children, about the capacity of the young to survive—is a little too clever in the context, and Charles does not quite give the scene the visionary quality called for. A more effective conclusion would have been a reversal to Miss Rachel, reading a story to her children among the stars—the story of the film itself perhaps, now a part of American legend.

Despite its flaws, *The Night of the Hunter* remains one of the few uncompromised masterpieces of the American cinema. Unappreciated at the time, it has now become more correctly viewed as an American classic. Charles's direction at its best is as individual in its evocation of a legendary world as Cocteau's in *La Belle et la Bête*. He uses Stanley Cortez's stylized, Germanic heavy-contrast photography, much as Welles used it in *The Magnificent Ambersons*, to create a formalized, abstracted feeling of a world out of time. Unlike Agee, he does not root the story firmly in the Depression, though the gingham dresses and flat shoes and wide-brimmed hats of the women, the baggy suits and fedoras of the men are all wonderfully authentic. Instead, he evokes a timeless atmosphere which might as well have been of the middle nineteenth century, a feeling reinforced by Lillian Gish's Griffithian presence, and the Griffithian use of landscape: children glimpsed against a long white fence, a tall church, a huddle of swine, a menacing herd of cattle, spear grass by a sluggish river; women making jam under the shadow of an elder tree; men spreading out in a harvest field through stalks of corn, an almost Russian effect with luminous cirrus clouds, a washed-out sky, a winding white fence, a dark roof, the pursuing figures forming a triangle as the Preacher nervously waits in a barn.

This is, above all, the film of a man who loves paintings—each composition, though never reminiscent of any specific artist, is devised to excite the eye and keep it moving, a constant fluid succession of evocative patterns, geometrically precise yet alive with significant detail. The film's plastic qualities have been equaled only by Welles in the American film. The full vocabulary of the cinema—fluid cutting, even an old-fashioned iris out, wipes, sudden transitions in lighting, a delicately recorded sound track in which every whisper or footfall is isolated and made particular—is conscripted into service here by a master hand. The performances reflect Charles's patient and sensitive guidance. Robert Mitchum, usually a somnolent and shambling figure, visibly bored with his work, here plays with a ruthless charm which exactly conveys the predatory nature of the Preacher. His acting of the wedding night scene is particularly effective: the sanctimonious softness in the voice as he forgives his bride's feeling of desire, his expression of disgust in the flesh, are conveyed with great skill and intensity. His pursuit of the children and his animal moans and screams when he is cornered suggest a dangerous beast of prey. He is at his best in his evangelical arousing of the local townspeople, using his sexual attractiveness, his sheer physical presence, to enslave the lonely wives and spinster women of the neighborhood.

Shelley Winters is very fine, suggesting a simple-minded, emotionally overheated girl who will fall for anyone of smooth talk, whether salesman or parson. Her almost voluptuous declaration of faith at the prayer meeting, her sexual frustration on the wedding night, and her still, passive acceptance of death are beautifully played. Lillian Gish is flawless as Miss Rachel, a figure at once tough and saintly, forbidding and adorable. And the children are excellent: the tough, resilient, illusionless little boy, the obnoxious little girl who's caught between a nervous evasion of the money's hiding place, and a cowardly disclosure of it. Charles's guidance of the supporting cast is unerring: James Gleason's senile river captain, the kind or shrewish local women, a tired-out stripper whom the woman-hating Preacher watches with murderous hate, the casually heartless hangman, cheerfully glancing at his prospective victim's neck.

At the completion of work on the film, Charles and Paul Gregory obtained the rights to Norman Mailer's famous war novel, *The Naked and the Dead*. Charles called Mailer, asking him to be available for a few days for discussion following the New York premiere of *The Night of the Hunter*. Norman Mailer wrote to Elsa in 1968, from his home in Columbia Heights, Brooklyn:

> We worked, I remember, for four or five days in his suite at the St. Moritz going through the book page and paragraph discussing every aspect of the movie. I was enormously impressed with him and I indeed don't think I've ever met an actor before or since whose mind was so fine and powerful as Laughton's. No aspect of the novel passed unnoticed by him—he wanted me to explain every last single point he did not clearly comprehend for himself.
>
> In the process, I would often discover a point I thought simple was not at all simple. He gave me in fact a mar-

velous brief education in the problems of a movie director, as he would explain to me, sometimes patiently,
sometimes at the edge of his monumental impatience,
how certain scenes which worked in the book just
weren't feasible for the movie.

But what I liked best about him was that these discussions were always open. He had a great ability to listen
and on occasion my arguments would change his mind,
which was no easy matter, but altogether satisfying when
it happened since his mind was so wide and so powerful.
About the second day he suggested I start making drawings of the characters and when I said I don't know how
to do it, he snorted and said, "Nonsense, Mailer, anyone
can draw. You go ahead and do it and that will give me
some idea of what you have in your mind that you can't
express." So the drawings began and in the process I discovered all sorts of varied enthusiasms and insights about
my characters. It proved to be a splendid way of
stimulating me to talk, but indeed that was just one out
of twenty subtle devices he must have used.

Toward the end of the week, when we were getting a little bored with each other, Charles looked up and said,
"Mailer, let's get out of here. I feel like seeing some art."
And we went over to the Oriental Room of the Metro-
politan where he was, of course, well known, and I was
introduced that day to Hiroshige and Hokusai, a pleasure for which I'm still in his debt.

Charles was at once fascinated by the book and repelled by it.
He admired Mailer's writing but was put off by the central figure,
a sergeant based on Mailer himself. He could not understand the
sergeant's character, and wrote Mailer from Hollywood about it.
Mailer sent him a sheaf of correspondence, written by Mailer to
his wife from the battle front. The letters contain revealing
comments on the men who formed the basis of the characters in
the book, and say a great deal about the complex character of
Mailer himself.

Early in 1955, Charles began working with the Sanders brothers
on the script. They struggled with the material for weeks, both at

Curson Avenue and at the Sanders' house. Charles often splashed around in the pool at Curson, shouting out ideas or standing by the edge, legs spread wide, rapping out instructions like Captain Bligh. In the meantime, a Philadelphia businessman named William Goldman became involved in the property, enthusiastically backing it, and Stanley Cortez left for Hawaii to scout locations. Finally, Charles broke with the Sanders brothers and proceeded to write the final-draft screenplay himself.

With weeks and months going by, and still no final pages ready, William Goldman became impatient. Paul Gregory did his utmost to pacify him, and to hurry Charles along, collecting more and more money from Goldman. After almost a year's work, the cost of writing and of sending Cortez to Hawaii escalated to $320,-000, and Goldman began to be desperate.

At last Charles had a script ready. It was a brilliant, powerful, and intense version of the novel, full of inspired touches, and Norman Mailer enthusiastically approved it. More overtly and unambiguously pacifist than the book, it provided a poetic, lyrical evocation of the lives of men at war, and if Charles had directed it, the picture would have emerged as a masterpiece. But two things militated against the project. First, *The Night of the Hunter* had suffered not only poor reviews but also a total public indifference. Released at the beginning of the CinemaScope era, a quiet black and white picture on a minor scale had little chance for success. Paradoxically, the huge public which had embraced the novel in part because of its "poetic" tone rejected the film because it was more genuinely and most personally a poetic work. The other problem lay in the impossibility of the three-way relationship between Goldman, Gregory, and Charles.

Paul Gregory told Elsa:

> Charles finished the script and it was sent back to Philadelphia. Bill Goldman called me and said, "It's a little thick, isn't it?" And I said, "Yes, it is. Everything except the kitchen sink is in it, but it can be edited." I talked to Charles and asked him how long did he think it would take him to get a shooting draft of the script. He said, "It will take at least another year, old boy."

Learning that Charles would need another twelve months, Goldman became very doubtful whether he could continue to finance the writing. Finally he showed the script to George Sidney, who had directed *Young Bess*. Gregory adds:

Sidney told Goldman it would cost twenty million dollars to make it and that it was a lousy screenplay and this and that. Well, I had no defense. No defense at all. And Goldman stopped the money. It was over. There was no salvaging it.

Later, Gregory took the property to Warner Brothers, had the Sanders brothers write an entirely new script, and arranged for it to be directed by Raoul Walsh, with very inferior results.

In order to prop up his own, and Charles's sagging finances, Paul Gregory at the very end of 1955 arranged for him to narrate and act as a consultant on CBS's Ford Star Jubilee presentation of *The Day Lincoln Was Shot*, a re-creation of the historic event starring Raymond Massey, Jack Lemmon, and Lillian Gish, directed by Delbert Mann, from a script by the Sanders brothers. Charles also appeared, at the beginning of 1956, on the Jimmy Durante Show, and at a reading in Big Spring, Texas; also he began planning a production of Shaw's *Major Barbara*, his major venture of that year.

The producer Robert Joseph had obtained the rights to the play several years earlier in partnership with Roger Stevens. At the time Joseph approached Charles to play the leading part of Undershaft, the munitions manufacturer, Charles was thinking about a role offered him by David Lean: the role of the army officer later played by Alec Guinness in *Bridge on the River Kwai*. He finally decided against playing that role because it involved several harrowing months in the tropics of Ceylon, and because of the somewhat warlike, militant nature of the story. While he was visiting New York for the Durante show, Joseph approached him with the idea again at the St. Moritz. But he said flatly, "I don't like the play. And I don't want to play Undershaft."

Joseph begged him to reconsider. Charles at once reread the play very carefully, and changed his mind. He told Joseph by long distance from Hollywood: "Come out to California. I've been thinking of people to play Undershaft, and I have decided I'd better play the part myself."

First produced in 1905 at the Court Theatre, with the American actress Annie Russell in the title part—her national origin caused a chauvinist furor in London at the time—*Major Barbara* formed the final part of the great trilogy which had begun with *Man and Superman* in 1901. In its powerful pages, Shaw provided a dramatic confrontation between Undershaft, whose very name suggests a mechanical device, and who is the representative of brute mechanical force in his life's role as an armaments tycoon, and his daughter Barbara, who represents purity, self-sacrifice, and modest decency in her vocation as a Salvation Army officer.

As in *Don Juan in Hell* and the play of which that work forms a part, Shaw does not provide us with an easy and uncomplicated confrontation of good and evil. He detests the Salvation Army's organized piety as deeply as he despises the drab conformism of heaven. He wrote in his preface, "This play is not a choice between opulent villainy and humble virtue, but between energetic enterprise and cowardly villainy." He makes it explicitly clear that the reason industrial power can triumph over the common man is that the common man is intellectually weak, pleasure-loving and self-indulgent, unaware of his own nature: that he is in hell. The Devil rules over hell: Undershaft can defeat the saintly adherents of the Salvation Army because it is weakened by blind faith and a sentimental adherence to lies. In his final confrontation between Major Barbara and her father, Shaw delivers a passionate argument for pure reason as the only product of nature which may enable man to survive his destiny.

Following his original rejection of the play, the purity and beauty of the Shavian ideal attracted Charles, forcing him to reconsider it. He must have seen that by again playing the Devil—reincarnated in the suave and accomplished Undershaft—he could paradoxically show his own intellectual position, standing firm against hypocrisy and cant, against self-indulgence and lack of discipline as well as the crushing forces of the industrial world. He accepted the play at once.

Paul Gregory was not involved in this venture. After five years, his partnership with Charles had finally and irrevocably broken up. The reasons are complex, and deeply personal; suffice it to say that Charles rightly or wrongly disbanded his partnership with him in one swift stroke during the course of an afternoon.

The finality of the gesture was typical of Charles. He had recently rejected his companion, Steve. He had also renounced another young man, Victor, an actor and a typical parasitical type, with whom he had experienced a brief and disastrous relationship. Even when David came back from New York, he found no full consolation. Though they remained friends, the entwined emotional threads of their lives together had snapped for good.

It was an unhappy time, and it is fortunate that Charles found a degree of escape in preparing *Major Barbara* for the stage. In June 1956 Charles began casting *Major Barbara*. First, he chose Cornelia Otis Skinner for the part of Lady Undershaft. Miss Skinner recalled later that she dropped over to the house on Curson and went swimming with Charles in the heated pool, discussing the play over gin-and-tonics and nibbling cucumber sandwiches. To her amazement, Charles didn't ask her to read the lines, but read them to her instead—then cheerfully offered her the part.

He chose Glynis Johns to play Major Barbara; in several conversations at the pool he gradually overcame her severe objections to the part, and to Shaw's work as a whole.

In New York to cast more actors, Charles began editing the play, partly in consultation with Herman Wouk. Together, they cut every line at the end of the second act after Major Barbara says, "My God, why hast thou forsaken me?" in order to achieve a more powerfully effective curtain. Charles cut a scene out of the third act and combined it with a piece in the second scene of the third act in order to convey the feelings of village life after the noise and glare of the armaments factory. He ended the play on Major Barbara's "Glory Hallelujah!" because the rest of the scene seemed anticlimactic, and he and Wouk combined the second and third acts. In New York, Charles hired Eli Wallach to play the clownish comedy role of Billy Walker, and Burgess Meredith as Major Barbara's fiance.

Charles used numerous daring touches in the production. In the first scene, he showed Lady Undershaft's drawing room assembled before the audience's eyes. Lady Undershaft stood motionless and cold while her servants prepared the room for the evening; she looked hard at them as they arranged the curtains and plumped up the cushions, disapproving or approving without a word. It was a very effective symbolic opening, perfectly conveying Lady Undershaft's contemptuous use of rank and privilege.

Charles also employed a cinematic device: when an actor had finished delivering a speech that actor became immobile, as in a "freeze frame." A most powerful scenic effect occurred in the second act, when five of the characters descend into the hell of the industrial world. They were shown in black silhouette against scarlet clouds of smoke, steam rose up, and the cold vertical steel of a modern city framed them against an artificial sky. By this device, more than any other in the play, Charles conveyed Shaw's equation of the inferno and the factory, a daring symbolic device that came close to his poetic concepts of cinema. The realism of the scene had an odd side-effect: the factory hooters made so much noise that the management of *Long Day's Journey into Night*, playing in a theatre back to back with the Martin Beck, complained.

In casting and recasting the form of the production Charles again achieved the kind of purity and balance achieved in *Galileo*, *John Brown's Body*, and *The Caine Mutiny Court-Martial*. Aided by Donald Oenslager's admirably inventive scenic design, he created a multipurpose set, with maps and stands and wooden levels, and without conventional scenery. This austerity, entirely typical of Charles, echoed the purity and cerebral cogency of Shaw's concept. The play, contradictory, alive with humor, angry and contentious, spiky and resistant, emerged without frills. Charles's abstract designs conveyed drawing room, village, and Salvation Army slum headquarters with equal felicity. He used scrim curtains, transparent maps, block props, all with great dexterity.

The play opened at the Boston Opera House prior to Broadway, on October 11. At the final Boston tryout, the curtain was rung down accidentally after the first act, when Charles had specifically ordered it to be left up until the end. Furious, Charles stalked out on the stage and, to the audience's delighted surprise, condemned the technical deficiencies of the theatre.

The notices were mixed, several critics remarking that Charles's direction was too cold and detached, and that Glynis Johns's playing was uncertain. Unhappy, despite Charles's painstaking coaching, Miss Johns was replaced after two months by Anne Jackson.

Elsa was in New York during the run of the play, and she and Charles took a small apartment for six months in Greenwich Village, leased to them by a sculptress who lived on the lower floor. Charles liked her collection of Greek sculpture, and, often touching them, pointed out to Elsa and friends the beauty of the forms.

Charles and Elsa grew closer at that time than they had been for several years, sharing many pleasures of New York, exploring museums and art galleries, walking in the park. The only blot on this renewed happiness was that Charles suffered from severe back pains and had to be sedated with injections every night during the run by a doctor.

The Laughtons returned to Hollywood in late May, making firm plans for the future. They were happy to accept an offer for a new film, *Witness for the Prosecution*, from the play by Agatha Christie, to be directed as well as scripted by Billy Wilder.

Wilder personally chose Charles for the important part of Sir Wilfred Robards, the famous Queen's Counsel who has to defend a murderer, Leonard Vole, in a trial at the Old Bailey. He cast Elsa as Sir Wilfred's relentlessly brisk and cheerful nurse, Miss Plimsoll; Tyrone Power was to play Leonard Vole; and Marlene Dietrich was cast as Vole's German wife. The story was a farrago, the characters mere paper cut-outs or mere caricatures, the plot development so convoluted that it finally became laughable, but audiences at the time accepted it. The work had been a huge success on the stage.

Wilder, acidulous and tough, and Charles, genial and perfectionist, hit it off splendidly. From the moment he began to prepare for the part of Sir Wilfred, Charles sank himself so deeply into it that he gave the broad, even crude portrait a measure of realism and depth. He added—from the character he had played in *It Started with Eve*—the witty touch of Sir Wilfred's infantile secretiveness over the hiding place of his cigars. He managed to create a character—in part suggested by his London solicitor, Florenz Guedella—at once petulant, childish, and ruthless, seemingly frivolous, but in fact fiercely honest and bent on finding out the truth. As conceived by Agatha Christie, the character is impossible. After this great advocate's lifetime of shrewd legalism, we are supposed to believe that he can fail to see that his client is guilty, that his client's wife is lying to save his life, or that she is disguised as a Cockney in one scene. It says a great deal for Charles's sheer technical skill that he could overcome the manifold deficiencies in the writing. From first rehearsal, he gave a bravura performance that left everyone breathless. Billy Wilder says:

> He took on the dimensions of a barrister. We had heated arguments but they always led to something positive. We would have fifteen or more readings and each time the interpretation of the lines was different. He was like a musician looking for variations in a theme. You can tell how good an actor is by looking at his script. If he's no good, it will be neat as a pin. Charles's was filthy, it looked like a herring had been wrapped in it. He had obviously digested it and regurgitated it—whole!

One of the few elements of Sir Wilfred's character which made sense was that Sir Wilfred was a heart patient, constantly being badgered by his nurse to take his medication, promising emptily to take a holiday in Bermuda. Charles took his part so seriously in fact that one day, while he was swimming in the pool at North Curson, he had a "false heart attack," and Elsa, and David, who was visiting, had to drag him seemingly half-dead, into the house.

Witness for the Prosecution earned both Charles and Elsa Academy Award nominations, and a very enthusiastic press. Charles's big courtroom scene was especially admired. Moving from triumph to defeat and back to triumph again, fiercely condemning Mrs. Vole, the surprise prosecution witness as an "unmitigated liar!" his voice rising from whisper to a tremendous roar of fury as he uttered the words, counting his pills at a moment of quiet, or thrusting home for the kill when he feels he has his victim trapped, he was a marvel of histrionic agility, and the reviews were ecstatic.

After *Witness for the Prosecution,* Charles left for Europe to join Billy Wilder and Tyrone Power on a tour of France and Austria. His plane ran into a blizzard and severe engine trouble forced it to make a crash landing near Frobisher, Newfoundland. Most of the passengers were compelled to sleep on mattresses in an army barracks; Charles was given an officer's room to rest in. Delighted to find a captive audience, he kept the passengers up most of the night by reading them excerpts from his repertoire of the classics. Next day, the replacement plane was not quite ready for departure. An army man told Charles he should go for a walk in the snow, where it was so silent "you can hear your own heartbeat." Excited by the poetic image, he strolled off into a vast white expanse under a leaden sky. He walked for a while, overawed by the scene. Then suddenly he saw something which almost made his heart stop beating: two black marks like coals burning against the snow. They were the eyes of a white fox.

TWELVE

While in England, Charles was offered a new play, *The Party*, by Jane Arden. The producer Oscar Lewenstein had bought the rights from the author; an agent at MCA showed the play to Charles, who fell in love with it immediately. He arranged a meeting with Oscar Lewenstein and an associate of Lewenstein's, John Beary, at the Great Western Hotel, Paddington, where his brother Tom had booked him; and he astonished his visitors by reciting a long excerpt from Thomas Wolfe. Discovering that they liked Wolfe's work, he warmed to both men at once.

His role in *The Party* was to be that of an unhappy and unsuccessful London solicitor who has taken to the bottle because of repressed incestuous feelings for his rebellious and equally unhappy daughter. When he returns from a mental home, his daughter cancels her plans for her birthday party; she is afraid that her father will become drunk and ruin the occasion. Elsa, Charles felt, would be perfect in the part of a neighbor who runs a dress shop specializing in nylon goods. Lewenstein cast her.

Delighted at the prospect of acting in the production, Charles continued on his European jaunt in more than usually high spirits, appearing just before he left London as the compere of a variety show, *Chelsea at Nine.* He joined Wilder and Power in Paris, and traveled with them to the baths at Bad Gastein to rest and renew his vigor, returning to America on November 16, 1957.

In January 1958 Charles signed the contracts with Oscar Lewenstein. He left for London to work with Jane Arden on the final draft of the script. And in March, Elsa flew over to join him at the rehearsals.

Before her arrival, Charles began a tour of the provinces looking for suitable actors and actresses to make up the supporting cast. His first objective was to see the remarkably gifted Albert Finney, then playing Macbeth with the Birmingham Repertory Company, whom he felt might be ideal for the part of the young man in the play. Finney told Elsa later:

> He came to see me. Naturally, I was excited. But then he said, "Well, you were really awful." I didn't feel bad about that. I knew he had acted Macbeth himself at the Old Vic and had been a flop in it. I was surprised, though, when he called and told me I could play the boy in *The Party.*

On his talent hunt tour, Charles took with him a new—platonic—friend, a skillful actor and former member of the Grenadier Guards, James Stevenson. He had carefully trained Stevenson in a one-man show he was giving, at a rented flat in a huge complex of apartments on the bank of the Thames, Dolphin Square, before leaving to look for the supporting cast. They traveled to Stratford, and walked in the Cotswolds picking flowers; they enjoyed the trip to Birmingham to look at Finney; and they returned to London to consider Maggie Smith for the part of the daughter, finally selecting Ann Lynn instead. Stevenson remembered later:

> I think of his love of mimicry. I used to find that at every opportunity he would give a private demonstration of Queen Victoria sitting on the lavatory at Windsor. The seating of Charles in a restaurant was somewhat like the maneuvering of troops into battle. The chair had to

be carefully placed so as not to be too obvious but
equally not too hidden. One particular time in the Midlands a waiter came to him and said, "If you have
chicken, Mr. Laughton, you won't throw the bones over
your shoulder, will you?"

Although Charles retained an enthusiasm for *The Party* which
now seems excessive—both throughout the rehearsals and during the six-month run at the New Theatre—Elsa did not admire
the play equally, and she was not happy with its performance.
The reviews were mixed, distressing Charles with their constant
reference to the alcoholism of the central figure he played. With
his continuing contempt for drunkenness, stemming from the old
Scarborough Hotel days, he was annoyed that this aspect of the
character was so heavily and unnecessarily emphasized. Convinced
that Jane Arden was a very promising Angry Young Woman of
the British theatre, and that she would eventually rival the great
success of the famous Angry Young Man John Osborne, he overrode everyone in insisting that he had uncovered a remarkable
talent.

During the run, he and Elsa lived in a flat in Dorset House in
London. They commuted regularly after the show, and at weekends went to Brighton, thinking they might rent a cottage there,
and enjoyed the bracing sea air and the warm golden light on fine
days. Charles enjoyed some pleasant moments that year: attend-
ing, with Elsa, a garden party at Buckingham Palace given by the
Queen, visiting Stratford-Upon-Avon, where Glen Byam Shaw
offered Charles the part of *King Lear*, and appearing as a narrator
at a Son et Lumière exhibition at Greenwich Palace. He made
several BBC TV appearances, and, in October, signed the contract to appear as Lear, and as Bottom in A *Midsummer Night's
Dream*.

Glen Byam Shaw later recalled the circumstances of his acquir-
ing Charles for Stratford:

I asked him, "Why don't you come and do a season
here?" He didn't answer, and said he must be going. We
said our goodbyes. He left. Two minutes later he popped
his head around the door and said, "If you asked me to

play *King Lear* here I should find it hard to refuse." He
shambled off down the passage.

In discussing the hundredth Stratford season with John Gielgud, Glen Byam Shaw discovered to his great distress that Gielgud would not be available to appear in it. In his stead, Gielgud
recommended Charles. Shaw called Charles at his flat and arranged lunch at a club. Charles was depressed and ill-tempered
over drinks and suddenly announced, "I *hate* London clubs!"
They went to a restaurant instead. As they finished lunch Glen
Byam Shaw said, "You *must* play *Lear*. You owe it to the British
public—and the American tourists!"
Shaw continues:

> Charles left, saying in a rather surly manner that he
> would let me know. Next day, my secretary told me that
> Mr. Laughton was on the line. "This is it," I thought.
> "He's decided not to do it."

But in fact Charles had decided to act in *Lear*. "And will you
do Bottom as well?" Shaw asked him. "Yes," Charles replied. "If
you think it's all right."
Charles told Byam Shaw that they must meet at once and discuss the plays. They must also visit Stonehenge and Beachy Head
to work themselves into the atmosphere of *Lear*.
"Meet me at Stonehenge tomorrow," Charles told Byam Shaw.
"All right," Byam Shaw replied. "At noon."
Next morning Glen Byam Shaw drove all the way from Stratford to Stonehenge. As he reached his destination, the famous circle of Druid stones, it began to pour. "Oh, damnation, this is
going to be hell!" Byam Shaw said out loud.
At the stroke of twelve, Charles arrived in an enormous black
limousine with a chauffeur at the wheel. He climbed out of the car
with a long multicolored woollen scarf wrapped around his head
and tied under his chin, looking like an old washerwoman. Byam
Shaw adds:

> We walked through the rain, and made our way to a
> pub at Amesbury. Charles seemed to enjoy the atten-

tion, had some gins, and a good lunch. He autographed menus and chatted cheerfully with the landlord. He was in very good form. Suddenly he said, "I want to read the play to you!" *"King Lear?"* I asked him. "All of it?" "Yes, all of it. We'll take your car to Oxford and I'll read the play to you." "But you don't have any overnight things," I cautioned him. "It doesn't matter," he said.

Dismissing his limousine, Charles fitted his bulk into the passenger seat of Shaw's miniature two-seater and they drove off through the rain to Oxford. Charles took rooms in a hotel, sat down in the huge and cheerless sitting room of their suite, and Charles plucked a ragged copy of the play from an overstuffed pocket of his shapeless coat. He began reading, his glasses perched on his nose. At two o'clock in the morning he was finished; but now he wanted to go over the play scene by scene with his colleague. Heaving himself on top of a battered upright piano, he said, "This scene calls for me to be seated on a crag!" Once he climbed down, he seemed to want to proceed with the discussions, but Byam Shaw was utterly exhausted, worried about Charles's performance—which he didn't think very good—and desperate for a night's sleep. He said good night.

Two weeks later, the discussions continued at the Royal Crescent Hotel in Brighton. Charles urgently suggested that Byam Shaw should engage Albert Finney as Edgar for the hundreth season, and Byam Shaw, who had barely heard of Finney, reluctantly agreed.

After lunch at the Royal Crescent, Charles got his second wish; he succeeded in persuading Glen Byam Shaw to come to Beachy Head to help his Learian mood. Shaw recalls the occasion:

It was a beast of a day. A very high wind and it was raining. I parked the car, and we struggled to the top of the cliff. I hate heights and stopped well short of the edge but Charles staggered on until he was within a few feet of it. Standing there alone battered by the wind and rain, he looked remarkably like Lear. When he came back to where I was standing my hands were sweating, but he was wonderfully happy and excited and on the

way back to Brighton he chatted away about his life in
Hollywood, his personal life, and his love of pictures
and flowers.

"I shall, of course, grow a beard," he said. "I can't stick
on a beard for *Lear*." "What about Bottom in the
Dream?" I asked him. "Oh, that's all right. I shall paint
it ginger," Charles replied.

Back in Hollywood in the winter of 1958–59, Charles began
discussing the play in depth with Elsa. They left for Hawaii in
December, and talked over the work each day very thoroughly on
the enchanted island of Maui. They stayed at the village of
Hana, where the local villagers believed in the Gods and spirits of
the islands—an ideal atmosphere for studying *King Lear*.

Returning in February, Charles began discussing *Lear* with
Christopher Isherwood, who had become a great friend. Isherwood recalls the weeks in which Charles talked over the play with
him:

> I remember his telling me that it was very important for
> him to have in his head the high note of the storm. A
> characteristic note to which he related the sound of his
> own voice. In other words, he wanted to create the effect
> of the storm in his own speaking of the verse. He said
> that he had heard this characteristic high note while
> crossing the Atlantic with Elsa on a ship in the 1930s.

Charles told Isherwood that his interpretation of the part of
Lear was against the thrust of traditional thinking on the subject;
that in his view Lear did not become a madman during the course
of the action, but instead became sane. Charles pointed out that
when the play opens, Lear is mad, crazed with lust for power. But
that his loss of his kingdom, his expulsion from human company,
his desolation on the heath and in the storm, clears his reason and
makes him feel compassion for suffering humanity. When he
addresses the Fool in Act Three, Scene Two with the words,
"How doth, my boy? Art cold?" it is with the deepest pity and understanding.

Charles, unraveling his thoughts in profound conversation with

Isherwood, stressed Lear's vulgarity at the beginning of the play, his gross exhibitionism, like that of a Hollywood tycoon ("Cecil B. DeMille, for instance. He used to make his girls scramble for gifts."). Lear, Charles said, was a megalomaniac humbled.

Isherwood remembers:

> I asked Charles how he would make his first entrance, and he said, "You know those old men in clubs? The kind of men who live in clubs for a very long time? Who go there every day? They have their own chair, their own place, their own newspaper, and resent every infringement on this. They enter the room in such a way that even if there's a grand piano in it they'll advance without the slightest hesitation."

Elsa had very distinct views about the interpretation of Lear; Charles was indeed so grateful for her help that he bought her a Lincoln Continental as a thank you gift. She felt that King Lear was

> the vehicle that Shakespeare used to cry out against injustice. He called upon the Elements, the Gods and all Nature's Animals in a verbal display of vengeance that has never been matched. Anyone who calls for help against injustice must first be unjustly treated, or collect injustices, or create them. King Lear in his colossal and soul-shattering scream against rejection by his daughters first is made to wish and maneuver himself into a position where he is rejected. That the tragedy of King Lear is primarily based on a fault, a petty human weakness, cannot be denied and therein lies the problem that all actors face. Shakespeare's King Lear is not Kingly. He wears a crown, and he sits on a throne, but he is full of pomp and misguided generosity and from that springboard the actor must invest him with grandeur.

While the discussions went on with Elsa and with Isherwood, who proved to be a most sympathetic friend and adviser, as well as a kindred spirit, Charles still had to earn a living. When he was offered a part in Stanley Kubrick's top-heavy and grandiose epic *Spartacus*, based on the novel by Howard Fast, he accepted at once. He only had to work for thirteen days, and he was paid just over $41,000.

Money had indeed become very tight in those days. Charles's period of major Hollywood stardom was long since over, and two years earlier the Renoir, the Rouault, and others of the great art collection at North Curson Avenue had been sold. Charles accepted the loss with tranquility. He believed in a saying of Gertrude Stein's, that after a time paintings disappear into a wall, that one is no longer aware of them. But he did go ahead and spend money adding to his collection of paintings by the reclusive and mystical Morris Graves, responding to Graves's sensitive capturing of nature, especially birds. He also acquired a further number of stone and terra-cotta pre-Columbian figures, some of which he set in Aztec-like structures built by Lloyd Wright, who had also designed the pool, in the subtropical garden of the house.

In *Spartacus*, Charles played Gracchus, the wily leader of the Roman senate, who attempts to wrest the power of government from the immensely rich and important Crassus (played by Sir Laurence Olivier). The writer, Dalton Trumbo, came over to Curson to discuss the part of Gracchus. Charles's was an impish, sly, and consistently clever performance which received almost uniformly excellent notices. During the picture, Charles renewed his old and somewhat awkward acquaintance with Olivier. Discussing their odd relationship over the years, Olivier wrote to Elsa in 1968:

> I was always very conscious that I was nowhere near up to him intellectually. We got along quite spendidly on *Spartacus*, though I was a bit distressed at what I considered to be his discourtesies on the set, and I told him so. I have always loathed temperaments and tantrums and anything of that sort in an actor. He asked me to direct *King Lear* and I refused, partly because Glen Byam Shaw was an intimate friend, and more specifically—and this I did not tell Charles—because I really did not believe that he and I would get on as I never could really understand what he said to me—which meant that I was

not intellectually his equal. I never really felt on quite the same level as he. What the hell would be the use of *my* directing *him* if I felt like that.

I think I did not admire Charles as much as many people did and I think this worried me. I think, as you say, that there was a possible envy about my playing roles he was denied on account of physical appearance, and that there was a mutuality in this feeling in that I felt in his appearance possibly lay the root of what people considered his genius. I think the most formidable element of obstruction towards our friendship and understanding probably lay in that wartime business [Charles's remaining in Hollywood while Olivier returned to Britain— author]. I remember telling him during *Spartacus* that if he wanted to play Lear he must go to the top of the hill on your estate every morning when the sun rose and breathe and shout the lines until he was exhausted. He rather pooh-poohed this idea and I thought then that his Lear was not likely to be much—a feeling which was confirmed when I saw it, I am afraid.

I only know that whether you liked it or not something extraordinary happened while he was acting and it was always well garnished with fabulous touches of originality. I often think of these, copy them and shall probably go on doing so, as I have no shame about being a copycat.

Making *Spartacus* was a disagreeable experience from the beginning. Charles only worked three weeks, but he disliked every moment. According to the late John Dall, Kirk Douglas, playing Spartacus and producing as well, proved to be a difficult taskmaster who fired the director, Anthony Mann, after six working days and replaced him with Stanley Kubrick. Dall said that Douglas was constantly late on set, keeping Charles, Olivier, Peter Ustinov, John Gavin, Tony Curtis, and Jean Simmons, among other actors, needlessly waiting around. Charles ignored the many petty squabbles on the set, simply giving the best performance he could under the circumstances, and thinking he would at least be well paid.

In late May, Charles and Elsa left for England by plane, and traveled to Stonehenge and Wales in order to steep themselves further in the physical atmosphere of the play. Rehearsals began at Stratford on June 2. Identifying deeply with Lear, Charles began to suffer nightmares and to feel a strong presentiment of death. In these rehearsals, under Glen Byam Shaw's direction, he created a Lear who was subdued, gentle, ruminatory, not at all the thunderous oppressive figure Olivier had played. Elsa observes about the interpretation:

> The theme of remorse and guilt was part of Charles's nature. Lear was Charles and Charles was Lear and the pursuit of each other in a mirror as it were became an obsession with Charles. It was clear that his mistakes and anger towards others were really only angers towards himself. But this unconscious identity with Lear was not a solution. At every performance he really reached out and stretched to solve the mystery of the crucifixion of Lear, but he never did quite touch on that ecstasy. He saw, he felt, he knew what it was about, but he was still not the transmitter of the mystery of the tragedy.

Christopher Isherwood, who saw the performance, adds:

> The scene on the heath was absolutely unforgettable, with the fool clinging to Lear's enormous skirts. And he was wonderful toward the end of the play, especially in the great speech "Never . . . never . . ."

Zoë Caldwell, who played Cordelia, remembered Charles years later:

> I was romantically involved with Albert Finney, who played Edgar, and I think Charles disapproved of this. He was a very talented child. He wanted the complete devotion of all of us in the cast. I found him abrasive. There was tension on the stage both in rehearsal and full performance. But his abrasiveness was exciting and stimulating.

Both fellow players and critics agreed that Charles, despite all of his many months of work, never quite "got" the part of Lear. The rehearsals were bad enough, but during the run Charles was irritable, testy, and in pain with his back. According to Glen Byam Shaw, he began telling members of the company that Shaw had lost control of the play:

> We had an unholy quarrel. He was wonderful at dress rehearsal. But on the first night he started badly and did not recover until the last third. I began to realize he was ill only when it was too late. My heart bled to see him struggling through evening performances when there was a matinée the same day. Charles also bitterly objected to the presence of someone in the cast I won't name. He threatened to leave the production if that man was not replaced. I refused to tolerate the threat. Charles stayed on, but he was very unhappy.

Despite the audience's great enthusiasm, the reviews were largely unfavorable. Harold Hobson's in the London *Sunday Times* was particularly devastating and merciless. Most critics agreed that Charles's delivery of the verse left much to be desired, that he could not always be heard, and that he seemed defeated from the outset, not a king brought low. The very qualities of humility, warmth, and accessibility that he brought to the "mad" scenes annoyed critics, who longed for grandeur and fiery display.

Charles's Bottom in *A Midsummer Night's Dream* was not much better received. Elsa recalls that he was wonderfully alive and funny and antic in the part, but Kenneth Tynan was cruel in *The Observer*, and the *Times* critic was lukewarm, talking of "amusing patches" and a good "Pyramus and Thisbe" scene, but otherwise saying little that was good about his playing. J. W. Lambert in the *Sunday Times* remarked on the tenderness and grace of Charles's scene with Titania and the fairies, but on the whole dismissed the performance with the faintest praise.

This overall response dealt a terrible blow to Charles. He had invested close on to a year to studying these great parts; he felt that he had at least come to grips with the role of Bottom, and had provided a new interpretation of Lear; but the failure of the

British press to appreciate either performance must have been like a knife thrust in his heart. He had attempted the utmost pinnacle of British theatre, and in the eyes of many he had failed. No wonder, then, that his illness worsened, that he felt more crushed than he had been for years—after the triumphs of the early and mid-1950s, the great readings, the dazzling direction of both theatre and film presentations, the outpouring of his genius in fruitful and personally rewarding ventures. There was only a single consolation that summer. When Elsa was back in Hollywood he met Bruce Ashe.

Bruce Ashe was a successful young photographer's model who had aspirations to be an actor. He was tall, sturdily built, with perfectly proportioned features, and a smooth, convincing, quite polished manner. His smile was bright and reassuring, giving an impression of extreme self-confidence. He was very much an English outdoor type, reminiscent of Roger Moore or Stephen Boyd. He did not have any striking depths or resources: he was a freebooter who lived by his wits and his looks.

Charles, as always fascinated and captivated by beauty, found Bruce aesthetically pleasing and a relaxed, amiable companion. He was to a small degree more impressive than the other friends Charles had enjoyed. He at least had the gift of conversation. He was not ignorant of food, music, books, and the theatre and film. There was always something to talk about.

Charles fell very deeply in love with Bruce. He had not fallen in love with David Roberts, and certainly not with the succession of masseurs and obscure actors with whom he had been involved in the period following David's departure for New York. Now he was in the grip of a profoundly shaking and disturbing emotion, in which he became to a great extent emotionally dependent on Bruce, in which he could lose the pain of his own existence in the rapture of experiencing vicariously what it meant to be young and strong and beautiful. It was a passionate feeling of commitment in which the other's silences and absences were agonizing, and the other's expressions of affection, and presence on the scene, were causes of intense and almost unbearable joy.

It was, from the first, an adoption of the heart. The two men met at an art gallery in London. It was an odd, antagonistic meeting. Charles said to Bruce, who was standing looking at a painting, "Beautiful, isn't it?" Bruce irritated him by replying, "Yes, I suppose it is, but what do you do with it?" Charles said sharply, "Hang it up on a wall." A moment later two old ladies came up to Charles and one of them said, visibly star-struck, "Oh, Mr. Laughton, we met you on the Isle of Wight in 1930." Charles replied coldly, "Madam, I have never been on the Isle of Wight in my life."

The two men left the gallery together and went to lunch. Their sexual relationship began almost immediately. Charles had long looked for the perfect image of an English son, and Bruce ideally fulfilled his needs, moving in with Charles to an apartment in Dolphin Square, Pimlico. Charles taught him to understand paintings, indicating tiny details of which Bruce was utterly unaware. When Bruce visited *King Lear* at Stratford, he was most awed and humbled by Charles's playing. When the season closed, they were together constantly, Bruce learning assiduously so that he could pursue a career as an actor.

In the fall of 1959, immediately after the run of *King Lear*, Charles felt a need to show Bruce the glories of the classical world. In their Socratic relationship, and in the classical body of Bruce, he had already discovered an appropriate parallel. He accepted a part in a film, *Under Ten Flags*, to be produced by Dino di Laurentiis, a film so bad it would be a kindness to Charles's memory to overlook it. But the great advantage of this job was that the picture was to be shot in Rome.

Charles enjoyed showing Bruce the sights of the ancient city. He returned to America with Bruce firmly established as his paid companion and devoted pupil. In March 1960 Charles appeared with Elsa on the Academy Award telecast singing, with great style and charm, "Baby, It's Cold Outside," a song originally composed for an Esther Williams musical. Then, in Santa Monica, he began intensive discussions with Christopher Isherwood on preparing a theatrical version of the Dialogues of Plato, based on the life of Socrates: a direct link with his relationship with Bruce Ashe.

Isherwood's memory of the experience is clear:

> At the beginning, Charles wanted to study an Italian play which existed, dealing with the life of Socrates. And he had this play translated. We found that it didn't con-

tribute very much. What we needed was something
much less formal and more improvised. We began to
work on the Dialogues.

Unhappily, in the midst of work, Charles became ill with a severe gall bladder problem. In May he suffered a heart attack, and
he was in the Cedars of Lebanon Hospital for several weeks. He
had to diet for three months, and in the fall underwent two unpleasant gall bladder operations. He was intensely depressed by
this indication that his robust health was, in his early sixties, at
last beginning to fail.

In June he began to work with Isherwood again, and to make
plans with Elsa to buy the house next door to Isherwood's on
Adelaide Drive, Santa Monica. It had a lovely, sweeping view of a
canyon and across to the Pacific surf. At last the dramatic presentation began to assume a coherent form. Act One was to contain
Plato's political ideas and indicate the reasons for Socrates' position as the leading political philosopher of his time. Act Two
would show his concept of love, and the ideal relationship that
could exist between master and pupil. Act Three would contain
the great drama of Socrates' imprisonment and death. Meetings
continued all through July. Charles evidently found Isherwood a
good, refreshing and cleansing presence; Isherwood was fascinated
by Charles. In the meantime, Charles could enjoy the classical
physique of Bruce, swimming and sunbathing with him in the
gardens all that summer at Curson.

At first, Charles proved to be a poor sight reader of the classic
Dialogues, but he soon outdistanced Isherwood, who wrote to Elsa
later:

I want to stress how much fun we had. When it came to
cutting pieces out of the various paperback books and
pasting them into an album for the rough draft it became a kind of nursery atmosphere.

They laughed together constantly; they had fun. Often, when
the work became exhausting or boring, Charles would break off
and provide comic readings, in particular one which Isherwood
never forgot, a passage from the Book of Job with God talking

like a Nazi gauleiter and Job like a stage Jew. Occasionally they quarreled. As Isherwood says,

> Elsa, in the kindness of her heart, used to try to warn me not to be victimized by Charles, and I always replied that, after all, I'm a monster, and quite able to take care of myself with other monsters—such as Charles undoubtedly was. And as I told her, monsters are very loyal to each other in their own peculiar way. And she wasn't to be afraid that either was going to eat the other.

In August and September, the months of his gall bladder operations, Charles was very sick indeed. Bruce Ashe had gone back to England for some modeling assignments and only just returned in time for the first operation. Charles recuperated with depressing slowness, looking old, shaky, and gray, "like a punch-drunk fighter," as Isherwood said. He continued to work more listlessly with Isherwood, much of his old fire gone, and still badly shocked by an experience in the hospital in which he had suffered from an infected scar and it had to be cut open and sewn up under local anesthetic. The summer heat also troubled him more severely than usual. Nevertheless, he devoted himself to work as much as ever, teaching Bruce, toiling on further problems with Isherwood, and helping Elsa to prepare a new one-woman show.

In October, Charles was violent and suicidal. He became afraid that his health would never recover. When Elsa presented the first tryout of her show at Stockton, California, he had to make an almost superhuman effort to attend the performance. He improved somewhat en route, stimulated and revived by the beauty of the California country he loved. Elsa recalls that he kept wanting to stop and buy fruit, and to pick flowers. But once he got to Stockton he had to lie down and rest all afternoon in the hotel room.

The tryout was a great success. After it, Charles made many valuable suggestions for improvements, to some extent losing his own sense of personal misery in the process; but finally the strain of his whole life brought about a serious nervous breakdown in the fall. Elsa says:

> It was the day before I was to appear in my show at

UCLA. Charles was having lunch with David—Bruce had gone back to England. Without warning, Charles began to shout that he wanted to take pills, to kill himself. Then he threw himself to the floor. He began to cry. He went to the front porch and seemed to be about to throw himself down the steps. David and I tried to overpower him but could not. We dragged him into the schoolroom. Filled with tension and hostility and determined to break through his fit of depression, I slapped his face. Charles suddenly grew calm. "Thank you," he said.

In October, Charles left for Japan with Bruce, who had returned from London, to make an appearance in an episode of a television series, *Checkmate*, shot in Hong Kong. Everyone agreed that the trip would refresh him. He had owned Japanese prints for years, and longed to see the famous Temple Gardens of Kyoto.

The bustle of Tokyo, the razzle-dazzle of its night lights, the still beauty and perfection of Kyoto and Nara enthralled and revitalized Charles. At last he could walk the streets of a city and not have people recognize him. He liked the thrust and vitality of the immense crowds. He was enchanted by the exquisitely modeled countryside, the rolling hills, the romantic mists, the sudden unexpected glimpses of water which Hokusai had captured. He visited temples and talked to priests in saffron robes. He became more tranquil than he had ever been in his life.

And he had the additional joy of seeing his handsome friend respond to Japan, not perhaps with equal understanding of its culture, but with equal vibrancy and pleasure in its aesthetic loveliness. Bruce, to Charles's delight, entirely appreciated beauty. Charles forgot the weakness and pain he felt. He could look at a sky over Kyoto and tell Bruce how it had been reflected, stilled and subdued forever, in the formal mirror of Japanese painting.

It was a miraculous experience, the last happy time of Charles's life. Hong Kong was not aesthetically pleasing, but Charles again enjoyed the crowds, the noise, the bustle of an Oriental city. He returned in November, where Elsa, who had been in Canada on her tour, joined him on the fourteenth.

For the Christmas holidays, Charles, Elsa, and Bruce all went to Palm Springs together. On January 22, Charles appeared on the Dinah Shore Show in Los Angeles, and a few days later he appeared on the Jack Paar Show in New York. Elsa opened in her one-woman show, which Charles created and directed, at the 49th Street Playhouse, to wonderful reviews; the New York *Times* said that "only she could take the public's mind off 17 inches of snow."

In April, Charles went on an extensive reading tour through the south with Bruce, then proceeded to Washington, Philadelphia, Montreal, and Toronto and back to California through the Middle West. He enjoyed enthusiastically showing Bruce the beauty of the American countryside. That year he had seen to it that this passion for the life and landscape of America would be immortalized for a second time in an anthology, *The Fabulous Country*, a companion piece to his earlier omnibus, *Tell Me a Story*.

The Fabulous Country, published by McGraw-Hill in 1962, was, following the earlier book, an extraordinary demonstration of Charles's pride in being an American. He included descriptions of New York by Gertrude Stein, Thomas Wolfe, and Truman Capote; Emily Dickinson, Robert Frost, and Sinclair Lewis on New England; Sherwood Anderson and Stephen Vincent Benét on the South; George Ade and Sherwood Anderson on the Middle West, among many writers on many places. He summed up his feelings about America in richly evocative images which throughout the book indicate the responsiveness and warmth of his spirit. He described the exact moment of truth when, sometime in the early 1930s, he had realized he wanted to live in America:

> I was the guest of the Savage Club in London, and Sir Austin Chamberlain made a speech. I was sitting next to Nelson Doubleday, the publisher. Sir Austin was polite and polished and imperturbable. At the end of the speech Nelson Doubleday said to me, "Charlie, however thin you cut it, it's still baloney." And I suddenly wanted to get on a boat and get back to New York so bad I could taste it.

This, and other introductory passages for the excerpts, were very well written indeed. Charles gave glimpses of many cities, and of his appearances on his tours. He even contributed a long and luminous descriptive piece of his own—on readings in Alaska, an unexpected evocation of Charles's love of the life of the snow country:

> We had been given high-waders, and I found out why when we got there. We waded from the float of the plane to the shore. There were moose and bears—we didn't see any wolves—and ducks and swans and arctic terns, which must be the most beautiful birds in the world. I had never hoped to see a bird whose flight is more beautiful than the flight of a sea gull. The arctic tern has a black head and neck and a body of pure white feathers. The tail and wing feathers spread like a fan and they hover upright like humming birds. And there were swallows, the bluest swallows I have ever seen. The swallows were friendly and swooped around our heads and dived in front of us, and lighted on the ground a yard from our feet.

Sometime early in the summer of 1961, Otto Preminger, the bald and fierce-tempered director of *Laura* and *Bonjour Tristesse*, dropped over to Curson Avenue to discuss a new part for Charles: Seab Cooley, the bigoted Southern senator, in a version of Allen Drury's novel *Advise and Consent*. Preminger had seen Charles in *Don Juan in Hell*, *Galileo*, and *Spartacus* and knew that he would be perfect as Cooley. For Charles it was, once more, a chance to play the part of someone who symbolized everything he hated. By showing the full horror of the character in the playing, he could by inference make clear his own contempt for bigots of every persuasion. And here he had a double motive: in this declining period of his life, he had ceased to be a maverick homosexual. He no longer wanted to live his life away from others of his persuasion, as he said to Elsa; he felt he wanted to "be with his own kind." A very important feature of Cooley's character was his hatred of homosexuality. This Charles played with a biting edge, indicative of his own dislike of men who were prejudiced against the minority to which he belonged.

Charles studied the part intensively, grappling with the particularly awkward problem of a satisfactory Southern accent. He studied a record of the Southern Senator John C. Stennis' keynote address to the Democratic Convention in 1952, and with the help of a voice coach Ben Bard as well as his research assistant for his anthology, *The Fabulous Country*, Bruce Zortman, he finally licked the problem.

Shooting began in Washington in September and continued for six weeks, with three weeks at the end in Hollywood. Charles especially liked Don Murray, playing a young senator haunted by a homosexual incident in his past. Murray, in his turn, was fascinated by Charles's ability to work his way into the heart and soul of a character. Charles was surpassingly energetic in his playing of scenes. Despite his ill health, his sheer stamina reasserted itself. In the stifling and humid heat of Washington in late summer, he was so caught up in his part he seemed to the other players barely aware of any discomfort. He added all kinds of unexpected touches to his characterization. In a long and devastating address to the Senate, he played the lines in a manner which went entirely against Preminger's concept. The conventional approach would have been to start quietly, then build to an impassioned, very loud outburst at the end. Instead, over Preminger's objections, hysterically voiced, Charles began the speech loudly, gradually lowering his voice to a near-whisper as he uttered the final words.

During the shooting, Charles had several conversations with Allen Drury. He pointed out the ways in which Otto Preminger had made changes in Seab Cooley's character, lighting him from below to make him sinister, photographing him from bizarre angles to emphasize his evil. This, Charles pointed out to Drury, made it all that much harder to give the character delicate ambiguities and shadings which would make Cooley believably human.

Otto Preminger, for all his outbursts of rage and his extravagant old-fashioned behavior on the set, came to appreciate what Charles was doing to give depth to the playing. He knew that

Charles deliberately made Cooley warm and attractive in certain aspects of his character, so that the senator's rear-guard behavior would be all the more shocking in the final scenes.

Old friends were in the cast: Burgess Meredith, and Franchot Tone, who was dying of cancer and was courageously playing a President dying of cancer in the picture. At times, in the midst of acting Seab Cooley with immense relish, Charles did feel a presentiment about his own physical condition. Concerned that he might only have a very short time to live, in his anguish, despite doctors' warnings, he began to drink martinis very heavily, and to eat excessively. Even as he worked with all of his old fire and brilliance, his constitution finally began to wear down.

He was not helped by the presence on the set of Henry Fonda, playing the part of a nominee for the President's office. Charles told Elsa that, as in the days of *The Caine Mutiny Court-Martial*, Fonda continually behaved with angry contempt toward him. Charles was considerate of the unhappy Gene Tierney, playing a Washington hostess. Knowing of her long history of mental disturbances and personal tragedy, he gave her great tenderness and protection, shielding her from Preminger when the director bullied her.

A pleasure during the shooting was a visit along with other members of the cast to the White House, to lunch with the Kennedys. Later that day, the group went out to the Presidential yacht on the Potomac, where they dined and danced under the stars.

Advise and Consent received excellent notices. This was a plain, straightforward film, on the whole quite well directed and played, yet with a script which was much less penetrating about American politics than it should have been. Charles's performance was among the most distinguished of his career. He created a character at once sly and childlike, devious and amusing, ruthless and charming. Played largely in a surprisingly minor key, Seab Cooley became an accessible and human figure, with his loose, shambling walk, his drooping badly ironed tropical suits, his eyes alive with mischief. Despite Charles's sickness he acted the part with great resourcefulness, especially in his climactic scene, when he gave an astute portrait of a corrupt Southern Republican on the rampage.

Advise and Consent seemed to absorb the last of Charles's strength. He threw everything he knew into the performance. But the difficulty of playing the part in a hot and sultry Washington made drastic inroads into his failing health. In the late fall of 1961, Billy Wilder invited him to portray Moustache in a film of *Irma la Douce*, with Shirley MacLaine, and Charles accepted at once. By December it was clear that he would probably not be well enough to play in the movie. He was again being cared for by doctors, and he was in bed that month being treated for severe pain in his shoulders and right knee.

Somehow he managed to summon up enough strength for another reading tour with Bruce Ashe in January 1962. Bruce's sheer physical handsomeness, his health and strength buoyed Charles up and seemed to be transmitted to him. He was elated as he drove off with Bruce for the tour, but seeing him go, Elsa had a premonition she would never see him healthy again.

In Flint, Michigan, on the tour, Charles slipped and fell in a bathtub and broke his collarbone. His road manager, Bob Halter, and Bruce Ashe rushed him to the Flint Hospital, where he lay in intense pain for ten days. At Otto Preminger's insistence, Bob and Bruce took Charles to New York, where he was treated at the New York Hospital.

Elsa flew to New York. She was told by doctors there that Charles had cancer of the bone. Now, she knew, she must give Charles a feeling of optimism about his early recovery, a recovery she knew could not possibly take place.

In his drug-induced state, Charles firmly believed that he had won the best actor award at the 1962 Cannes Film Festival. Although his Oscar for *Mutiny on the Bounty* had meant little or nothing to him, he was exhilarated by the thought of this new imaginary honor, and that he would be traveling to Cannes to receive it. Elsa was so determined to sustain the illusion they would be traveling to France that she bought a new white hat and dress, new leather luggage, and even underwent a smallpox vaccination, her arm swelling up severely.

It became very expensive for four people to stay at the St. Moritz—Charles, Elsa, Bruce, and Bob Halter. Loyd Wright, the Laughtons' attorney, felt it advisable for them to return home. They took eight seats on the plane—four to be made in a bed for

Charles to lie down, and an extra one for a male nurse. Charles was taken to Curson Avenue by ambulance and was made comfortable in the schoolroom. He was sedated for the entire journey.

In Hollywood, Charles spent some time on Curson Avenue, and at the Cedars of Lebanon Hospital. Elsa recalls:

> I was sitting in Charles's hospital room one night. Among other flower arrangements I had put a particularly perfect rose by his bed in his ordinary bathroom glass. He only had a few weeks to live and was under constant, heavy sedation—if awake, in pain; if under drugs, dreaming.
>
> He woke up for a lucid second or two and said, "You know that"—looking at the rose—"is beautiful, in fact more beautiful than anything you and I saw in Japan." I said—how badly my honesty served me—"But I was not in Japan with you, you were with Bruce." His face distorted into a thousand crinkles. He wept tears for about twenty seconds then slept as if nothing had happened.

When Charles came home, Elsa gave out interviews that he was wading at the shallow end of the Lloyd Wright pool with a nurse assisting him, that he was pottering about in the garden, and studying for the part in *Irma la Douce*. She showed him these news items, knowing they would cheer him. He never openly admitted that he had cancer.

His brother Tom came from Britain for two weeks—all he could spare from his duties—and then Frank Laughton arrived to help Elsa give Charles a sense of reassurance. One night, leaving Frank and the night nurse to be with Charles, Elsa attended the Ballet Folklorico of Mexico. Frank seized the occasion to call in a priest and have Charles given extreme unction. Next morning Charles said half-humorously, "Well, they've got me back in the Gang." When the priest asked Elsa if she were happy about his being received back into the Church, she said, "According to the Church we were never married. We were married in a registry office!"

Letters poured in, from Allen Drury, Agnes Moorehead, Lillian Gish, Iris Barry (then in the South of France), and Robert Siod-

mak, among many other friends. The doctors did not want
Charles unnecessarily disturbed by visitors either at Cedars or at
home, knowing that it was dangerous to overexcite a patient who
was under drugs. But when Albert Finney was in Los Angeles on
his way to Australia, Elsa told him that Charles would want him
to visit the sickbed. As an actor, he must be able to see everything, including dying and death, so that he could draw from this
experience in the future. Finney sat by Charles's bed for half an
hour, but Charles never knew he was there.

The painter Charles admired so deeply, Morris Graves, sat by
Charles's bed and held his hand. On this occasion, Charles did
wake for a moment and said, "You have been an enormous help
to me." And Graves replied, "And you to me."

Charles died on the night of December 15. He was in the
schoolroom, where he had taught his beloved pupils, surrounded
by his favorite paintings, with the lovely subtropical garden visible
through the windows. Elsa was sitting in the anteroom when
Frank and the night nurse came to tell her he had gone. She went
upstairs to her bedroom, and a few minutes later saw his face on a
silent television set. Someone had already given out the news to
the television reporters; she never found out who it was.

The funeral was held at Forest Lawn, conducted by the non-
denominational University Chaplain of U.S.C. The organist was
Raymond Henderson, who had been Elsa's accompanist and ar-
ranger. David Roberts, who had been devoted to Charles until the
end, was among the pallbearers, along with Raymond Massey,
Charles and Elsa's attorney Loyd Wright, Charles's former agent
Taft Schreiber, and Jean Renoir, who had substituted for Billy
Wilder at the last minute. Elsa had brought a small posy of wild
camellias, grass, and ferns from the house, and, impelled by a
sudden intense feeling, placed them on the coffin at the last minute before it was set into the crypt.

Throughout the service, Elsa could only feel an overwhelming
relief that Charles was released from his suffering. She could not
pretend a sense of sorrow that his misery of the past year was over.
She wrote in an essay:

I could have sung. At the funeral I stood with the nurses
and laughed with them. If they did not feel like it, they

knew well that there was cause for happiness for me. I felt very close to them. Charles's life was lengthened by modern medical care—his over-prolonged agony is what is called progress—but that is another story.

Elsa herself selected lines which Christopher Isherwood quoted in his final oration. They came from Prospero's speeches in *The Tempest*. She had at last understood, more than a quarter of a century from the time she and Charles had appeared in the play at the Old Vic, the full meaning of the lines in relation to Charles's life.

Isherwood's eulogy is given in full:

Someone who loved him said of him the other day, "He was such a powerful person," and this word "powerful" comes back to one's mind again and again in thinking of him. He had a natural "power" which he carried into all his projects, into his art, and into the work that he did with young actors, which was so very much a part, especially, of his later life. Most of the great parts that he played were power figures of one kind or another. But, beyond the subtlety, the incomparable art, the powers of characterization, and presentation of a character, there was something more. You felt about him that he was not only powerful, but a vehicle of power, something through which power passed, and was transmitted.

During those readings, on which he traveled all over the United States and got to know this country and its people so well, and made himself so much beloved by them, you felt that here was something more than the mask of acting. Something was coming through him which was uncontaminated, even by any egotistic kind of personality, and, I think, this was most noticeable also, in one of his very great performances—the *Lear* which he gave at Stratford-on-Avon about three years ago. There you felt that you were in touch with something that seemed almost to be the very inspiration of Shakespeare himself. And he might well have addressed the spirit of Shakespeare in those words by John Donne, and said, "Thou art the Proclamation, and I am the trumpet at whose voice the people came."

I have been asked to read three extracts from another of Shake-

speare's plays, *The Tempest,* in which he also appeared, some
years ago now, during the Thirties, in the part of Prospero. These
three extracts are all from speeches by Prospero, and they form a
kind of threefold farewell. The first is the speech which Prospero
makes, after he has conjured up a magic scene, a magic play, for
the entertainment of his daughter and her lover. Prospero, when
he speaks of "my art" means, of course, his *magic* art. But this
word "art" links Prospero to the figure of the artist, and it has
been often remarked that in this play we seem to see the artist
laying down, saying farewell to, his art.

> Our revels now are ended. These our actors,
> (As I foretold you) were all spirits, and
> Are melted into air, into thin air,
> And like the baseless fabric of this vision,
> The cloud-capp'd towers, the gorgeous palaces,
> The solemn temples, the great globe itself,
> Yea, all which it inherit, shall dissolve,
> And like this insubstantial pageant faded,
> Leave not a rack behind: we are such stuff
> As dreams are made on; and our little life
> Is rounded with a sleep.

Then, a little further on in the play, Prospero speaks again of
all that he has accomplished with his magic, and here again we
can well take this as the allegory of the actor speaking about his
great roles, and about the magic which he has wrought upon the
stage. And here Prospero abjures this magic, and says goodbye to
it:

> . . . I have bedimm'd
> The noontide sun, call'd forth the mutinous
>   winds,
> And 'twixt the green sea and the azured vault
> Set roaring war: to the dread rattling thunder
> Have I given fire, and rifted Jove's stout oak
> With his own bolt; the strong-bas'd promontory
> Have I made shake, and by the spurs pluck'd up
> The pine and cedar: graves at my command

Have wak'd their sleepers, op'd, and let 'em forth
By my so potent art. But this rough magic
I here abjure; and, when I have requir'd
Some heavenly music (which even now I do)
To work mine end upon their senses, that
This airy charm is for, I'll break my staff,
Bury it certain fathoms in the earth,
And deeper than did ever plummet sound
I'll drown my book.

Then, at the end of the play, in the Epilogue, Prospero appears before us bereft of his art, a human being, fallible and weak, appealing to us for our compassion and our love and our prayers. He says:

. . . But release me from my bands
With the help of your good hands:
Gentle breath of yours my sails
Must fill, or else my project fails,
Which was to please. Now I want
Spirits to enforce, art to enchant;
And my ending is despair,
Unless I be relieved by prayer,
Which pierces so, that it assaults
Mercy itself, and frees all faults.
As you from crimes would pardon'd be,
Let your indulgence set me free.

Index